INDIA ABLY SERVED

A GOOD GOVERNANCE STORY

SECRETS OF AN IAS KARMAYOGI

PRASANNA KUMAR HOTA

notionpress.com

INDIA • SINGAPORE • MALAYSIA

Notion Press

No.8, 3rd Cross Street,
CIT Colony, Mylapore,
Chennai, Tamil Nadu – 600004

First Published by Notion Press 2020
Copyright © Prasanna Kumar Hota 2020
All Rights Reserved.

ISBN 978-1-64951-803-3

COMMENTS OF EMINENT MANUSCRIPT READERS

Jagannath Patnaik former Cabinet Minister, Odisha

Three recurrent themes: Concern, Determination and Ready-Wit. Narrated in poetic language it details out what contributes to delivering good governance with chosen emphasis on 'effectiveness and efficiency'.

Statesmen are rare now... Hota's suggestions for Hospital Corporation and 10000 E-based Saathi Centres one in each Block aim at making every ordinary Indian a Statesman. Flow of Bank finance through PPP leveraging Govt. Budget to expand social sector goods of health and information-empowerment are truly revolutionary.

Any young civil servant willing to outshine others in serving the people should not give this book a miss.

Surendra Singh, former Cabinet Secretary

Hota has critically examined the concepts of good governance and demonstrated ways of practising them, deriving from his experience in the IAS...

Prabhat Kumar former Cabinet Secretary

I was not aware of the fact that Hota was an accomplished storyteller as well. His memoirs are illustrative of the ordeals faced by an IAS office, in the course of her or his career...I look forward to read the book in print

Mr. M. Mahapatra Former CMD Syndicate Bank

I wait for the book to appear in print. I suggest for an audio version too! Laced with anecdotes and humour, the book is going to be a treasure trove of critical life lessons in management and self-development for all leaders. Mr. Hota deftly demonstrates how the spirit of entrepreneurship trumps obstacles anywhere, from industry to healthcare, urban development to public administration and personal life to public negotiation."

Lt. General C.B. Vijan

Hota leads from the front.

K.N. Bhagat (Social Work)

Service to man…service to God. This IAS showed in action. Sadly not many others… Love all-serve all.

Ms. Bina Malhotra (Educationist)

Scintillating stories-all true- IAS Karma Yogi… Humour as art of administration.

Upendra Behera (former Addl. CS, Odisha)

Role-model colleague, pro-poor & pro-public sector. Book- a 'Must-Read' for the Officers & aspiring civil service candidates.

Wing Cmdr. Nanda Samal

What an achiever- more for common people less for himself.

Dr. N.K. Arora former Professor AIIMS

Unbelievable public health Game-changer. Women from common homes for hospital delivery up from mere 5 lakh to 1.05 crore in a year!

D. Chhotray, former Secretary GoI

Hota always superb performance-based storyteller. IAS aspirants and Public Administration professors must follow this saga of Governance in Action.

Prof. Dr. Vinod Sethi

An essential reading for all aspiring to a public service/sector career.

Dr. R.C. Deka ex-Director AIIMS

What a performer! Hota put life into all Govt. Medical Institutions. Hospital Corporation is a Wake-Up IDEA for Indian health care.

Bulbul Ganguly (Entrepreneur)

Book, serious, humorous and always vigorous- like generous Hota in work life. All 8 PSUs in loss turned to profit by him.

SS Gupta former Addl. CS Meghalaya

Hands-on Experience eloquent but cogent & pragmatic. An Officers' Work Manual in challenging times.

Syed Mqbool Ali (Social activist)

Most talk, Hota achieves. His Saathi Centres – antidote against Corruption; empowering common people to the centre of the economy.

Rajiv Goyal Sr. Partner

Using skilfully the CAs and finance guys & changing losses to profit… only a few IAS know the art.

Bijaylaxmi Senapati [Odia poet; elder sister]

Prasanna…often bed-ridden and quiet childhood…Seldom ate… Started reading stories; soon devoured one book a day…Later seen IAS Prasanna work 6.30 AM to 11.30 PM all days of the year… no holidays for him.

Malay Chatterjee, former CMD Kudremukh Iron Ore Co Ltd

An IAS who respected PSUs and encouraged them to reach their profit potential. Led all 8 PSUs where he was deputed from loss to profit. Scooters India miracle is a case study in Kellogg School of Management.

Upma Chawdhry former Secretary and Director LBSNAA (IAS Training Academy) Govt. of India

Candid and captivating, the book captures the reflections of an officer who re-defined the bureaucratic workspace and simultaneously seeks to re-orient the IAS ethos to 'I-Ably-Serve'. A must read, especially for new recruits to Civil Services. Book- a great resource for training Public officials at different stages of their career.

Brig. PC Das

Remarkable resilience in varied and challenging situations and assignments. Book is full of lessons for Civil Officials to rise up to each occasion to serve people without concern for personal comforts.

Dr. B.M. Mishra Faculty Harvard University, USA

Proper administrative conduct for good governance was the foundation for India's opulence until it was shattered by foreign occupation. I congratulate Hota to have revived the fundamental analysis with anecdotes from his forty-year experience in the service.

Prof. Dr. Tanmay Panda, Toronto. Canada

Value based and practical approach to public governance". Value is to serve the people and practicality is to get your task done effectively and efficiently with a smile. Hota's book brings in a plethora of his real life experiences as a learning lesson to new public servants. A must read for all those in public governance.

R. K. Bhandari former Engineer Member DDA

Book respects engineers and their contribution. Hota a true colleague and a leader, got the best out of technical officers, particularly, Civil Engineers. Engineers would understand IAS better and vice-versa if all read this book.

Yashbant Das Senior Advocate Supreme Court

Passionate description of the career of a hard-working civil servant. His suggestions on judicial reforms depict the agony of a citizen…Brainstorming mandatory.

A.K. Bhowmik Senior Advocate Mumbai High Court

Hota always focused on common man. Suggestions for Judicial reforms are to the point and must be adopted for immediate results.

Manoranjan Patnaik

Hota dislikes publicity; but his simple but effective suggestions for speedy disposal of civil and matrimonial cases deserve public debate.

Tathagat Satpathy Editor Dharitri and Odisha Post and former MP

Mr. Hota is a true Karmayogi

PREFACE

Welcome to a gripping tale of what it takes for a sickly bookworm to become a great administrator – leading always from the front, often dramatically and always with impeccable homework, planning and attention to details combined with sheer slogging hard work. Prasanna Hota describes both lifting up the common man and facing down rabble-rousers and interfering politicians and inflated egos in fascinating detail, a roadmap and must-read for serving and would be IAS officers and other leaders of men.

Few of us know that less than 5000 serving IAS officers, almost 30% promoted from State civil services, implement national policies to administer our nation of one hundred thirty five crore fellow citizens and indirectly run our lives and futures. Annually just 100 are chosen for IAS training, from 1.5 million applicants. No wonder so many adorn themselves with undeserved haloes. Yet only 5-10% of them are outstanding and take the country forward, like my heroic but self-effacing IAS hero SR Rao, Surat Commissioner who converted India's dirtiest city to its second-cleanest one in 18 months, proving that such change is possible.

What all these star performers have is the will to perform and ways to find creative solutions to problems, as described in this book. Hota is one of these outstanding officers, aware of his brilliance but wearing it with modesty and humour. His avowed mission in writing this book is to illustrate by example the meaning of Good Governance GG - an initial discussion of the theory and then it is GG unfolding in action. Of all its aspects, Hota's lodestar has been the prompt and efficient delivery of goods and services to benefit the common man. In this, he has succeeded in every one of his postings and varied careers, in unusual and innovative ways. Believing that delay is the root of corruption, his speed of decision-making and disposal of files is exemplary. This is in stark contrast to the inordinate judicial delays and backlog that he bemoans. Retired Justice Roshan Dalvi's book *Tangible Justice* contains gems of incremental improvements. Hota's suggestion of an All-India Judicial Service cadre deserves attention.

Interwoven in these stories is an indirect picture of less-than-perfect administration by imperfect performers or needless egos and automatic promotions. Good governance and high performance are still very person-specific and often do not outlast the frequent transfer of high achievers. We need, nationally, an inviolate undisturbed tenure of 2-3 years per posting to allow IAS officers (and mayors) to make long-term plans and systems.

There are cautionary examples of what to avoid, how not to be. We need frequent peer sharing and learning where Navaratna administrator-managers can regularly teach each other many practical ways to exercise available powers within the existing framework. We need a system of reward for merit and a Perform or Perish work culture and systems like the private sector, promoting efficiency.

Delegation of fiscal powers and more efficient 'tender' system will hugely improve grievance redressal, on-road efficiency, productivity and costs. A culture of faith must replace a culture of mistrust, urges Asiad Jyoti S K Chawla, Chief Engineer CPWD. Each person assigned any responsibility should automatically have some financial authority to go with the respective post. A discretionary spending imprest of a day's wages for the lowest workers, of a weeks' pay for their supervisors, and imprest equal to a month's salary at every higher level would improve problem-solving and governance speed and efficiency enormously.

Our public sector enterprises, which could have been shining models of industry, are often depressing examples of how not to run a business. Hota highlights what ails them and how sincerity and dedication can find creative ways to turn around even the most hopeless cases, if the will is there, with integrity of purpose.

Hota also shares three sweeping ideas - opening the governance hierarchy to lower-level departmental participation and the advice of outside subject experts and ideas of Hospital Corporation of India; and IT-enabled Saathi Centres in every Block headquarters of India to empower the common man, provide space for constructive citizen suggestions and greatly reduce information-seeking litigation and issues of access. I commend these ideas to the highest levels of government for consideration.

Mrs Almitra H. Patel M.S. ((MIT) USA

Member, Supreme Court Committee for Solid Waste Management.

National Expert, Swachh Bharat Mission.

www.almitrapatel.com

Introductory

India Ably Served - Good Governance - Secrets of an IAS Karmayogi

The book is an interesting story of a wise and pragmatic bureaucrat who has no grudge against the given political set up and its leadership. In various narratives, the author has shown how one can still work in the existing steel frame of administration with efficiency and effectiveness – indeed a path breaking leader showing the way to future generation of bureaucrats. The book is all for bringing Good Governance to the central stage of Indian Administrative System with efficiency and effectiveness as its key drivers.

Be it Mashal (Fire Stick) rally of students of Ravenshaw College, high voltage Industrial Relations incident involving death of a workman in Steel Melting Shop (SMS) of Rourkela Steel Plant or flood management with MLA, MP & Revenue Minister of Odisha, or piloting in RBI and SBI a near-impossible loan for a PSU in distress, clearing backlog files in the house of Union Minister of Health, the author has demonstrated how "out of box action" swings the situation from adversity to positivity. Rightly in his book he has diagnosed meticulous planning and hard work are the mantras for success. It is result-oriented work and more work for the people that give him the energy.

As a turn around manager he could revive SIL, HEC, Housing Board and other five PSUs where he had worked and as an outstanding bureaucrat, he achieved excellence in Public Service, no wonder JRD Tata wanted to airlift him to include in his team and latter he got Knighthood.

Replete with anecdotes and quaint situations, the book once read will make you read it more and more. Each of his career experience is a treasure house of learning lessons, his words of advice, "one should be above reward and insult in career" will continue to ring in the ears of bureaucrats and corporate leaders when they achieve success or meet failure.

Dr. T.K. Chand,
Former Chairman,
NALCO

CONTENTS

1

INTRODUCTION

It is my avowed belief that Good Governance –GG– is the missing headline in Indian democratic discourse and GG will yet come from dedicated group dynamics of a team effort by civil servants –serving and retired- led by political leaders, supported by multiple of professionals in Government, Public and Private sector of India. In turn, the civil servants must not see themselves as the high priests of GG, but as creators and facilitators of a countrywide process to draw out the lessons in GG and create a multiple set of platforms-preferably e-platforms- for the dynamic and continuous unfolding of GG to serve the wide and varied strata of Indian society enabling it to reach its optimum potential.

The biggest challenge to fast-tracking GG is the inability and unwillingness of top-notch IAS officials to come together and believe in and operationalize GG as one of the topmost Agenda for the rapid development of our country. IAS, a senior colleague had once remarked jokingly, hunts alone not in packs. In the final stages of a career in IAS, most of the officers tend to forget group action and principles of merit. The lure of 'important' postings and the possibility of post-retirement jobs corrode many. Many Secretaries and officers of different Departments bring about a lot of changes, in working methods, etc. in their respective work fields which contribute piece-meal to GG. However, there is no coordinated effort by a group; there is no wide participation in creating a process of GG or 'reforms'. I understand that the Central Government has now created Groups of Secretaries to deliberate and improve coordination between the Departments. It is a very welcome step. I hope there is a specific Group of Secretaries constituted for Governance Reforms. Economists trained abroad with very limited experience of implementation continue to be the High priests and pronounce on the required 'reforms' which refer mostly to bank rates, taxes, foreign investment liberalization, and the like. These are important issues, but these contribute only in a limited manner to improving 'GG'.

Independence and Expectations

India gained its freedom from its colonial rulers; there was heightened expectation from the Government. However, nascent India had huge challenges and limited resources. Its mining, railways, shipping, automobile, communication, food production, availability of potable water, heavy and light engineering sector, technology, education, health indices, particularly high MMR and IMR combined with high birth rate threw up tremendous challenges. The intelligentsia of the country was trained more in Non-Cooperation with Administration, and the Administration was trained in denial mode, and was oriented to maintain the status quo. The Five Year Plans were an expression of the determination of leadership for planned and rapid development in the desired sectors. However, the implementation of successive Plans showed a lot of failure in the administrative machinery. The growth of the population overtook and exposed the deficiencies of all development work. Control-Permit Raj prevailed in the name of equity.

Ghosts of the Bade Sahib

I may be permitted some facile categorizations to bring to the readers a flavour of the time. The first 8 years after 1950, the 'Bade Sahibs' continued to head administration. The next 8 years saw 'Sahibs' continuing by clinging to the stiff upper lip era of the predecessors. The next 8 years saw some better availability of resources to implement schemes, and officers still ruled. However, the politicians had started asserting themselves and particularly after 1967 when the hegemony of

Congress got challenged in elections in different States, the new breed of politicians started calling the shots in administration. The next 8 years saw officers facing distinct diminution of stature; administrative powers definitely had to be exercised under political supervision. It was followed by the proliferation of 'Civil society' institutions- the NGOs, who demanded a share in public resources and lobbied for accountability-answers from Administration leading eventually to the 'Right to Information Act'. Later Coalition Governments in the Centre and some States made life difficult for officers. Finally, the prevalent atmosphere of graceless and combative federalism has made life impossible for officers of some cadre these days. However, the expectation from the people still is that the IAS should, must and will deliver.

I am writing this book to plead for better governance in which the civil servants definitely have a role. So, instead of a textbook on the theory of Governance, my book will be a discussion how Governance must give way to Good Governance in India, Notwithstanding the onslaught from febrile Political system, unaccountable Judicial system, competition from the private sector, Civil Societies and Consultants of different hues, the civil servants can still work in cohesion to facilitate the creation of goods and services in volume and improve the delivery of public services, particularly for the large segment of common people,

The 'I' Syndrome

There will be an autobiographical note as I unfold my views on GG.

One thinks to a great extent within the context of one's life. Therefore, I shall initially start with my background as a person and then go on to analyse GG at each stage of my career as an IAS officer and more so in the concluding chapters of my career. My holistic thoughts on GG evolved and took shape in the last few years of my work-life after my retirement from Government service.

The I.A.S. suffers inevitably from the 'I' syndrome; I could also be a victim of this even if I deride its excesses. The reason is that the narration to be authentic, has to be told as I saw it. I have to be forgiven for referring to my experience excessively.

My caveat is that 'I' would never mean I alone. It is always Teamwork and utilizing valuable lessons learnt from other stalwarts in the Government, Public and Private sectors. Knowledge and analytical skills acquired from competent Bankers and Chartered Accountants in the early stages of my career benefitted me immensely. I learnt from many bold and public-spirited civil servants and personalities beyond the IAS. I have tried to acknowledge the lessons I have learnt in the respective chapters of my narration. However, I want to acknowledge two stalwarts of Odisha cadre [there could be many more, I am only recording here with whom I worked]. Mr Gyan Chand taught me the lesson of coming to meetings thoroughly prepared. Mr. Rabi N. Das never had a file on his table whenever I entered the chamber of the Chief Secretary. His speed of disposal of files and the ability to judge the calibre of a colleague were remarkable. In the Central Government I came across many inspiring persons. The most inspiring mentor was Dr. APJ Kalam who somehow developed a liking for me and would ring me up over RAX occasionally.

In fact, I was always considered the simpleton among eight siblings. My mother despaired whether I could cope with adult life. So, I have no inherent credential to brag.

I have to be forgiven further if I state that the 'I' element in my narration could still be visible too often because of the inefficiency that pervaded most of the governance as I saw it around me in my career-mediocrity masquerading in the guise of 'brilliance' which hated to be challenged and stifled dissent. Quite a few colleagues covered their unproductivity through PR skills. Some others made a fetish of their 'honesty' and delayed all decision making indefinitely. In the Public and Government sector, our traditional governance stops often at granting 50% weightage to Merit, and the rest to nepotism or such other non-merit considerations.

Merit Quota

An anecdote will set the tone of my book; Mr. D.P. Bagchi IAS (1966) of Odisha cadre got posted as Joint Secretary in the Department of Commerce in the '80s. Many happy younger and contemporary colleagues from Odisha cadre in Delhi rushed to my eldest brother, Mr. Purna Chandra Hota IAS [1962] to ask him about this miracle – Mr. Bagchi's posting in the coveted Commerce Department- happened [posting in 'important Departments in Government of India was then believed to be entirely based on lobbies and nepotism]. My eldest brother is a born raconteur. He said, "I understand that the young Prime Minister [Rajiv Gandhi] apparently has said, 'We have many kinds of quotas in India; let there be also a 'merit' quota'; Bagchi might have 'sneaked in' through this." We burst into laughter. Two years passed, Mr. Bagchi was transferred from Commerce to the 'less glamorous' Dept. of Personnel a. More or less the same group of colleagues again rushed to Sri P.C. Hota and asked him for an explanation for this unsavoury and unusual transfer. This time the eldest brother looked at us straight and rolled his eyes in despair and said triumphantly - "You boys are immature to understand Delhi! This is the ultimate proof that Bagchi was initially posted on merit quota. Merit does not survive for long in India!!"... On with my story!

2

GOOD GOVERNANCE

Good Governance has now international connotation and nuances. We must discuss ab initio what is meant by the phrase – Good Governance! However, while delineating the current discourse, I shall try to accord my own emphasis to what the standard texts on Good Governance pronounce.

The notions of Governance and GG have developed simultaneously. After the 1980s, the discourse on Governance [G] started emerging. And as soon as G started getting discussed GG became the paradigm. As observed by Prof. Ninad Shankar Nag and as felt by me personally throughout my career "… sovereign state finds it difficult to admit any fault in its own political and government system and to recognize its failure to achieve." But the discourse on GG emerged from policy intrusions made by the international institutions dealing with development aid under the euphemism of 'structural adjustments'. The disintegration of the former Soviet Union and the pro-democracy efforts elsewhere in the world brought to centrality the inherent incompetence and limitation of paraStatal institutions and bureaucracies to manage the human and economic resources of the country in an efficient and effective way. It is unfortunate that Indian intellectuals had to wait for foreign multinationals to lay down a discourse for defining Good Governance. While, there was piece-meal study of reforms in some sector, and while the voice against corruption and residual feudal trimmings of bureaucratic and political arrogance of Administration in its interface with citizens in day to day administration got talked and written about there was no attempt of an Indian discourse on GG to the best of my knowledge.

World Bank Discourse on Good Governance

The World Bank set out its definition of governance. This term is defined as **"the manner in which power is exercised in the management of a country's economic and social resources for development"**.

The essence of good governance was described as predictable, open and enlightened policy, together with a bureaucracy imbued with a professional ethos and an executive arm of government accountable for its actions. All these elements were to be present in a strong civil society participating in public affairs, where all members of the society act under the rule of law.

Elements of Good Governance

Good governance comprises the existence of effective mechanisms, processes and institutions through which citizens and groups articulate their interests, exercise their legal rights, meet their obligations and mediate their differences. Its essential characteristics are mentioned by World Bank as:

a. **Participation.** All men and women should have a voice in decision-making, either directly or through legitimate intermediate institutions that represent their interests. Such broad participation is built on freedom of association and speech, as well as on the capacity to participate constructively.

b. **Rule of Law.** Legal frameworks should be fair and enforced impartially, particularly the laws on human rights.

c. **Transparency.** This concept is built on the free flow of information. Processes, institutions and information should be directly accessible to those concerned, and enough information should be provided to render them understandable and monitorable.

d. **Responsiveness.** Institutions and processes should serve all stakeholders.

e. **Consensus orientation.** Good governance should mediate differing interests in order to reach a broad consensus on the best interests of the group and, where possible, on policies and procedures.

f. **Equity.** All men and women should have equal opportunity to maintain or improve their well-being.

g. **Effectiveness and efficiency.** Processes and institutions should produce results that meet needs while making the best use of resources.

h. **Accountability.** Decision-makers in government, the private sector and civil society organizations should be accountable to the public as well as to institutional stakeholders. This accountability differs depending on the organization and whether the decision is internal or external to an organization.

i. **Strategic vision.** Leaders and the public should have a broad and long-term perspective on good governance and human development, together with a sense of what is needed for such development. There should also be an understanding of the historical, cultural and social complexities in which that perspective is grounded.

It shall be my argument throughout this book that point (g)- 'Effectiveness and Efficiency' should be the single-most paradigm determining even the outcome of all other elements mentioned from (a) to (i) above. It is time that Indian governance discourse has the confidence to create its own emphasis amongst the various elements of GG bandied about by international institutions. We should catch the bull by the horn; an all-round improvement in efficiency will pave the way to all other elements of GG.

3

STUDENT DAYS

I was somewhat of a 'miracle' child -ever sickly and unimpressive in demeanour. I was so sick at the age of 6 years that after a prolonged bout of typhoid lasting about two months and then dysentery, I could not even stand erect; I had to crawl on all four like an eight-month-old baby. I never studied from Class 1 to class 3. I was provisionally admitted to Class-IV. I started indifferently; I got one tight slap from Purohit Sir, wetted my shorts, and stopped going to the school. It took some time for my father to discover this due to the large number of siblings crowding home. He brought four thin books 32 pages each, and each costing four annas [1/4th of a rupee]. The year was 1954. I was 8 years old. These were stories of the lives of great Odia leaders. He handed these to me and ran his hand affectionately through the hair on my head. The miracle took place; I devoured the words in the slim books again and again, and roamed around in our own home, and in the homes of neighbours, etc. for more storybooks. I was hooked on reading. I read whatever came my way. In the half-yearly examination I topped in the class and seldom looked back. I owe everything to my father, a stern disciplinarian; however, he never used a harsh word when I used to fall sick [I did not study entire Class V and then Class IX] and he tended to me in all my sickness. I owe a lot to my eldest brother Mr. P. C. Hota (who retired as Chairman of UPSC) who was the Role-Model in the family and spent considerable time getting me good books, encyclopaedias and guided me all through. I am beholden to my mother who always secretly thought and asserted to her close friends that I was a gifted child even when I used to be bedridden for months sometimes; equally kind and nurturing was my eldest sister Smt. Bijay Laxmi Senapati who would get me a storybook each afternoon when she returned from school;

I studied in an Odia medium school, Mission School of Cuttack town. The school was known for its prowess in sports and not in scholastics. Occasionally a star would shine forth – Mr. J.P. Das, IAS, one of the most outstanding IAS officers and winner of innumerable literary awards was an illustrious alumnus. I used to be compared by persons who liked me with J.P. Sir; I used to be always thrilled though I knew clearly that the 'Imitation' can never be as good as the 'Original'. I owe a lot to teachers of Christ Collegiate School like Sunil Patnaik Sir, Choudhury sir and Head Master Sri R.L Roy and Sri Chandra Sekhar Mishra who wrote the delectable poem 'Bahuda Bije'.

My first college was Stewart Science College, which perhaps never had a student with my high marks; Ravenshaw College was the College of choice for good students. I immensely benefitted due to each of the faculty lavishing attention and affection on me. Prof. Bimalendu Mohanty, handsome with a mercurial in temper doted on me and ensured that I never strayed into bad company. I did very well in Science stream and minus the 'fourth optional' I topped in the University. It was 1962; the I.A.S. results were out, and my brother Mr. P. C. Hota was selected for IAS. His name was announced in Radio as he was amongst the Best Ten rank holders. Immediately, I saw a shift in the balance of glamour in our home which was dominated till then by cousins and brother-in-law- all Civil Engineers. Sri Kashi Pradhan, attached to my father as Orderly Peon, explained, "Hey, hey; till now 'Babu's used to come home, now Collector Sahib will come." I was selected for I.I.T. (Kharagpur); I did not join and changed over to the Humanities stream and in Ravenshaw College to follow my eldest brother's footsteps. Ravenshaw then was the hub of intellectual excellence in Odisha; we students without access to important and up to date books etc. still thought that we were the centre of the world. And we were full of gumption.

After, topping in B.A. (Honours) in Political Science from Utkal University, I went over to the University of Delhi. Political Science was not the chosen subject of the best students of the University of Delhi; History, English and Physics apart from Economics were the more glamorous subjects. We were not to be denied; the Ravenshaw group in Delhi in Political Science soon became visible in all activities of the University. I was awarded the only Post-graduate scholarship. And then to Jubilee Hall, a veritable Civil Servant producing 'hostel' as I became a lecturer in Sri Ram College of Commerce, Delhi University with a princely salary of Rs. 728/- per month. The 'hostel' charges including food was about Rs. 130/-; the rest was spent in Coffee House, on friends etc.

Then the Civil Service examination! Late Himachal Som [later IFS] saw me at the desk in the Dholpur House examination hall of UPSC with the roll number 902. His illustrious friend had the roll number 901. I distinctly remember the look of pity on Himachal's face. True to his ebullient nature, he blurted out, "Hota, I feel sorry for you. My friend Singh is so brilliant that the examiner who will go through his answer sheets first will find your answers 'pedestrian' in comparison. You may suffer." I did not benefit from his sagacious advice; I did not fill up the forms for the Civil Service examination of the next year even though the last date for doing so got over before the IAS results were out. I also figured in the Best Ten list of that year's civil service examination; my mother, Smt. Basanti Devi heard my name over the radio and promptly got up from her sick-bed and climbed up each flat of the three-storied housing complex [no lift] and informed all eleven other households about my selection.

In spite of my promise to be brief about my personal life, I have recounted the studentship days in some detail. The purpose is to cull out a lesson – you are limited by your own thinking and lack of effort, not by the limitations of your circumstances! If you put in the planning, hard work, and keep your mind open to absorb new knowledge from all around, you are bound to do well. The other part of the lesson was that I did exceptionally well in the subjects for which I devoted attention; I performed abysmally in two papers where I was over-confident and under-prepared. This has been the running lesson of my life later also-planning and preparations have generally been rewarded; cockiness or overconfidence has often had a negative cost adversely.

An important Issue In Examination Reform:

Stray lessons in Good Governance would pop up as my tale unfolds. Here are some thoughts on examination reforms. The IAS is a career; each year a hundred may qualify ultimately. But to imagine that each year about 15 lakh students get obsessed with this job, makes me feel bad as a socially responsible person.

A colossal waste of young trained manpower during their productive youthful years is taking place in our country; and the politicians pathetically over-dependent [often without real electoral gain] on 'appeasement' are abetting the process unwittingly. The age limit for appearing in Civil Service is now from 21 to 32- and even more for other categories OBC[35] and SC/ST [37], physically handicapped [42]. And the number of chances permitted for Civil Service is 6 for the general category and up to 9 for some others. It is similar for recruitment to Public Sector undertakings and Banks etc. There are cases where a person joined IPS/Income Tax etc., and after spending 3 years in that Service, he joins IAS wasting all his experience only to retire ahead of his peers in the last stages of his IAS career feeling frustrated and contributing only a little to GG.

A worse situation is in Medical Education where there is no limit of age or chances for post-graduate courses. To produce a MBBS doctor costs a substantial amount of time and money – to him and the public exchequer. India is woefully short in doctors in many parts of the country. Yet these MBBS doctors after qualifying as doctors, instead of working sincerely and seriously, neglect their duties and keep on mugging textbooks [leading to deskilling in terms of practical hands-on experience vital to becoming a good doctor] to go on appearing in examinations for postgraduate seats in lucrative specializations.

Sad Story of MBBS

I was once invited by Dr. M.L. Jain, then Director of State Institute of Health & Family Welfare of Rajasthan to interact with twenty-eight new MBBS doctors who were recruited for State Medical Cadre of Rajasthan. I was alone with all these new recruits and chatted with them rather than delivering a speech. Soon they opened up. I asked them about choosing a career in Government. Barring older three, 25 young -each one of them- unhesitatingly said that they joined Government for special quota in PG seats, and that they would get leave of two months and eleven days. They have joined only to prepare for PG examination while getting a salary with less work. It is a pattern all across India leading to colossal waste. And our Public Health experts keep on spewing data of UNICEF and WHO, and some bureaucrats and leaders keep shedding crocodile tears about the shortage of doctors in the Public Health system in India.

I suggest that the age for appearing for the entrance examination to MBBS for all categories be reduced to 21 and 29 for PG. There are now enough successful students in all reserved categories to appear in the examinations and fill up the seats; thus there is no social cause served by stretching the age and number of chances. So also in Civil Services etc.; the entry age should be from 21 t0 25 for all Services and all categories [may be 28 for reserved categories], and chances limited to two for general category and 3 for all others.

4

TRAINING ACADEMY

The 'Training' Academy at Mussoorie was our first foray into bureaucracy. The training of IAS in our time was good, not great. A lot of improvement has taken place since then. However, the training does not emphasize on preparing a civil servant in life skills, in positive public relations, in the art of measured and polite conversation, in virtues of silence in handling sometimes a ranting politician and raving mobs; the training in 'attitude' is never considered important though it is as much needed as knowledge of rules regulations etc. Generally, not even one hour formally is spent in inculcating "the value of a smiling face for a civil servant even in most trying conditions". As an IAS officer, one picks up these by oneself through observation and introspection – sometimes, from mistakes of oneself and of other officials too, sometimes from the success of seniors etc. However, sometimes years pass and wrong impressions are created which take unnecessary time and energy to correct. Many of us are fresh from Universities when we enter the IAS; it takes a while to understand that we have become responsible officers. Training and discipline are serious matters. We are already being paid to be a full-fledged civil servant. OLQ – officer like qualities are sometimes referred to, but no genuine formal discussions take place. The process, however, could have taken much lesser time. At the Academy stage , a well crafted set of structured learning inputs should form part of the curriculum. These inputs must aim at helping the officers (both probationers ad later the mid level officers coming for refresher training) to understand better the roles and expectations of all stake holders of governance, particularly the common people. Breaking in the colt/filly to become a race horse is not an easy task! However, the training in Academy was and is very important; it needs continuous improvement to keep probationers as well as in-service officers abreast of new challenges to GG. The training in the Academy was coupled with 'field' postings at cutting edge levels like becoming a BDO or a Tahsildar for four to six months and then returning to Academy for a final spell of training. I appreciate the improvements in the Academy to improve both the content and methods of Training. However, GG never permits resting on laurels; it works on the axiom that even 'best' can be done better, and improvement need not be swaddled in clothes of finality, it must lend itself to continuous introspection and churning to remain fresh.

The First Job & Early Training- Study Abroad: I was posted as Charge Officer, in Berhampur, Odisha in the then Ganjam-Koraput Settlement Office. It was not a very busy job; I toured extensively to interior regions of Koraput and Ganjam Districts. However, like my childhood in Ganjam district, this spell in Berhampur also affected my health quite adversely. I suffered from indigestion continuously and lost a lot of weight. So, in about a year, I applied and got selected for a scholarship in East-West Centre at Honolulu, Hawaii. I went to Honolulu, joined the University of Hawaii for a Master's program in Public Administration. The democratic culture prevalent in the University life of U.S.A.; the access to unlimited number world-class reading materials, and above all, the freedom from diseases caused by petty infections which ruled my life in India all these combined to shape and broaden my approach to life and provided me a platform for continued intellectual curiosity about life and knowledge in general; it made me also a bit of non-conformist in later bureaucratic career. I could go into details about my American experience; but, I don't want to lose focus on the main issue of GG. It may suffice to give my readers a sample of the source of my non-conformism. One of the required course works in my course on Governance was to read Ken Kesey's epical book, "One Flew Over The Cuckoo's Nest" and write out a thousand-word critique on the book. This book was turned into an Oscar-winning movie by the same name, with Jack Nicholson running away with the Honours. It is a brilliant exposition of how petty officials seek power over the clients for whom the organizations have been set up by monopolizing interpretation of the rules basically to concede as little benefit as possible to the clients.

Nine months of secondment during this period from University of Hawaii to pursue MBA courses at Columbia University, New York expanded my intellectual horizons further. However, it also awakened me to the disparities that existed in American society between the rich and the poor and the simmering tension between races. There were other lessons too – some quaint, some enriching. The work ethics and discipline in American Government as well as private offices was remarkable; there was no moment of easygoingness. Even in the Universities, the required Coursework was heavy and demanded utmost diligence. There was interpersonal informality that released my mind from trappings of feudalism; but at the work output point, everything was formal and rigorous.

MBA and Tropic of Capricorn

MBA classes of Columbia University demanded utmost hard work and careful devotion to Course work to maintain 'A' grade. The library of Columbia University was a revelation. It had in its archives even a handwritten manuscript of John Locke – the great English philosopher of Liberalism. I may be pardoned for a digression- this is about the deprivation of authentic books and materials to the then Indian middle class (1960-70) leading some times to hilarious consequences. An extreme example may suffice. One day, during Delhi University days, a friend got hold of a slim book with a green/blue cheap cover. with the title of 'Tropic of Capricorn, the author- Henry Miller, an avant-garde novelist known for his controversial novels, Tropic of Cancer and Tropic of Capricorn. The friend scoffed at our praising Henry Miller and said that it was outright pornographic writing. Some of us aspiring to literary pretensions borrowed the book and read it trying to discover any literary value. It was borrowed by a senior who joined IAS earlier to us. He commented- "Great literary work, though controversial"! This remark broke us up into peals of laughter. We all knew that the books of Henry Miller were banned in the USA on grounds of obscenity. The matter rested there, till one day while studying at Columbia University, I had free time in between my class schedules, and I went into the library. I read up on some serious course material, and then got bored. Then it struck me that perhaps, I was too young in college, and might have lacked the required perspicacity to appreciate good literature. So I decided to have another foray into 'Tropic of Capricorn'. The book came; it was hard-bound and quite substantial in girth, I picked it up with some curiosity, checked the title and author and launched into it. What a fabulous piece of un-putdown-able literature!! It did have some graphic scenes and language; but, by no stretch of imagination, it could be called pornographic. It was indeed a literary magnum-opus. I was puzzled about this; soon the mystery was solved. One evening, I was in Central New York, I walked into a small store selling newspapers, cigarettes, condiments and the like; also some magazines and thin books with blue/green cover. I looked at the books; these had various titles including Tropic of Capricorn. It was the same classy pornography book of my classmate, which had adorned the drawing room book self of his illustrious brother. It then struck me how naïve we were; taking advantage of the ban on Henry Miller, some spurious books have been in circulation; and we in Delhi in 1967, read these bluff stuff and discussed its literary merit.

Internship: I worked as an 'Intern' in the State Government of Hawaii for four months. The experience of my days in the USA opened my eyes to the possibilities of much better goods and services that the mass of people can enjoy through superior technology and organizational skills. The discipline and accuracy of the public processes in the USA were remarkable. Discipline was subtly but firmly emphasized upon, but not through the feudalistic approach but through accountability. I was yet to fully understand my role as a 'public servant in India'. Going on deputation on this scholarship created first murmurs of a larger perception of what public service could be; my basic non-conformist instincts got a fillip on my return to India to my IAS career.

5

MY FIRST REAL JOB: DEFINING MOMENT OF MY CAREER

On my return from the USA in 1974, I was posted as Sub-Collector to Rourkela. My work limits included the Steel City; but, truly speaking my work was more in rural Blocks. My first recollection of the job is that one day, a law and order situation arose. The Dy. S. P. came to me saying that ADM was away; people along with local shopkeepers have become unruly and have created barricades to obstruct the main road. I was relatively new and without a clue. However, from the imploring words of Dy. S.P., I could understand that I was expected to bring the situation under control. I arrived at the scene; there was a restive crowd raising slogans against high-handedness of police. A constable had beaten up a cart puller who took a short-cut and violated the 'one-way' rule. It was 2.30 PM on a hot day of May in Rourkela; the road tar was melting and sticking to shoes. I waved my hands and asked the crowd to quiet down and explain the matter to me. I was pushed by one of the shop-keepers who did not know me from Adams for interrupting the slogans. The Police Inspector caught hold of him and warned him to behave properly with Sub Collector Sahib. I saw the cart puller sitting injured in the middle of the road, a streak of dried blood below his knee from the blow of police baton. I realized that he was the victim; all others were only concerned with their own agenda. I immediately walked to a road side 'Dhaba', got a can of water and made the cart puller drink; then I poured some water on his wound and ordered the Inspector to get me some spirit and cotton etc. In a matter of five minutes, I bandaged his wound, helped him to stand up, and got the police personnel to reload his cart with the spilled goods. I asked the offending constable to escort him to his destination removing the barricade. In less than ten minutes, people were won over and the normal life interrupted since three hours was resumed. Looking at the core of the issue and not wasting energy on auxiliaries was both my weakness and forte.

I learned a few things from my senior colleagues- both what to do and also what not to do. Each human being is unique and has his own style. I concede that; but, overall a Public Servant has to have a sense of proportion and has to be productive in essential matters within his jurisdiction. C.M. [Smt. Nandini Satpathy] came on a visit. Local leaders met her and made several requests for small and medium-size public work relating to water resources. Our Collector kept on saying that the accounts in Blocks have to be audited first to give a clear picture of money available. CM was getting exasperated. After some time she looked towards me and asked whether I could organize digging of three ponds and three wells in the 3 Blocks of my sub-division. I blurted out, "If CM wants some public work done, it will be done!" CM gave me an approving glance and told the gathering that all their requests for water sources would be attended to gradually but definitely.

I carried on my work with medium diligence. I had the habit of making quick decisions; whenever there was any large scale work involving a number of public, I would plan, mobilize my entire office and never allow long queues. And I hated procrastinations. I remember that once my 'Bench Clerk' [one who assists me when I acted as a Court] brought to me about thirty files to sign. These files were about Industrial sheds in the Industrial Estate of Rourkela. I immediately sent for the Additional Director of Industries Sri Jachak. I also requested for the Govt. Advocate Mr. B. Mishra. Both were men of calibres. I showed them the files; these have been dragging for four years. The case files were replete with meaningless noting like- 'SDO is on tour' or 'SDO is busy'. I had been to Industrial Estate and had noticed more than half of the sheds were lying closed. I discussed the matter, issued fresh show-cause notice with a date after fortnight, and requested the two colleagues to be present. On the appointed day none of the entrepreneurs of these sheds appeared. I on suggestion of Govt. Advocate granted another date. Then on the second date, again no entrepreneurs appeared. I pronounced the order of resumption in open Court. After three months or so, I visited the Industrial Estate; all closed down sheds had been re-allotted to waiting aspirants and were now humming with activities. However, I must confess that I thought that my work as Sub-Collector was routine and easy; unwittingly I must have given some signal of easy-going nature. Coupled with my unconventional manners, I was a sitting duck inviting disaster.

New Collector and Shock

The Collector was transferred; and a new senior colleague joined. He never berated me for my work or for any mannerism; but, once or twice my brother Mr. P. C. Hota [later Chairman of UPSC] who happened to be posted on deputation to the Steel Plant did pull me up for my casual manners in presence of the Collector. I should have listened to the voice of experience and wisdom. To cut the story short, I received a missive from the Revenue Divisional Commissioner to meet him. I went 200 kilometres and met him in his residence office. He looked grim and before I could gather my wits he threw a file with some papers at me, and shouted, "You are Mr. B.N. Hota's son and P.C Hota's brother!! And this is the remark you have got for your work!" I sheepishly glanced at the paper; it was my annual appraisal report. Collector had written, "He does not work hard. He does not tour adequately." I kept mum; I did not proffer any excuse or challenge Collector's assessment. I stood there with my head bowed. RDC Mr. Parija thundered, "You better improve. I am giving you three months' time. I shall be watching you. If you do not improve, I shall add worse remarks and send it up."

I stumbled out of the residence office of RDC feeling utterly ashamed of myself. Believe it or not, I felt no resentment against my Collector Sri P.K. Mishra. I never felt that he was unfair to me. On reaching Rourkela I was like a man possessed. I threw myself into work with my heart and soul. Instead of the routine approach to work,

Worshipping Work

I started taking pains to get into every detail, increased my touring, went into every aspect of my tasks increased the speed of my disposal. My tour notes became meticulous and included clear action points for follow up. At this point, a severe drought struck my sub-division and ordinary people – mostly tribal- were in dire straits for food grain and water. I visited each Panchayat of each Block, the B.D.O. generally accompanied me. We looked at every water source. There were good wells dug from earlier programs; but, in many villages the villagers did not use these wells mostly thinking that these wells did not belong to them. So, I held small impromptu meetings with some of the villagers, particularly women, parlayed with them, carried out some overhauling and repairs and handed over the wells ceremonially to the villagers. Thus with the minimum expenditure about two thousand wells were resurrected and put to use augmenting the water supply. The poor used to sell to 'country' liquor dealer wheat grain assistance given to them to tide over the hard time, and drink low quality alcohol in empty stomach and suffer badly health-wise. It took some doing to break this practice. All around things improved, lives, particularly of elderly male were saved.

Two months after the declaration of drought, during which I toured the interior areas extensively and improved the water sources and the public distribution system in each Panchayat, the names location and details of all work and task points were on the tip of my tongue due to constant familiarization, a 'review' meeting of the status of the drought and the measures taken was held by RDC. In the first hour, he focused on my subdivision and went on questioning me on each detail in the official Status Paper placed before him, and even beyond. My hard work of day and night paid off; I answered all questions with alacrity. After about fifty minutes of grilling, RDC looked at the Collector sitting by his side and remarked, "The young man seems to have improved and is doing some good work! What do you say?" The Collector gave a slight smile and nodded ascent. So, my career was saved. It was not only saved, but, then on I became a workaholic. I started enjoying productive work and got a 'kick' out of hard work and taking up challenges.

Public Servant

I stumbled onto the golden lesson of how to be an excellent IAS officer- one must be energetic round the clock, never tire of serving people and enjoy small and big achievements which help people.

My work life as an IAS Officer truly began. Work, more work, systematic work, vigorous management of public assets at my disposal to produce goods and services for people became the core of my personality. The more I worked, the more focused and energetic I began to feel. I had arrived at the work scene as a public official and I started taking immense pleasure in solving difficult problems, producing voluminous results, and being of use to people and my area. And as I had no indulgences like alcohol or tobacco etc. and was frugal in my eating habits, I could manage the self-invited heavy workload without falling sick in spite of my general frail health. My non-conformism in manners towards seniors reduced; but my interaction with my juniors remained slightly unconventional. I never pulled my rank; humour was my major tool to build up teamwork. Humour also helped in public situations including law and order when carefully used.

At this juncture, the Collector rang me up one day and said, "Congratulations! You have been transferred and posted as Managing Director of IPICOL." I had no clue as to what was IPICOL. But I realized from the next sentence of Mr. Mishra, that the posting was something to look forward to as he blurted out "I am jealous. Many of us looked forward to this post."

6

MANAGING DIRECTOR IPICOL

And I was off to Bhubaneswar, the State Capital to join my new assignment. IPICOL was the new Corporation of the State Government to boost the industrialization of Odisha There was a Chairman of IPICOL. He knew a lot about 'Who's Who' of Industry and Investment Banks like IDBI, IFCI and ICICI. IPICOL was supposed to be the catalyst, promote and implement an entrepreneur-friendly Industrial Policy with various incentives, and selective limited equity and loan participation in the proposed new industries. IPICOL was also the friend, philosopher and guide of the entrepreneur- from arranging infrastructure like land water electricity etc., arranging tie-up of his raw materials and so on. IPICOL was also to carry out first stage appraisal and was to help in preparing a feasibility report. IPICOL was also to plead for the financing of the Project before IDBI etc. in a professional manner through a twelve years cash flow analysis. My brilliant predecessor had assembled a fine team of professionals-engineers, M.B.A.s with loan appraisal experience. Three outstanding colleagues were Mr. G.C. Das an Odisha Administrative Service Officer who was so balanced and meticulous that one could always benefit from his sagacious advice. The other was Mr. Niranjan Mohanty from IIM, Ahmadabad. The third brilliant colleague was Mr. L. N. Barik who was an outstanding Civil Engineer of the State Government on deputation to IPICOL. The first ten days in IPICOL were all Greek and Latin to me; I did not know all that the Chairman was rolling out for me. IDBI, etc. were all strange acronyms. Somehow I survived by remaining silent and taking extra briefings from all colleagues. After a month, I gradually got on top of such difficult categories like discounted cash flow analysis, IRR-internal rate of return, capital to output ratio, and the various parameters for a Feasibility Report. I poured myself into all financial newspapers, magazines etc. Often in the career of a Generalist such challenges come up. It is better to admit the gap in knowledge and get proper and extra briefing rather than maintain a pose and distance from staff and be found wanting later.

IPICOL was a big challenge. Everywhere I went in the first month to meet seniors in the Secretariat; I found many indulging in back-biting about others IAS colleagues. Remaining silent and focusing on work-related issues was my best strategy. The extreme nature of some personalities left me stunned – some bluffed outright and instead of disposing of the matter before them, talked tall and postponed decisions on our matters waiting on their table. Most personally greeted me warmly, but spoke disparagingly of IPICOL. [There was an IDCOL with a non-IAS go-getter influential MD heading Industrial PSUs who looked at the emergence of IPICOL with disfavour.] IPICOL had a powerful Board of Directors; most of the important Secretaries of State were in the Board, like Secretary to CM, Industry, Finance, Revenue Secretary, Chairman Electricity Board, Chairman IDCOL, MD State Finance Corporation [OSFC]. Barring MD OSFC, the brilliant Mr. Girish Patra, I found most other colleagues stuck in the past stance of the then typical IAS governance - say 'No' to every proposal. Frankly, I found most senior colleagues warm towards me but not warm to the task of rapid development of the State. They were resistant to change per se, whether good or bad. Odisha was and is still to a great extent considered a less developed State, not particularly attractive to industrial entrepreneurs. All discourse on Odisha started with the same cliché- that it was a rich State with poor people. It had some good deposit of industrial minerals including precious metals like chrome, nickel, iron, aluminium, and coal etc. However, there had been only 36 large industries in Odisha from 1950 t0 1975. There was definitely a chance to do much more. However, the main stumbling block for rapid industrialization was the out-dated bureaucratic procedures, lack of cohesive action by the senior bureaucracy to improve infrastructure and fast-tracking decisions. Allotment of land from the Government for an industry was a herculean task. It made me once blurt out before CM in a review meeting that Revenue Department was manned by Kauravas – "We shall not part with an inch ['suchyagre medini'] of land without a battle-royal"- What is popularly known as 'Ease of Doing Business', was almost non-existent in Odisha. India was opening up; the competition amongst States to attract new Industries to their own State was tremendous. Odisha was a late starter. If by chance, a couple of proposals passed the muster from our Board, as there was practically no delegation of powers to IPICOL, our proposals would have go to the Government from table to table of different Departments for months. It was quite frustrating; on one hand getting a reputed industrialist to come to Odisha, and if any one showed some interest, then to pilot the proposal through the labyrinth of 'No' saying officialdom.

New Industrial Policy and the Old Bosses

I tried to formulate and put up a New Industrial Policy for the State to be adopted by the Government with some schemes for incentives and some delegation of powers to IPICOL so that decision could be faster. CM was quite keen for industrialization and chaired the meeting. I noticed this in the early phase of my career – the officialdom predominantly leaned towards status quo; the political leaders wanted development as they had to talk about their achievements to the people for votes. We tabled the proposals for further delegation of financial powers to IPICOL from the prevailing Rs. five lakh to only Rs. 15 lakh. This first proposal immediately met with resistance from Mr. B.K. Mishra IAS, Additional Development Commissioner, who always came to meetings reading each word of the agenda. He was the terror for the younger group; some colleagues senior to me but relatively young often came to meetings without preparation. They were easy targets for the brilliant Sri Mishra who had a sharp wit and an acidic tongue. So, Mr. Mishra was accustomed to dominate all large review or policy meetings. He explained to CM- "Madam, if Rs. fifteen lakh's power is delegated to IPICOL, then with another fifteen lakh by entrepreneur and Public

Issue and Loan, an Industry of about Rs. two crore could come up in the State without knowledge of Government." Promptly, I raised my hand, CM looked at me and I blurted out, "Ma'am, Government wants Industries or 'knowledge' of industries?" The gauntlet was thrown and the battle began. There were about four other Ministers and more than a dozen Secretaries. I was the junior most; in fact, the next colleague was at least eight years my senior. Mr. Mishra vehemently persisted, "Government has to examine so many aspects." I didn't give up, I said, 'Ma'am, all important Secretaries are on IPICOL's Board. Only Additional Development commissioner is not there. He could be in IPICOL'S Board for a single window clearance." I made this statement in all earnestness. However, the venerable Mr. Mishra- eighteen years my senior- was not amused. He shouted, "Ma'am, I have never been insulted like this before; I cannot continue in this meeting. He is daring to suggest that I am angling to be on his Board." He flounced out of the meeting. CM immediately intervened, shouted at me and said, "Hey, Prasanna, you don't know how to talk! Sit down! Yes, please record that what Sri Hota has said is the decision. Someone go and get Mr. Mishra back." That became the leitmotif of the entire meeting. The next agenda met with similar objection; I again replied aggressively. CM again shouted at me and said, "Prasanna, you don't know how to talk. Sit down. Yes, please record whatever Sri Hota has said is the decision." At this stage, the third agenda began; the then most powerful officer, Secretary to CM, Mr. R.K. Rath intervened and literally shouted, "You are talking so much! What new industry proposals you have put forward." I was ready for Battle unto Death. I replied, 'Sir, you were very gracious to visit IPICOL the day before and give us valuable guidance. We really have not been able to do much. However, the two large new industry proposals we sent are gathering dust on your table since the last six months." At this, CM could not restrain her mirth; she laughed and said, "Prasanna, again, you do not know manners. Anyway, let it be recorded that Hota's proposals are accepted and the entire Policy brought before the High Power Committee stands approved." More than the new Industrial Policy, the meeting marked the end of a feudal era of Official Meetings. The discussions became multilateral; participation based on preparation was permitted. After a month of maintaining sulky demeanour, Chief Secretary Sri Dave, Sri B.K. Mishra and Sri R. K. Rath – all three brilliant seniors- forgave me my callow ways and lionized me in all official matters. 36 more large and medium industries came up in the State during my tenure.

Captains of Industry

In this phase of my job in IPICOL, I met several Captains of Industry like Mr Shankaran Chairman of Enfield Motor Cycles, Mr. Chowgule, [then the highest individual income tax payer] as well as a lot of top Bankers and learnt a lot from them. Most of them utilized their time purposefully, were focused on their goals and were always well prepared, I am sorry to say this – I noticed that many senior public officials, particularly the IAS were caught up in ego, sloth and lack of public purpose in their day to day work, their only preparation was to say a loud NO. Only some brilliant officers were ahead of me in thinking matters through and guided and encouraged me to improve processes to achieve industrialization of Odisha. In fact, in all through my career I found sincere, thinking and brilliant officers never felt threatened by my penchant for out of box but effective ideas; it was the mediocre group who raised apprehensions and canards about my proposals and working style.

This resolve to face opposition from powerful service seniors in course of carrying out large-scale official work stood me in good stead all through my career. However, bravery cannot be bravado; one should have burnt night oil to prepare meticulously, carry out cash flow studies, get all data tallying and ready, and remain focused on the larger vision and a Road Map of Action. CMs and PMs have the urge to achieve and so they would definitely support provided you are logical and well prepared. In retrospect, I should have been more persuasive and less aggressive; but what is done is done!

The Ministry changed. Mr. Nilamani Routray became the CM from Janata Dal. And for a few days my travails began. I carried the stigma of being the blue-eyed boy the previous CM, Mrs. Satpathy. The logic was simple, how else I was so outspoken, how so many projects were implemented and how [to some] I strutted about? This became a repetitive story of my career- the need to explain why I worked so hard and achieved during the previous government. However, each time, this would last for a short while, as the next Government also needed hard-working achievers. And, there were always some good people in society, who voluntarily came forwards, spoke to the Powers that be and restored my reputation with the new Government.

Gratitude to Good Samaritans

I must mention here some decent persons to whom I owe a great burden of gratitude, as they used their personal time to meet Powers that be, and reasoned with them to forgive my manners and look at my voluminous work. Sardar Amar Singh IAS(retired) and Sri Santok Singh- both leading doyens of Sikh community in Bhubaneswar, and both having received no personal favour from me ever, on their own initiative met Chief Secretary Mr. Dave [who was ailing, but was a humane leader and supported right causes] at his residence after my aggressive presentations in the Industrial Policy meeting and pleaded with him to see the goodness in me and my anxiety to achieve for the State as the word had started going round about my apparent non-observance of respect for seniors and that I would be 'taught' a lesson by Chief Secretary. Similarly, when Mr. Routray became the Chief Minister, my neck was in the list. I did not call on the new Chief Minister as I never thought that I was required to do so, as I was a junior person. Also, I had no specific work to plead. So I kept working in my assigned job as usual from 7 AM in the morning to 9 PM at night with some short breaks for food etc. On the fourth day, a stranger walked into my office, introducing himself as Sri P.K. Mohanty, and said that he had been watching my work, and that the State would benefit by my continuing in my job. He further added that he had access to CM; CM's son Bijayshree ji had apparently said to him that I was close to the previous Government and I should be thrown out to some insignificant post. I just looked at Mr. Mohanty and said that this was the prerogative of the Government. Sri Mohanty told me to be practical and meet CM immediately, as CM in his magnanimity was meeting one and all at his residence. I politely said that I just could not see me standing in a serpentine queue to meet CM when I had nothing to say to him.

New CM and Old Problem

Sri P. K. Mohanty didn't give up and said that at least I could phone Bijayshree and say 'Hello' to him. I yielded to him as Bijayshree studied in my school as my junior and we were marginal friends then. Mr. Mohanty phoned from my phone and made Bijayshree ji come on line. True to my ebullient nature, I started saying, "Hello, Prasanna Hota here. I understand that you think I am a bad officer." He was a bit perplexed, but said, "Why have you not come to meet my father when so many others have done?" I remember to have said that he should not tire out his father with so many visitors. But he said, 'You come!" And Mr. Mohanty true to his ability and agility smuggled me in straight to the presence of CM. Bijayshree ji was there and he introduced to me his father, "Father, this is Prasanna Hota M.D. IPICOL. He is a bright officer. He did a lot of work; he will support us now." I looked at CM; he was literally swaying with fatigue- meeting all the people continuously for three days by then. I folded my hands to him; I should have known better, but my training in becoming a seasoned officer was incomplete; I should have kept quiet. Stupidly I blurted out, "I always love to work, and I shall work hard for all development work for people." Luckily nobody made any issue of my words. Then began my second innings in IPICOL and several interesting twists and turns took place.

Bijayshree ji visited our office; I diplomatically told him that in future he could phone me and discuss anything that bothered him. But the damage was done; the news of the visit reached the ears of the Industry Minister. The Industry Minister started behaving in a hostile manner towards me. Mr. Buxi-Patra was a communist in his student days, later a socialist. But, when he became a Minister he became a Capitalist. He wanted me to be transferred. Bijayshree ji [he later became a Minister in Odisha] had become my fan due to the large number of industries promoted by IPICOL through my effort. The humane gentlemanly CM was caught between two extreme opinions about me. Mr. Routray was a seasoned administrator but had never dealt with Industry as a subject in his earlier responsibilities. He needed an independent, reliable opinion. So, he sent for one of his old acquaintances, Mr. Rungta who had a medium size concrete product unit. CM asked, "Aare Rungta, what is this IPICOL? Why is everybody talking against some Prasanna Hota there? Should he not be transferred?" Rungta ji apparently said, "You must transfer him immediately. The Industry Minister must be upset. If Hota continues there, neither the Minister nor you will benefit!" At this CM apparently smiled and said, "Our Babul [his son's nickname] has no experience of Government. Buxi Patra would not complain for nothing." Rungta ji triumphantly said, "See Sir, I told you. The Minister must be unhappy. I had been to IPICOL recently for a 'counter-guarantee' of Rs. fifty lakh for some temporary 'bridge loan' from my Bank as I had got a big order from Railways. I met the MD, Hota and gave him my written proposal with all documents. I was about to go after saying that I would be obliged for a decision within fifteen days. The MD made me sit, served me tea, read through all the papers, called his officers. They discussed some more. He asked them to issue me a 'Letter of Support'. After three days I was called by him personally over the phone to come to IPICOL with my office seal etc. I reached; documentation was done in half an hour and I was issued 'Sanction Orders' of IPICOL. If Hota does work like this without delaying matters, then nobody would come to Minster or to you. So, why keep him there? Transfer him." CM was quick to get the point. I was saved for the time being.

Chairman IDBI

However, the animosity continued, Minister kept on harping on my transfer. At this juncture Chairman IDBI came for a visit to Bhubaneswar. He was a tough personality, a seasoned banker, a thoroughly No-Nonsense type of professional. . All of us were ready the next morning at the State Guest House meeting chamber. MD IDCOL had the first chance to speak about his proposals for additional term loans for its Jute Factory, and Pig Iron projects. MD got up and said, "Huzoor, Odisha is very poor. Please bless us." Chairman IDBI was unimpressed and grilled him on the projects for fifteen minutes each, asking detailed questions on capital investment decisions, working capital details and the IRR etc. Sri Das Mahapatra again resorted to flattery, "Huzoor Maa Baap, you know everything." Chairman IDBI looked at him and said, "Come prepared. Answer questions. I am not here, some king meant to be flattered." Then came IPICOL's turn; we had four large industry finance proposals under consideration of IDBI. I remember that one was for a Calcium Carbide factory at the tribal district of Mayurbhanj. Chairman started with a statement, "Too many Calcium Carbide licenses have been issued." I immediately went up to his chair, unfolded a map, showed him the catchment area of this industry in terms of the possible consumers. As I had thoroughly studied the project report I could answer all his questions about debt service coverage ratio, the IRR, the manpower needed etc., And I added for his benefit that the proposal was viable as such; it was more so as it would be located in a Tribal district entitled to subsidies from Government of India though the proposed site was in close proximity of Jamshedpur. Chairman IDBI asked a lot of questions on other three proposals; again I was ready with all the answers as I had prepared myself thoroughly. Chairman finally beamed at me and said, "When you come next to Bombay meet me. We shall consider your proposals with an open mind."

All of us then went to the Office of CM for the formal meeting between CM and Chairman IDBI. The Chairman was aged but still a vigorous personality; he marched ahead of us, pushed open the door and started addressing CM without any preamble. Seated with CM were Industry Minister, Chief Secretary and Industry Secretary. Chairman IDBI looked at CM and boomed, "Chief Minister Sir! I was under the impression that your State was a backward State. I have now revised my opinion. As long as you have officers like Hota looking after industrialization of the State, your State has a bright future. IDBI will support your current proposals and requests you to formulate more proposals but with proper home work." CM burst into his beatific smile and looked slyly sideways at the Industry Minister who bowed his head down. Another crisis passed.

My office colleagues rejoiced. We threw ourselves day and night into professional work. At this juncture, a memorable event occurred; I had the privilege to meet Mr. J.R.D. Tata. But first story first. IPICOL tried to promote two important projects with TATA Group – a specialized Refractory project and a Sponge Iron Project. The first was a joint sector project with Belpahar Refractory Ltd, a TATA subsidiary. The project was progressing smoothly towards implementation, when an internal squabble between MD BRL and Jt. Managing Director TISCO [an ego clash, it happens in Private Sector too. One may read Iacocca by Iacocca to get a first-hand account by Lee Iacocca] held up the final investment plan. I was crestfallen; I did not know how to overcome this turn of events. The Jt. MD Tata Steel came with his officials to meet Industry Minister to convey the decision of putting on hold the investment in Refractory project. I was not called to the meeting; but, somehow I came to know of it from Sri N.K. Patnaik Chief Liaison Officer of TISCO at Bhubaneswar, a thorough gentleman. I rushed to the Industry Minister's office and pushed into his chamber; the meeting had just begun. I knew the project by heart. I started answering allaying all the anxieties of Jt. MD of TISCO about the viability of the project. Jt. MD, all said done was a top-notch professional; he did not contradict me in face of facts. Finally, he raised a legal point about obtaining a 'No objection' from the Govt. of India. I volunteered to get it within a fortnight which I did. The Industry Minister was initially uncomfortable at my bravado of entering his chamber without his permission; but, later he kept nodding assent to my submissions. After I left, he apparently said to his staff, 'Hota is really good. Only if the son of CM would not interfere with him, he would have been my asset.'

TISCO

I had some official work in Patna. I went from Bhubaneswar to Calcutta by train, and then to airport to catch a flight to Patna. In those days, so much security formality was not in vogue. I reached late and walked on the tarmac to board the plane. I noticed a tall fair gentleman surrounded by armed police going round the plane. I was bemused. Anyway, when I was sitting inside the plane this august gentleman came into the plane and occupied a seat in an empty row. He was Mr. JRD Tata who was also the Chairman of Air India's Board. The plane had only a few passengers. JRD ji was reading a newspaper. I mustered up courage. After the flight was airborne and stable, I went up to his seat to greet him. I said that I was MD of IPICOL, the State Corporation of Odisha for promoting industries. I broached the matter of investment in IPI-BEL Refractory project. He replied that there were too many refractory projects in the country already. I was ready with my data, and explained to him that only special grade refractory meant for the glass and cement industry would be produced and there was unmet demand in that catchment area for such refractory. I told him about the raw-material source, gave him details of grades and proven deposit of fire-clay, the lead and the carriage cost. He started asking me about the various financial parameters; I could reel these out effortlessly. He finally asked "What is the projected Capital to Output ratio?" I said it around 1 to 2 .5. He nodded thoughtfully, promised that he would re-examine the matter. As I was turning back to my seat, he politely asked me whether I was an Engineer. True to my stupid nature, I blurted out, "No Sir! I am a much-hated three lettered official." He said, "What's that?" I said with a wry smile that I was an IAS officer. At which he guffawed, and said politely, "No, no. There are really some very good IAS officers in India." I did not stretch my luck, and came back to my seat. Two days after, I took the 'return' flight from Patna to Calcutta. As usual, I was the last to board the plane. This time the plane was full to the hilt. Left and right; not a single empty seat! Finally, I reached the front row; the left extreme seat of the middle row was empty. I sat down. I looked to my left; JRD Sir was gazing at me with delighted curiosity. He burst out before I could greet him, "Hey young man why are you chasing me all over the Globe?" Pat I replied, "Excellency, the first time I met you it was my immense luck. But this time it is a divine direction to you to do something for my State." This pleased him. He kept talking to me throughout the flight till it landed at Calcutta. He assured me about the investment in the proposed Refractory project. Then he launched into various aspects of governance in the country, bemoaned the tardy decision making process and complained a lot about the 'steel' policy of the Government. He explained to me in some detail about the problems TISCO was facing, particularly in getting good grade coal. I saw my chance and slipped in a suggestion, "Excellency, you should think about a sponge Iron project." [I had read up avidly on the subject, I owed it to DR. P. K. Mohanty, a brilliant Odia engineer, promoter of Orissa Sponge Iron Ltd.] JRD Sir shook his head and said that the sponge iron making was not financially viable. I didn't back down, and said, "Excellency, you are a pragmatist but also a visionary. The future of Steel making will be 'continuous casting process' and sponge iron is the feed material. You mentioned low grade of coal, Indian coal's ash content will continue to be high and the grade of iron ore must use the 'blue dust' ore to avoid unscientific use of iron ore." He then assured me that he would re-study the entire subject of Sponge Iron. And then we parted ways at Calcutta airport. Two days passed; it was a Sunday, and as usual I was in the office working. The phone rang; it was a call from the Office of Chief Secretary. Chief Secretary came on line and said, "Hota, what have you done? Mr. Rusi Modi [MD, TISCO] is sitting in front of me. He has come with the TISCO plane. Mr. JRD Tata wants you to resign from IAS and join the TATAs. You are to fly back with Mr. Modi." I said something to the effect that such decisions needed a bit of time, and formal acceptance of resignation might also take some time. I would get back to Mr. Modi through the Chief Secretary in due time. Anyway, it was not to be! My father and eldest brother dissuaded me saying that serving common people had its merit. However, the Refractory and the Sponge Iron projects went through. In life many turns come, 'If only I could have taken the right decision at the right time!' – remains an eternal regret. After about four year's tenure in IPICOL, I was down with viral pneumonia and was at home for a month. Then I thought that enough was enough; I went and met the Industry Minister and requested him to speak to CM about my transfer. Industry minister was mollified. I was transferred as Collector, Cuttack.

Pet Dog & Collectorship

Cuttack then comprised Kendra Para, Jagatsinghpur, Jajpur and Cuttack Central. It had 46 Blocks and more than 50 lakh population and was considered a prestigious posting. When I came to learn of this order, I called on the CM and pleaded for posting as Collector to Mayurbhanj, a quieter and decent district of my childhood. CM heard my impassioned plea; he had a single word answer –'Cuttack!" So I came away from his chamber slightly crestfallen. Bijayshree ji phoned and said, "Do you have a pet dog?" I replied in the negative. Then he added, "Bapa [father] has said not to keep a dog while you are the Collector, Cuttack!" I was bemused; but, I was perceptive enough to understand that CM has alerted me to the need of being completely accessible to people if I were to succeed as Collector, Cuttack.

I want to acknowledge a large-hearted senior IAS colleague who protected me without my knowledge. Chairman IPICOL wrote some nasty words in my Annual Confidential Reports and sent it to the Government. It reached the Special Secretary of the General Administration Department, Mr. A.N. Tiwari IAS. He rang up the Chairman and asked him to meet him. When the meeting took place, Mr. Tiwari with his infinite tact and wit made Dr. Mishra tear up his assessment and sign up an assessment prepared by Mr. Tiwari and kept ready for use. All should believe when I would say that I had been stupid enough not to have formally called on Mr. Tiwari earlier other than meeting him occasionally in official meetings. A high calibre IAS officer should not wait for any petty formalities or sycophancy; he must try to do justice at all times, and particularly protect the innocent and the hard working! I bow to Mr. A. N. Tiwari and his sense of right and wrong.

7

COLLECTOR AND
DISTRICT MAGISTRATE, CUTTACK

I joined as the Collector, Cuttack. Anyway, in a matter of days I could realize that being Collector of Cuttack was altogether a different cup of tea than being MD IPICOL. As MD IPICOL, I frequently met top-notch personalities; my preparation had to be immaculate and my answers immediate. Here, I found a stream of influential visitors dropping into my chamber and making all sorts of liberal comments like "We know that you have been brought by the Chief Minister as Collector to do his bidding." Now, I realized that it would be foolish on my part to answer the querist either in the affirmative or in the negative. Nor can I manifest annoyance. So I learnt the art of a beatific silent smile. Some of the visitors would offer you a paan [betel leaf with tobacco etc.]. I would fold my hand in salutation and excuse saying that I did not chew paan. Then the visitor would guffaw and say, "If you do not take paan, how would then you manage Cuttack?" Listening to this several times a day for ten days or so, I succumbed. I also had to keep my mouth shut; a paan might help. So one day I accepted a paan, opened it, cleaned it from excess tobacco and calcium paste and popped the paan into my mouth. Immediately it hit me, I saw the stars at day and sun at night. I rushed to bathroom to spit all out, drink several glasses of water to recover my poise. But a stupid bravado took hold of me, I would master paan.

The initial months at Cuttack were full of pleasant activities. I had proficiency in Odia literature. So the scribes lionized me and I was frequently in vernacular newspapers, mostly published from Cuttack. A small anecdote would give the readers the benefit of ready wit. There was a Hockey Tournament organized in city. Mr. Rabi Patnaik was the Secretary of the District Hockey Association and I, ex-officio President. The 'Final Match' took place. Prizes were to be distributed. Dr. Mahtab, the Editor of newspaper Prajatantra and a host of other journals, the ex-Chief Minister of Odisha and always a political heavy-weight, creator of important landmarks like the Hirakud Dam, Barabati Stadium, author of History of Odisha and score of novels etc. was the Chief Guest. The prize ceremony started. Rabi ji read out the Secretary's Report. While doing so, he addressed Dr. Mahtab as the most distinguished Odia leader and 'Kula-Brudhha'- an 'elderly Statesman'. My turn came to speak as the Chief Guest was to speak the last. I started with a bold statement that Rabi ji had conducted an excellent tournament; but, I could not agree with his conferring the title of Kula-Briddha on Dr. Mahatab. I distinctly saw a bit of consternation among the seven hundred strong audiences. Subdued murmuring started. Who was this young pretender trying to lower the dignity of Dr. Mahatab!! I did not stop my flow of words; I said that Rabi ji had not reckoned with the multifarious personality and achievements of Dr. Mahatab; I recounted quickly Dr. Mahtab's achievements, some of his literary works and his busy daily routine of public life. I said that it would be more appropriate to take into account the youthful fountain of productive energy of Dr. Mahatab and call him as 'Kula-Shrestha" [the Best Odia]. The entire audience clapped lustily and Dr. Mahatab beamed at me. In fact, after a few months I met Dr, Mahtab at his invitation. He said that I should consider joining him as Editor of the English newspaper published by his organization. He said that he had produced three Chief Ministers of Odisha; He had noticed some spark in me. I could do well in public life. I consulted my father; he left the decision to me. I did some introspection and realised that political life was very demanding and chancy. And I was weary of the extremely costly political process and its need of amoral pragmatism. I decided that the IAS offered me a steady opportunity for rendering public service; I decided not to jump into the uncertain cesspool of Indian politics.

Constitution and Collector

In 1980, General Elections were announced. News of Indira ji's coming reached. Our CM who had never interfered with my work any time phoned me. I knew what he was going to ask – I should not permit Indira ji hold public meetings at Cuttack. [She was flying on a very small plane and the pilot Capt. Mishra who was a close acquaintance phoned me for landing permission and 'aviation' fuel. I had no clue under what authority I could prevent Mrs. Gandhi from landing with the aircraft and where from I would access aviation fuel]. However, as an IAS probationer I had been administered Oath of Allegiance to the Constitution of India, and that in a democracy, I could not be choking the normal public meetings etc. of any leader even when she was not in power. CM kept ringing two three times; I avoided the telephone telling my staff that I was on the roads of Cuttack city supervising law and order arrangements. Captain Mishra landed the plane on a Highway and was adroit enough to arrange aviation fuel also, using my name. I never knew the details and did not bother to pry. Janata Dal lost at the Centre. The continuance of Mr. Routray as Odisha CM became untenable. The Central Government dismissed his Government. The Governor Rule was imposed again. Sri B.D. Sharma, a leader of Haryana was the Governor. Some friends and foes thought that my days as Collector were numbered. But, the fact was that from the time I became Collector, I never was vindictive towards Congress politicians. To the great credit of CM Mr. Routray, he never asked me to misbehave with Congress functionaries. I maintained civil and proper behaviour whenever Congress delegations came to submit some memorandum etc. Those days, Cuttack was still the hub of political activity.

At this juncture, a routine administrative measure became big news. It was found by my Civil Supply staff headed by the capable Mr. Asutosh Das that the leading business families of Cuttack were indulging in profiteering in sugar which was a 'controlled' commodity under the Act. Their obvious mistakes and written records and overtrading in stocks established a clear chain of profiteering. I issued detention orders against twelve richest traders of Cuttack. It created headlines in local newspapers. The local Congress leaders thought that it showed Congress in good light. Mr. J.B. Patnaik emerged as the leader of Congress in Odisha. He became a Central Minister. Whenever he came to Cuttack [his residence], I would make immaculate police arrangements along with S.P. with whom I had cordial relations. So, Mr. J.B. Patnaik started seeking me out and consulted me on various things. I never indulged in politics or back-biting; avoided tactfully political questions and concentrated on a development agenda of scale for Cuttack city and district as and when Mr. Patnaik would become CM of Odisha. The writings were on the wall. Congress was on its way back.

Ending Bus Permit Corruption

An interesting administrative incident happened then. As per law, the various Committees were still in force even if the Governor's rule was on. One of these Committees was the District Road Transport Committee [RTC] which dealt with issues of bus routes and road permits to bus operators. Apparently, for such a large district, there were only 8 regular route permits and 16 temporary weekly permits and RTO/Collector had the power to issue daily permits. I was aghast. On my insistence RTO explained that the RTC was dominated by M.L.A.s [about three or four were Members in RTC]; they did not want to throw open routes as restriction of routes was a source of money for them. My blood boiled, I saw a chance. I asked him immediately to bring out an advertisement as per rules inviting applications for 48 new permanent routes and issue notice to hold a meeting of the RTC. RTO was demurring, saw my stern eyes and immediately issued the notice. The meeting was held at some Inspection Bungalow. When I arrived for the meeting, I found a crowd. The S.P. was also a Member of the Transport Committee. I asked him to beef up police deployment and started the meeting. The MLAs were lame-ducks; but they tried to obstruct diplomatically saying that the Collector would be having so much other work, this meeting would take time; I could leave; they would discuss and draw up the minutes. I said – 'Nothing Doing. All discussions are to take place in my presence; all decisions are to be on merit.' The MLAs looked at one another helplessly. One of the applicants- two sisters- having buses for a long time, came in and openly alleged that they were being bled for money every week. They did not trust the objectivity of the Committee. The

MLAs hung down their heads. I announced without any ado that as women applicants they would definitely get permanent route permit for which they had applied. They were taken aback and burst into tears. I kept on rushing through the agenda, of course, discussing all pros and cons and kept on announcing decisions on a set of criteria discussed and recorded. The MLAs realized that it was a lost battle. Suddenly, there was commotion on the outer veranda, in front of our room. I heard someone shouting that rascals were inside and trying to take wrong decisions. I came out of the room and said that regular office work was going on; I would hear any grievance right after the meeting. Then I rushed back and resumed the meeting. The substantive part of the meeting was over. Again a voice shouted from the veranda that the Collector was a thief and was in cohort with MLAs. When I heard this I lost my cool and charged out roaring, "Who said this?" All scattered beyond the boundary wall of the bungalow, but one tall dark fellow held his ground and confronted me. I thought that if I pinpoint the matter he would retreat. I asked, "Did you call the Collector a thief?" He did not back off and repeated his sentence. I just lost my senses; I caught hold of him by his collars; he was taller than me; I don't know from where I got the strength; I lifted him clearly off his feet. He was non-pulsed. I shouted for the SP to come out. I asked SP to arrest the person. By that time, I had left the collar of the person, but firmly held him by one hand. SP looked at the person and then at me. He was hesitant, mumbled something about a written order. I firmly told him to carry out my instructions first. Then I completed the meeting, thanked the MLAs who had also witnessed the whole drama. They also kept looking at the person whom I had handed over to SP and were whispering to one another. Anyway, by evening I knew that I had arrested the MLA candidate of Congress from an important constituency. He was released on bail by SP, and rushed to CM-designate, Sri J.B. Patnaik. Sri Patnaik heard his demand for my immediate transfer, tactfully got all the details out of him. Mr. Patnaik apparently knew RTO Cuttack personally and rang him up. RTO spoke out about my boldness to end corruption in the bus permit sector. Mr. J. B. Patnaik told the MLA aspirant that I should not be transferred as it would harm the image of the Party.

To be a good Collector, you must be able to use words suitable to the occasion, but not to be in a rush to reply. Patience, fortitude and being a good listener will help. You must be honest and carry such a reputation by your conduct. [You should not be seen drinking in public and social gatherings]. You must have strong common sense and you must be both decisive and also have a sense of proportion. As Collector, you exercise sometimes a lot of power, but better to be careful – power must not get to your head. There was never a dull moment as Collector, Cuttack – for good or for bad. There were close encounters with impending disaster; but, common sense, hard work and good luck saw one through. There was some foolish moment too.

Paan and Pain

The paan chewing had started and become a habit. But neither did I have the health nor the ability to deal with tobacco juice; I had to spit out the juice two three times in the first five minutes for if I were to swallow it, my stomach would churn and my head would reel. But like a fool I persisted to show to the Cuttack public that I was man enough to eat a tobacco laced paan. It once led to an acutely embarrassing moment. Agriculture Secretary and my boss RDC once held a meeting with officials of Jagatsinghpur to explain some new agriculture scheme. The meeting hall was packed and I sat between the two seniors. I was tightly sandwiched. The meeting was old style and traditional. There was no Presentation; not even charts and graphs. It was a monologue from Secretary Agriculture who went on and on. Without participation I started feeling sleepy. I put my hand into the pocket, and found a paan. I took it out and quietly popped it into my mouth while pretending to wipe my face with the handkerchief. My agony started. I realized that the tobacco juice was too strong and I could not swallow. I kept holding it in my mouth; soon the volume was too much. The speech of the Secretary continued. I put my handkerchief to my mouth to mop up the juice. It got soaked, Red juice started dripping onto my white shirt which became red. Finally, the speech the meeting got over. I rushed to the bathroom, took out my shirt, cleaned it in plain water, twisted it to take out excess water and wore the still wet shirt. Some lunch had been served, so I joined it sheepishly. The senior colleagues neither mentioned my paan nor berated me, and the juniors pretended not to have noticed. However, I felt thoroughly chastised. I stopped eating paan in office hours. But it took many years to give up eating paan. Tobacco is a pernicious habit. All indulgences are bad, and these are particularly so for public officials.

Student Agitations

Every week there used to be some incident or other where I had to play perforce a leading role and bring normalcy back. A few are worth mentioning not to show off my ability but as these contain some universal lesson for young officers. The new Government ran into student agitation. It started as usual from some trivial cause; some students got into a fracas with local Marwari traders in Western Odisha. However, it could not gather an All Odisha identity as students of Cuttack did not take part. The student leaders from Western Odisha sent them missives.

A Carom Gamble at Ravenshaw College

The effort of the Western Odisha students to involve colleges of Cuttack went unabated. After fifteen days, SP informed me that 'Intelligence' had got the news that Western Odisha student leaders have sent bangles to Ravenshaw College [the largest and the most important College of the State, and my alma mater] leaders deriding their 'manliness'. At this, the student leaders of Ravenshaw College decided to strike and paralyze the city roads with procession etc. It was nearing evening. I requested the SP to accompany me in plain dress. His car followed with a reliable Havildar with two concealed loaded pistols. SP was worried that the students would grab and lynch us. But having been a student leader myself I knew the routine. Aggression starts after strike; before that a lot of 'jackal gathering' [clustering and yapping within the college by the core leaders to mobilize the hostellers, a captive crowd]. I told SP that from my experience that the students would have assembled at the back at New Hostel. We drove to New Hostel. About forty students stood near the entrance of the hostel in semi-darkness. I saw simultaneously, two students playing carom at the entrance lobby. Some from the student group rushed at us as we got alighted, asked, "Who is there?" The leader types hollered, 'Sir, this time we are not going to listen to you. You cannot trick us this time." Pat I replied, "Nobody can fool the bright Ravenshavian. I have come to enquire after your wellbeing." "You are welcome, but not the person behind you"- they said. I replied that I had come as an old Ravenshaw alumnus; Mr. Senapati [SP] was also an ex-Ravenshavian. I continued that I never knew that old Ravenshavian were not welcome to drop by in the college. At this they were a bit embarrassed and said, 'But we are not going to do your bidding this time.' I thought in a flash and said, "I have come to play carom. Call your Hostel champion. I shall defeat him by a 'Nil-game' [a contest so one-sided that my opponent would not win a single board.]" This got their goat; even the leaders forgot the possible danger and hollered, "What! You will defeat our Champion by Nil-game?" I said that I wagered a bet that I would do so; if I would fail, I would give them a feast and never ever interfere in their matters. And, just per chance I might win, I would ask for my prize later. They took the bait- hook line and sinker! My confidence came from the fact that I had noticed that there was no boric powder- no professional carom player would play without this basic prop. I took out some money and sent some students to the adjacent market, get boric powder and plenty of potato chops and 'bara's for everyone's enjoyment. The students were just loafing, trying to work up some enthusiasm for an 'imported' strike. So, they wanted some fun! Within twenty minutes everything was over, the powder and the hostel champion came; so did the snacks. And before they could finish the last 'bara', their champion had been defeated by Nil-game. [I was champion in carom in Cuttack at the age of 15 defeating a person who was 34 years old. We used to play top level carom.] And then the commotion started amongst the students- "See, I told you. Collector ji was up to some tricks. He would now prevail over us to do his bidding". I smiled and said that I had no such intention or ability. I said that we came to enjoy with our student friends. I could never believe that the alert, bright and all-Odisha leaders studying as Ravenshavians could ever be dominated by outsiders and even old Ravenshavians. I told them that I was also a student leader; the Ravenshaw group always made its own intelligent decisions. Then we left. It had the desired result. The students of Ravenshaw wore black hand-bands, marched for half an hour within the college; but did not spill over to the city. However, this was not the end of it.

Playing with Fire

Again fifteen days later, close to evening SP rang up that news had come that students of Ravenshaw were going to march out that evening with burning flame sticks to show solidarity with Western Odisha students. Now a march of even a hundred students with fire sticks was fraught with grave consequences. I asked SP to cordon off the College square area and deploy force all across the opposite side of the road facing the college boundary. I specifically requested him to ask the force to fix polished bayonets to their rifles, so that these would glisten even in darkness. We rushed to the College square; I saw heavy force about four platoons deployed with their bayonets shining. I requested the SP to ask the force to take position; he didn't flinch and shouted out orders. And then we saw the students within the eastern gate side of the college slowly coming with fire sticks. I told SP to be near the force and issue 'loud orders' to the Force to take position and aim; but under no circumstances, he would order 'Fire'. He would keep looking at me for further signals. I told the most efficient Inspector of Mangalabag P.S. Mishra ji to take out his revolver and accompany me. I told him that I might behave rudely, but only for drama. As the students reached the eastern college gate and started coming onto the street, I winked at SP and he shouted, "Force, fix bayonets. Take position. Stay ready to fire!" And all traffic had been dispersed. The road was empty. I walked towards the students, the Inspector following me with his raised revolver. Just as we reached the middle of the street, it was the decisive moment. I turned and stopped Mishra ji in open view and shouted, "Who has authorized you to come between my student friends and me. Go back!!" The students- three abreast about a hundred fifty or so- from the East Gate got halted watching the scene of Collector stopping mid-stride a burly Inspector with a raised revolver. I quickly walked up to the front of the student procession. I told them to give me a fire stick and that I would march with them to protect them. They were totally bewildered at the Collector joining their procession. Anyway, I took a fire stick from a frontline student and started marching but very slowly. Per force they kept pace with me. I kept on talking loudly to them, "See, SP may think differently; he may act tough. Do you see the rifles with bayonets? He may attack, fire and charge; but, he cannot do so as long as I am with you." The students slowly marching behind me saw the heavy police arrangements with police force on their knees with rifles raised and aiming at us, the bayonets glistening. It must have brought some fear of God onto them. They trudged after me, I leading the procession. I remember giving some slogans like –Student Unity Zindabad- to keep the students totally trusting me. We walked about a hundred fifty yards on the street. Then we reached the street near the Main Gate of the large college campus which was luckily open; I walked rapidly into the college, the procession following me. I knew from experience that the real ring leaders would be at the back of the procession to avoid the first baton blows of the police. The whole procession entered back into the College; a verbal hell broke loose. The leaders of the back rushed to the front and shouted, "Who has brought the procession in?" By that time I took advantage of the darkness and scaled over the college wall and was back with SP who embraced me out of fellow-feeling. We moved even more police force to both the gates and showed our determination not to allow them to come out by making a mike announcement, declaring Sec. 144 around the college exit. Anyway, the students had started quarrelling amongst themselves and had lost their zeal. They gave vent to their frustration by abusing me with choicest dirty words; then they started abusing my family. SP got very agitated and wanted to let go a volley of bullets; I merely laughed and said that let the students indulge themselves; thus they would have something to say to save their face the next day. The CM sent for me the next day and said that the IG had complained to him about my extreme bravado, that the police would have been blamed if the Collector would have been set on fire. I remember that I got up and saluted CM and mumbled that I couldn't have 'not' tried to protect the students and also minimize the fall-out to the Government, and left his Chamber.

In Front of Raised Rifle

The next major 'police action' took place soon after. One Sunday morning, I was out for a morning walk in my large residential compound; two press reporters who had become friendly but loyal to their profession never to miss the smallest incident of police excess from being highlighted were seen at my gate. At this moment, the telephone rang repeatedly. First it was the Chief Secretary telling me that some big incident had taken place at early morning at Barang [about twenty km away] Glass Factory and firing had taken place. I should go and control the situation. The second call was from SP with similar words. I told him to come to my home and that we would go together. I told him to mobilize APR [Armed Police Reserve] and bring about four platoons. I invited the two press friends to hop into the car to see some 'live' action first hand. It was about 6.15 AM, we reached by 6.35 AM. It was a horrific sight though the place was deserted. Apparently, there was a negotiation meeting between the Union and Management the early evening before. Some mischief-maker cut the electrical wires; and then pandemonium took place. A section of police deployed outside rushed in to protect the Jt. MD Mr. S. Jhunjunwalla. The crowd of labour indulged in heavy stone pelting. Somehow, the Jt. MD ran away by the back door. Police had fired into air at night a few rounds to scare the mob away. The result was opposite, the mob in darkness could not see if the bullets had hit anyone. The ammunition finished early morning; mob rushed in and attacked the seven policemen. One was killed when someone snatched his rifle and stabbed him with the bayonet. Others ran and hid in nearby bushes. When we arrived, seeing us the injured policemen crawled out from the wayside bushes. The villagers and labourers had united and were standing at the entrance of the adjacent village looking restive. Soon two platoons of APR arrived. I started hearing their loud breathing and hissing when they saw the dead body of Havildar ji and injuries of their fellow policemen. I immediately sent the dead body of the policeman in SP's jeep away to the Bhubaneswar hospital which was about 12 KMs away. The villagers were pelting stones, the jeep driver was afraid, so I had gone with my car to escort him about a kilometre away from the scene of the mob. When I returned I saw a macabre sight. The new force which had joined us took law unto their hands and attacked the villagers one of whom had raised and aimed the police rifle snatched early morning. It was a word-painting befitting Gabriel Garcia Marquez to describe. A young man was lying writhing on the ground injured by a police bullet. One of the Press friends saw me and burst into tears folding his hands at me beseeching me, "Where have you brought me?" The other press colleague was twirling in circles raising his hand and shouting, "Fire! Fire!" The SP ran towards me to explain, stumbled across the railway cables and fell on ground totally flat. A policeman ran to him. Instead of extending his hand to help SP to get up, he saluted the SP and waited for orders. I rushed towards the villagers; one of them had the snatched rifle pointing at me, I reached the young injured person. I shouted at the villagers that I had come and I would control the police as the Force was very agitated at the unnecessary death of their senior colleague. The villagers better should melt away. I talked to the young man pretending that he was only marginally wounded, and told the villagers that I would immediately remove him to hospital for treatment. I called SP's and my drivers, picked up the injured and put him into a police van. Then I saw Death ending a life. Nothing could be and was to be done. I sent the vehicle away with the body. **First principle in all such situations is to remove the body/bodies because as long as the bodies would be lying around these would become the centre of excessive emotion and exacerbate violence.** I talked to the force after SP assembled them to order. I explained that they had opened firing without Magistrate's order and it has caused a death; this would mean grave trouble for their jobs and career. But, I was their friend. I would help them. I asked them to prepare a short report and put it up to SP seeking my orders to open fire. I told them to count their ammunition to account for the rounds fired. All this I did to distract them, restore sanity amongst them and engage them in some routine. The situation would not die down as more new platoons arrived and the dead Havildar had apparently belonged to one of the new platoons. So throughout the day, it was a battle of wits between the restive Police Force who were disobeying orders of SP and demanding that they would enter the villages and arrest the wrong-doers – it was basically to let themselves loose on the villagers. And all along, I was breathing hot and cold at the villagers who were in case not present there. I was abusing the villagers, but, simultaneously, telling the force that I loved my police colleagues, I could not expose them to further danger. I kept on saying that when the evening would come, we would enter the village. I said that I would not leave the place without avenging their colleague's death. Thus the whole day I stood in the sun, ate from the food that had come in cans for the force in their presence. The force saw that I was with them all the way sharing all their travails. Anyway, the day passed, IG [no DG system then] came, and he was also heckled by the restive force. Only I was tolerated by them. I briefly whispered my request to IG to send 3 platoons of Odisha Military Police at 11 PM assuring him that I would by hook or by crook bring back the APR. Early evening APR force came to me asking for the plan to invade the villages. I told them that they should rest. I would wake them up at midnight. Most of them went to sleep. The OMP with their large vans arrived. I hid them. I shouted at the sleeping APR force to get up, I abused the imaginary Management and the Villagers in a loud voice; and said that we would come back very early morning, properly equipped with riot gear and attack the villagers. The sleepy forces were bundled into the vans which I had taken the precaution to keep on start [ready to move] and whisked them away. The DIG Odisha Military Police came, congratulated me at my presence of mind, deployed his OMP platoons, and I exited.

Unprecedented Floods

The floods were another story. The District Emergency Officer-DEO had briefed during the meeting about our flood preparation measures briefing me that floods were not a major worry any more. The Brahmani river system where there was no dam had 37 boats in strategic areas for rescue and relief. The 'chooda' [parched rice] making mills had enough capacity. The October day started as usual. Around 2 PM DEO rushed to me saying that a wireless message had come that a flood was expected at night as there was heavy rainfall on the upper catchment of Hirakud Dam. The rainy season was practically over, so the Dam was full to the capacity for use of water later. I got out of the office and drove on the Mahanadi-Kathajodi rivers embankment; the flood water had started reaching with ferocity, I felt alarmed, rushed back and rang up the SP and Irrigation, electricity officials to mobilize their all staff as a big flood was expected. At about 6.30 PM DEO came to me with another bunch of wireless saying that the flood could well go over 12 lakh cusec. And he added that the infamous Daleighai flood of 1955 had reached a flood level of 13 lakh cusec. I told all that I would stay in the office throughout the night. Those days, communication systems were inadequate. Telephones were unreliable. I rang up Mr. Khirod Mohanty, SP in charge of Police Communication, explained the emergency and requested if he could help me with a VHF set. Within half an hour the VHF set came and was operational. Around 8 PM, Hirakud dam started trembling with the force of water, electricity generation briefly went off and we all sat dismayed. Luckily electricity came back and with it the news that the flood water was expected to cross the volume of 15 lakhs cusec. My phone started ringing constantly; Politicians of all hue except CM kept ringing. At about 1 AM, VHF informed the first breach downstream. I asked for a large map of the district and pinned coloured flags showing points of breach. By morning, 143 breaches were flagged. By the next day noon the ferocity of water subsided having flooded an extensive area including Jagatsinghpur town which had never seen flood even during the historic Daleighai. The middle class families of Jagatsinghpur were frantic as flood water had come to the floor level of all ground floor rooms. Each one demanded boats for rescue; and there were none in the Mahanadi river system. I called for the Engineer in charge of the boats; he politely but clearly said that he had the ability only to shift one boat a day to the Mahanadi system I improvised, bolstered his logistics but he could raise it only to four per day.

Roti MP MLA

At about 8 AM, MP Sri A.K. Panda invaded my chamber with about twenty of his followers. He started banging my table loudly and shouting at me for paralysis of action, and not helping the distressed. I kept cool and looked at him unperturbed. My officers including Civil Supply Officer-CSO- were near my chair. Suddenly I had a stroke of inspiration. By 7 Am I had sized up my priority- I had calculated from the map and breach points that about 8 lakh hungry children, women and men would be there from the affected villages as water would have overrun their hearth. They must have taken shelter on the highways which were at heights, unaffected by floods. DEO had already informed me that all 'chooda' mills were in rural areas and had been overrun with flood water. I had to improvise. I asked the CSO if Atta [wheat flour] would be available. CSO said that the famous Cuttack Malgodown was intact and was full of stock. The MP lost his cool at my talking to my officers when he was banging the table, and shouted, "How dare you talk to others when I am speaking to you on urgent matters?" I looked at him in the face and said, "MP Saheb, please take 2.5 quintal of Atta. Aap roti beliye [a process of using a wooden pin to shape a roti from the dough], prepare chapattis; put a small candle , a match box, two boiled potatoes, a small lump of gur, some salt in a paper packet so that it does not mix up and a chlorine tablet with two chapattis, all into a plastic packet. If self-locking plastic packets would not be available, please tie the packet with a rubber band; you have so many able followers, you can do it, all materials including firewood will be supplied by us." At this MP Ji began to literally froth at his mouth and thundered, 'I, MP will roll roti??" The District Public Relation Officer DPRO was standing nearby. I said to him, "Arrange photos of MP Saheb when he rolls out the first ten rotis. It should go to Press immediately with the caption that Cuttack MP has dedicated himself to the flood affected, preparing rotis with his own hand to send food packets!" The MP stopped mid-stride, and immediately folded his hands to me and said, "I and our boys will do it, Thank you!!" As soon as he left, CSO came near me and whispered, "Master stroke Sir! Why spare the MLA- MP's rival?" And so I rang up the MLA and told him that the MP had come and forcefully taken away 2.5 quintal of Atta to prepare food packets." MLA ji roared on phone, "I am Cuttack MLA. I shall mobilize a thousand households. Give me a ton of Atta gradually throughout the day; please help me with materials and initial logistics. I shall flood your office with food packets throughout the day." And lo and behold, food packets started pouring in starting at 10.30 AM or so. Trucks and vans were requisitioned. Trip-loads of food packets started heading to interior areas flood affected areas. I never went home. Never ate anything except plain soda and two biscuits. I was organizing the work and answering phones. Waves of disgruntled visitors came; they were mostly irritated about lack of boats for rescue. I must admit that I had no answer. But luckily, no large-scale of lives [barring may be three or four through accidents] were lost. The disgruntled people would sit for about twenty minutes initially shouting then gradually calm down seeing my non-stop working. CM never rang up. His people must have told him about my all-out effort. He arranged air-dropping of food packets from Bhubaneswar Airport. At about 2 PM, I went home for half an hour, freshened up and rushed back before my absence would be noticed. I took my key officers into confidence and told them to go home, freshen up and be back promptly. Around evening 6 PM, the crowd temporarily thinned from my chamber. I took a tour of my office. The front rooms were full of food packets touching almost the roof. I went out of the office; I found five trucks lined up and in the starting position, their 'dala' [back goods space] empty. I went up to the drivers and learnt that they were ready to go, but were waiting for labourers to load the food packets. The labourers were tired having worked from morning and had gone for tea and snacks. I quickly calculated that if the labourers were to take 30 minutes for tea, then another 30 for loading, it would cross 7 PM for the trucks to move. And it would be past 10 PM by when the trucks could reach last points. People in darkness would have gone to sleep. And the food might be wasted. I just came back to the rooms and picked up about a dozen food packets in my hands and made an improvised open bag from my shirt pulled out from my trousers. I walked back to the trucks and put the food packets in. I had seen from the corner of my eyes that some curious press reporters and onlookers had surreptitiously followed me to know what I was up to with the food packets. I went and picked up another load of food packets and carried them to the truck. This time I found a dozen others started carrying the packets to the trucks. The third time, I was half way when the food packets were taken away from my hands; a hundred hands came forward and the five trucks were loaded and ready. Just then the labourers returned and the trucks were off. I was carried back to my upstairs chamber on the shoulders of admiring emotional audiences.

Office Table as Bed

For seven days I continued to sleep on the office table and work often through the night. Each hour of the 7 days had tales to tell. A few salient points only. I went to Jagatsinghpur on the third morning arranging about twenty truckloads of relief materials in tow. I knew that the affected Jagatsinghpur town people would be waiting to jump on me.

And it was so. Seeing the number of trucks, the crowd got distracted temporarily but within a couple of hours all materials were finished and the fresh wave of mob swarmed the SDO's office. The SDO was in a bad state, he had not been allowed to leave his chair for close to 36 hours, his face and feet were swollen, eyelids puffy and drooping. The mob now directed its attention to me. The State Government had sent four reputed senior OAS officers to help me; I had brought them all to Jagatsinghpur. They saw the mob and lost their nerves. One developed chest pain and was admitted to the local hospital, two simply ran away and the fourth kept me company initially with his head between his hands. It was an unnerving situation. I kept ringing the CSO to keep on sending more supplies; he took a lot of time. People were getting restive. Luckily, on my request Paradeep Port authorities sent some boats. CSO came with some supplies; I immediately sent him back to organize much more. Around 2.30 PM, Mr. Pratap Chandra Mohanty –ex Revenue Minister barged in and started shouting like others. But in a minute he fell silent, pulled a chair close to me and just sat nearby without uttering a word. He saw my untiring sincerity, and kept me company hoping that he could prevent my being lynched. Assisted by my Tahsildar of Salepur, Sri Gopi Nath Mohanty OAS [later IAS], I restored semblance of order and started planning for Block-wise relief. Mob kept coming and would force me to talk to them, disrupting my work. After an hour one kurta wearing person with a sharp 'katuri'- a iron tool used for cutting coconut etc. [He was initially shouting when he came to the room and then had fallen quiet.] took out a thin towel, tied it around his waist, raised the katuri and stood guard at the door loudly declaring that if anyone would come and disturb Collector, he would cut him up with the katuri. [He was a postgraduate and a Sarpanch of an adjacent Panchayat].

Suspension to Commendation

Work started in earnest. At about 4.30 PM there was a small commotion; some important leader type persons came into my room and said that the Revenue Minister whose constituency it was had arrived by helicopter. He was in the Inspection Bungalow and had asked me to come to him. I folded my hands to the leader-types and requested them to inform the honourable Minister that I was busy setting up the work and would come after 30 minutes. Hardly twenty minutes would have passed; this time there was a huge commotion on the veranda. The Revenue Minister burst into the small room where I was sitting and organizing work [including creating a group to keep detailed accounts]. I got up and saluted him. He hollered without any preliminary, "What nonsense is going on! You are having tea and chit chatting and not doing any work." The responsible elements knew that from morning 7 AM, I had not drunk even some water, much less tea or any snack. Before I could know what was on, the mob surrounded the Minister and shouted, "What, you fool, you dare misbehave with our most sincere Collector!!" In a minute, the mob had torn all clothes off the Minister; he was standing there overwhelmed with fear in his undergarments. I jumped through the mob, put my arms around the Minister, and told the gathering that any further misbehaviour would mean that I would go away without doing work. I whispered to the Minister that I would take care of his people and constituency, it was an inappropriate time for him to come; he could come after a day after I would have saturated the area with relief and other basic arrangements. He left grumbling. I came back and resumed work. I returned late at night, asked the CSO to keep up the flow of materials especially to Jagatsinghpur town. Apparently, Revenue Minister felt personally affronted and carried a note to suspend me to the Cabinet meeting [the Cabinet met every evening to review the flood situation.] During the meeting he voiced his proposal to CM. CM looked at other Ministers. Some Ministers objected loudly; not one supported. CM looked at Revenue Minister and said he would still fulfil Revenue Minister's request, but the Minister should pause and think whether after Hota's suspension, he would be able to enter his constituency. The Revenue Minister calmed down and tore up the proposal. However, wily CM would not let go of the matter so easily. He called for his Private Secretary, dictated a note as if it was from the Revenue Minister, made him sign it and CM counter-signed it. The communiqué arrived in the next few days- it read something like that the Government of Odisha was pleased with my extraordinary devotion to public service and the Government was commending me.

The intense period of work of relief and rehabilitation lasted at least for a week; I never went home to sleep, and managed on the office table. There were many highs and very few lows, memories of those days would run into pages as in most flood affected sub-divisions SDOs and most junior officials were overwhelmed. Some of them had deserted station of duty. I had to go to each Sub-division headquarters and to some Block headquarters and re-establish the authority of the District Administration. There were some touch and go situations – restive crowd waiting to pounce. But in a dramatic five minutes by demonstrating humble sincerity in action, the crowd could be own over. The lessons were –Never to run home leaving work aside, never show tiredness, never eat heavy food, never breakdown in face adversity, always there is a solution, improvise and manage resources to make an impact, remain calm and smiling in face of provocation or insults; if you continue to work purposefully the most abusive mob would notice your sincerity and become your supporters; consider no work small, always set personal examples. And be particularly sensitive to the weaker sections, children, and women particularly of SC and ST segment who suffer more in any large disaster. A simple piece of data was my eye-opener. 29000 houses were washed away in the floods. The Scheduled Caste population in Cuttack District was 20%. However 19000 [65%], of the fully damaged houses belonged to Scheduled Caste. [I did not chew paan during the period of Floods.]

There were some really dramatic moments like the time the Durga Puja Idols immersion procession and Bakrid [Eid-al-Adha] happened to be celebrated on the same day. It was adroitly managed without any untoward incident. And as Chairman of Cuttack Municipality [additional charge] I did advance planning and kept all equipment ready, and responsibility of each official fixed ahead. The rainwater clogging of the city which had become an annual feature throwing the city life into chaos never was allowed to happen during my tenure. One small but great achievement has to be mentioned. DPRO had invited me to preside over Utkal Dibas – 1st April of each year when Odisha had become a separate province. I went to the meeting place at 5 minutes to seven, the Chief Speaker also arrived. To my constraint I found an audience of four only, even if declared a State holiday. I felt ashamed as an Odia, and decided that the coming year there would be a separate story. In October, I presided over several meetings to promote Durga Puja and later Kali Puja. I gently persuaded that Cuttack was at the forefront of separate Odisha province movement. So each Mohalla Puja Committee would contribute ten percent of its collection to a Common fund to be managed by them only. On 31st March there would be competitions to shortlist the Sahis ['mohallas'] who would put on show their theme on Odisha [any distinctive historical or cultural aspect] on 1st April evening in the large ground near Saheed Bhawan. The Municipality would bear all the cost of lights, decoration, chairs etc. So next 1st April was a thundering success, more than 10 thousand people congregated, 'Bande Utkal Janani' was sung together by the entire crowd. Respecting common people always would yield uncommon dividends for a District Administrator. I was sad to note that many young IAS even if they were otherwise talented assumed a lot of self-importance (and so some adverse comments from the intelligentsia and even their colleagues) during their Collectorship.

Development Work

Readers must have started wondering is that all I was doing- public posturing round the clock!! I was alert to my responsibilities as a Development Administrator. I toured all Blocks extensively, mainly to encourage BDOs to take up more and more public work, development projects, pisciculture, lift irrigation points, groundnut cultivation and the like. I took full advantage of some sagacious seniors having engaged a Consultancy organization to help draw up a District Credit plan where all BDOs, SDOs, and Bank Managers participated. I found that in the previous year the credit uptake was a mere Rs. 16 crores. I reviewed in the meeting each Block and gently prodded BDOs and SDOs to come with a more courageous plan; a spirit of competition ensued and soon we had a District Credit Plan of Rs. 64 Crores which eventually was exceeded in the field. Additional Development Commissioner complimented me profusely in a Collectors' Conference. Then unto my role as Collector- head of District Revenue Administration. I set strict standards for revenue collection and there was record revenue collection.

Too Good to Last

Good things however, cannot last forever. A series of coincidence and small mistakes and carelessness snowballed into a major situation. Member, Board of Revenue, set his program to inspect one of my Tehsils. I took all the care to prepare for his visit. But on the day before CM rang me up to accompany him to his constituency [he had chosen to contest from a constituency in my district apparently after assessing that image of governance in Cuttack District was the best]. I called on Member and put the matter before him; he advised me to attend CM's program. [My mistake, I should have attended to Member first] Then a few malcontents from the Janata Dal like Srikanta Jena and Ashok Das who were slighted by SDO Jajpur, nurtured anger against me- in spite of my telling them that I never played any partisan role and considered them as my respected friends. They were joined by a suspended ACSO [suspended for corruption by me], and a disgruntled Editor of the newspaper Pragatibadi [here the mistake was clearly mine; when I was MD IPICOL he came to my office for a courtesy call with appointment. Stupidly, I delayed calling him to my chamber, he left in annoyance. I rang him up to make up, but, he was wounded and never came on line.] and a rich Iron/steel rod etc. dealer of who mistakenly thought that I had targeted him for some survey of the stock of goods in his godown. They often met for drink parties, and hatched a plan to humiliate me. Cement was in tremendous short supply- people needed cement for building houses etc. I had withdrawn all powers of allotment and had kept in my hand to give cement to bona fide users. So if any known genuine applicants used to come to me I used to sign an order for release then and there. I would get hold of whatever piece of paper etc. available and would write a slip to the CSO who would prepare a proper official note and get my orders later but would give a permit against some dealer immediately. My goal was to avoid making people go round in circles for a few bags of cement. The suspended ACSO managed to get a few pieces of 'slips' written by me to CSO. Fundamentally, it was no irregularity; but he told the group of malcontents as if it was a big thing. So there was a big Headline in Pragatibadi- 'Collector Cuttack surpasses Antulay' [who was embroiled in money-making from cement scarcity] in Cement Corruption. And the two MLAs Das and Jena moved an 'Adjournment Motion' in the Assembly demanding a special discussion and reply from CM. I felt angry but I did not clarify to anyone about my conduct; I had this faith that if I had done no wrong, no harm could come to me.

Peekay Hota Hai!

At this critical juncture something unforeseen happened. The poor suspended ACSO had a massive heart attack, was hospitalized and realized that he was going to die. He expressed a desire to speak to DG Vigilance Mr. G.C. Senapati IPS. The DG heard that it was some kind of a last wish of a dying man and rushed to his bedside. God's Will works in inscrutable ways. ACSO made a dying declaration that Collector Cuttack was a decent person and he had done no wrong in cement allotment; the ACSO was stricken by God for conspiring against Collector by joining with the MLAs etc. He was seeking Collector's forgiveness. Mr. Senapati was a veteran; he immediately reduced all this to writing and got the ACSO to sign it. And unfortunately, the ACSO Sri Rath died soon after. DG went to the Assembly when the Adjournment Motion was going on; Ashok Das was in full flow saying, "Ye Collector Cuttack kyon aisa hota hai, kyon ki O PEEKAY Hota hai!' Hardly had he finished this witty alliteration on my name creating great amount of merriment all around [notwithstanding the fact that I did not drink] the DG managed to enter the Assembly and pass on the dying declaration to CM who looked at it, raised his hand to stop Das in his full flow of oratory. CM read out the 'dying declaration'. The Speaker immediately disallowed the Motion.

I probed into the real state of affairs of cement. And soon enough, ADM rushed to me within days showing documents that as many as 15 Dealers had procured cement form Andhra Cements Ltd, in each 'check gate' on the highways this cement load and truck numbers were recorded; but the entire cement arrival was not reported to CSO office and was disposed of by the 15 cement Dealers in black market. All fifteen cases had similar documentation, we as an abundant precaution got confirmatory messages from Andhra Cements about the release of cement to these 15 dealers. I prepared detention orders. One of the Dealers was a prominent city congress supporter, Khiorod Sahu. Khirod ji after the Pragatibadi publication thought that I was done for, and in presence of many he had publicly abused me in vulgar language behind my back. The MP was his bosom friend, CM used to go to Sahu's residence on Durga Puja for a goodwill visit. Unfortunately, for Sahu, the Cuttack MLA who was rather partial to me was also present during Sri Sahu's absolutely unnecessary outburst. He informed me all the details. The Cement black-marketing now boomeranged on the real rascals. The detention orders were ready to be executed, I had called for the city Additional S.P. Mr. Surendra Swain without divulging the purpose to come by 8.30 AM to my residential office. Still the matter reached the ears of the MP. He rang me up at midnight to inquire! I pretended and replied in a manner that he became complacent; otherwise he would have spoken to CM and I could have been perhaps embarrassed. I also rang up the SP and apologized to him for not telling him earlier and explained the position and the assignment to Addl. SP. And by 2 PM all 15 were arrested under MISA. I learnt of CM's unhappiness, but he never spoke to me. The funniest judicial experience then came by my way. There was an Advisory board of Judges to review the MISA orders. This Board examined the papers, heard me and released seven of the detainees as 'Not fit case'. The fifteen had also moved the High Court; the High Court declared that seven were 'not fit' cases; curiously the MISA Review Board and the High Court held only one common case to be valid; each released seven different dealers. The facts in each case were absolutely the same. Later I came to know that the young man who found no favour from the judges was from Tirtol area and was a known detractor of Basant Biswal, a Minister of State in rank but the de-facto- Dy. CM. People in general were very supportive of my action and the tar of cement scandal could not stick on me. I was posted as Director of Industries.

Adverse CR

Soon I got in writing from Special Secretary, General Administration a communication of an 'adverse' Appraisal Note- Member Board of Revenue wrote "He does not do case work." Chief Secretary had concurred though both of them had praised my other accomplishments. Both must have got irritated at my larger than life image and [unwittingly] hogging news headlines in local Newspapers each day. They must have thought that as I was some sort of a debonair, always moving, I would have definitely neglected disposal of cases. Anyway, the Bench-Clerk of Collector Cuttack was still a loyal colleague; he gave me the detailed figures of disposal of cases by myself and three of my predecessors. Lo and behold- I had disposed of more cases in my two years than all the three predecessors put together in five years. I always had dedicated one day a week to disposal of cases, asked the parties to come fully prepared and come with written briefs. I used to evaluate the proof in open court in a loud manner and pronounce the judgment then and there. Overnight, the draft judgments were kept ready and I issued them within a maximum of 48 hours of the hearing. I learnt later that not only the adverse remarks in 'Character Roll' against me were expunged, but the Member was issued a communication by Government to be careful and factual while writing the CRs of juniors.

I left Collectorship with many memories, including my submissions to Mr. J.B. Patnaik about strengthening the city's river embankments and also about developing Bidanashi after Naraz-Munduli barrage would come up as New Cuttack. CM had once attended a High School Golden Jubilee to which I was also invited. I gave a short speech emphasizing that school education must be improved, and meritorious students from ordinary families be given full scholarship to form the backbone of the intelligentsia of the country and requested the honourable CM to sponsor this proposal to the Centre. JBP was a Sphinx. One never knew his reactions. However, the Navodaya / Sarvodyay Vidyalay idea saw the light of the day within some months. I built a Deer Park, beautified the city with gardens and wayside plantations. JBP did all this later on a much larger scale throughout the State.

Losing My Head

I used to work from 6.30 AM to 10 PM everyday including Sundays and never felt tired; never kept files pending. The workload was heavy, but I delighted in getting on top of it. There were occasions of unethical political pressure, I never succumbed to it. CM then developed the habit of telling me his requests but not goading me about it, nor taking it to heart if I could not fulfil his request. I told him once that I got my job through merit and he would have to excuse me if I would not tamper with any selection process for any job. He did not misbehave. Basant Biswal Ji once said to me something about a revenue case that was pending with some Tahsildar. He wanted a particular person to be favoured. After a week he called me to his office at Bhubaneswar and wanted to know what I did about his instruction for the revenue case. I told him that it was a legal matter and would take its own course. All I could do would be to mention to Tahsildar to expedite the case. At this Basant Biswal ji lost his cool and screamed, "Don't talk to me about legality! I know all the illegal things you did to remain as Collector during the Janata Government." I lost my sense, lunged across the table and caught hold of him by his collars. Luckily, my most favourite role model OAS officer Sri G. C. Das had become Private Secretary to Basant Biswal. He knew me; he was watching us from behind the screen. He rushed in and separated us. But, credit to Sri Biswal- he did not rush to CM demanding my transfer or suspension. I also never talked about this [even to my father to whom I used to confide everything] till I had retired from IAS.

Still A Collector 18 Years After

There were innumerable other incidents like when a rogue tusker had been swept against the city embankments and climbed into the main bus depot area of the city; I arranged two special hunters at once who had .475 magnum rifles and supported them with logistic and a major situation could be averted. There was no 'Mohalla' clash during my period over Puja subscription and such other matters. And once I controlled the whole riot-like situation after pitched battle ensued between the Opposition sponsored Odisha Band supporters and the police personnel. I always led from the front, and my SPs never minded my participation as they benefitted from my presence of mind to handle situations. [I always was friendly with them; never any friction.]. I left the job in 1981; I did not hanker for any lost glamour. But I did not realize that I would be leaving such a lasting impression. Fast forward to 1999! I had published a short story volume, 'Jugal Bandi'. I was posted away to Delhi in the middle of the printing. The book needed lamination material to make a good cover page. I came on leave, went to

Cuttack to search for lamination material and landed up in a small but specialized stationary shop in Dagarpada. My father had passed away early 1999; I had shaved my head and was looking sad at the loss of my most revered father. Anyway as the storeowner was counting the 600 pages of laminated material, there was suddenly a very noisy commotion down the road. I tried to peep out from the store, could see nothing and generally said,' "Why such commotion?" The owner looked up and said that a grave 'free-for-all' was in many parts of the town. He lamented that there was no effective Collector as in the past when the town had an excellent atmosphere. Eighteen years had passed from my Collectorship; yet, I felt a pang of jealousy. I asked him the name of the effective Collector. He was busy counting. He took a pause and said, "Nobody can match our Collector Prasanna Hota; he was dashing in looks and effective in action." I could not help but laugh; at this the owner looked at me intently. "Sir, is it you? How dark-complexioned you have become!" And a small drop of tear rolled down his eyes. I was moved; I was never fair complexioned, but, my image in his mind was such!

8

DIRECTOR OF INDUSTRIES

The position of Director, Industries used to be a coveted for younger IAS officers earlier. With the coming of IPICOL, the importance reduced a bit; but still it was a good job. There were many outstanding colleagues posted as General Managers of District Industries Sector in different areas. In spite of that there was stagnation in the number of new small scale industries. We pulled our efforts together and established a hundred percent more small-scale industries in the State than the previous year.

I remember attending a meeting of the 'Full Licensing Committee' of the Ministry of Industries of Government of India at Udyog Bhawan, New Delhi. Four 'Letters of Intents' applied for by Odisha to set up new industries had been rejected by the Ministry of Industry, India. As per the procedure of federal structure, the Full Licensing Committee was called to finalise the rejections after giving the States a routine hearing. Everyone in the Ministry knew that the meeting was only a formality. The Industry Secretary was a cigar smoking, scowling personality with a formidable reputation for suffering no nonsense from the States. So, the meeting as far as I remember, was attended by no Secretary Industry of any State. The meeting started with the Director of the Ministry reading out the rejections one by one and the Industry Secretary concluding, "Okay, reject. The next!"… Not one State's representative protested as the alphabetical order continued. Then the alphabet O was reached, and the Director read out the title of the LOI. Before the venerable Industry Secretary could utter the 'Death' words, I was up on my feet submitting effective facts succinctly in support of our application. The Secretary to his eternal credit did not snub me or ask me to shut up. He might be getting bored with the lack of challenge from the minions. He started asking questions on facts, and I could reel out the relevant facts out sequentially and cogently. And the unthinkable happened; I argued one after another all the four cases; and the gracious Industry Secretary announced immediately that all the four of our applications were sanctioned. I was later told by some colleagues working in Udyog Bhawan then, that my name was mentioned approvingly by junior colleagues of the Industry Ministry both for my audacity and for my accurate presentations. I noticed some disturbing habits among my contemporaries in Delhi. On my tour to Delhi, I would visit a friend or a batch-mate; I would tell them that the real power over Industries was with the Financial Institutions at Bombay, and the IAS would do well to try for some deputation to these Institutions. Not one was interested; instead they would be monitoring who got which 'powerful' subject in work distribution in the Department and what happened to 'foreign' tour proposal that had gone up.

I had some pressing personal problems. I made a request to the Secretary to CM. I was posted to Rourkela Steel Plant on deputation as Dy. G.M.

9

ROURKELA STEEL PLANT DAYS

I joined Rourkela Steel Plant [RSP] as Deputy General Manager [DGM]. A new Managing Director had joined two months ahead of me. He was a vigorous leader, always on the go. Like many technically competent Public Sector Chiefs, he carried some animosity against the IAS. He also found the local ADM and Collector, Sundargarh not to his liking. It was an unfortunate tradition- It was always an ego clash and nothing more. Public officials behaving in immature manner and seeking opportunity to put one another into trouble was childish. I steered clear of this nonsense and concentrated on improving the general administration of the township. Steel cities were well planned. I had my memory of Sub-Collector, Rourkela days. RSP was allotted about 25 thousand acres of land. The State Government wanted back some land for expanding the civil township and auxiliary infrastructure. RSP did not want to part with any. The lease deed was never formally executed; and the whole land administration and land –based developmental issues were hanging fire. I went several times to Bhubaneswar. I mobilized all in a positive manner, made the MD call on CM to invite him to Rourkela. When CM came, I arranged a red carpet welcome in the Steel city; and in a public reception accorded to him made a respected local leader read out a small charter of demand which harped on the need of immediate execution of a land lease Deed which would pave way to all round development of Rourkela. I found to my horror and delight that under the constitutional arrangements, all land belonged to different

States; and RSP was the first public sector company in the country to get a proper land lease deed and legal ownership.

As DGM I was expected to improve and promote ancillary industries; but decades had passed; only some industries had come up. But during the time of my predecessor the addition to ancillary industry was nil. It remained so the first year of my tenure too. An opportunity suddenly came up. MD one day spoke to me to talk to SP and ADM to remove encroachments of casual labourers dotting the steel ash dump yard boundary. I requested him to confide to me the urgency. Then he talked about the collusion between some Plant officials and the coal-dust mafia which was buying coal dust from Plant at Rs. 263/- per ton for many years. MD had revised the price to Rs. 323/- per quintal. The merchants made a cartel and stopped buying. The Plant yards were overflowing with coal dust. It was a battle of nerves. MD wanted more area to dump coal dust for the next 15 days and break this cartel. I was quick to seize upon the opportunity. RSP because of some subsisting Agreement with Unions was supplying cooking fuel [high grade imported coal] at the rate of one quintal per employee for domestic use. It had 42 thousand employees. So high grade coal costing about 1650 rupees per quintal costing the plant about Rs. 70 crores per year was being spent. The distribution work was given to a Cooperative where the coal depot managers had become experts at coal mafia business. They would buy the coupons from employees, show delivery, and the imported coal greatly in demand in nearby foundries etc. would be sold at a high premium in black-market. This illegal money flowed in the veins of lanes and bye-lanes of Rourkela and law and order was always poor in Rourkela. And the employees- quite a sizable number- had developed the nasty habit of meter tampering and doing all their cooking on electric stoves inflating the township electricity bill. I made MD an offer which he could not refuse. I said that I would take 4 thousand tons of coal dust from RSP per month at the price already fixed by him-It would be an adjustment in books. I shall charge Rs. hundred twenty only per quintal as conversion cost and supply coal briquette to employees in place of imported coal. He quickly called a meeting and worked out the economics; I told him about the township electricity bill etc. Within 21 days briquetting and distribution started, the township electricity bill fell to Rs. 20 crores from 31 crores. And imported coal minus the cost of briquette to RSP was about Rs. 50 crores annually. And my balance sheet of ancillary industries showed a jump of about Rs. 20 crores per year. The law and order in the city improved. MD became friendly towards me and involved me with many major decision making processes. However, there was a PR guy who was a perpetual scoundrel creating and filling the ears of MD with all sly tales. He put it into MD's head that MD should try to oust the Chairman SAIL and become Chairman himself. It created a very embarrassing situation among the top managers of the Plant. I counselled MD, but he paid no heed. I thought that I would do well to concentrate on my job and avoid being any part of a poisonous process,

I am conscious that I am generalising in a facile manner and there are exceptions; but overall the PR Departments of our PSUs are terribly over-manned. And all they do is to pander to the ego of the highest level of Management and dissipate the energy of the organization. This PR guy in RSP was a combination of Machiavelli and Malvolio. Ultimately a very decent and competent Chairman like Mr. Samarpungabhan was ousted but RSP MD was left high and dry. Mr. Krishnamurthy of BHEL and Maruti fame became Chairman SAIL. My ethical stand must have reached the ears of Mr. Samrpungabhan; he wrote me a very nice personal letter commending my work and my sense of ethics and integrity.

I must say this much that the work ethics in RSP was way higher than that I experienced in State Government. But for his misplaced personal ambition instilled in him by the poisonous PR Snake, MD, Mr. Subramony was a Role Model of work ethics. He was thorough, very hardworking, went into details in review meetings and permitted participation by all levels provided that the participant was prepared to contribute. The PR guy tried once or twice to poison his mind against me; but, after the second time MD told him to lay off and said to him point blank that Hota was super-brilliant and would be part of his future Team if he were to become Chairman and the PR guy would do well to behave properly with me. Ironically the PR guy told me this himself.

Anyway to the positive and negative lessons of this period of my career:

New Tweed Coat

MD started doting on me for many reasons; a few samples would establish that it was because of my work. Once there was an accident in the Steel Melting Shop area. A casual labour engaged by a contractor died. RSP like other PSU steel plants had a set compensation procedure which in case of casual labour did not provide for appointment of a member of the family to RSP. And there was a demand to engage a kin of the unfortunate dead to a permanent job in RSP on compassionate grounds. The union leaders and some labour of the Steel Melting Shop area had managed to muster support of the workers working in that yard and had stopped working, holding a chanting of their demands sitting surrounding the body and not allowing the removal of the body for post-mortem. MD was about to board a flight to Delhi, GM (Works) assured him that the situation would be handled. Like an eager-beaver I offered to assist GM Works). MD in a moment of superiority of the Technical vs. the Generalist shouted at me, "You are not to meddle with matters within the Plant," I kept quiet. Now the situation escalated; a group of leftist trade unionists and others would not let the body to be removed or the work to go on. About twenty hours passed. The Steel Melting furnace could not take an unplanned shutdown beyond twenty four hours. At 11 AM the next day, GM [Works] must have rung up MD at Delhi who phoned me and started hollering, "What is this? You know you can solve it. Why you are in a sulk, please go and handle the matter." I immediately devised my plan, shared it with GM [Works] and requested him not share 'our' plan with anyone. He was to keep a team of experienced officers and technicians ready who could operate Steel Melting Shop. They should stay hiding at a 100 meters distance sharp at five minutes to two PM. I got in touch with DIG CISF and told him that he should remain ready for some operation within the Plant premises. He always liked me, never questioned my authority and waited for my arrival at 1.30 PM. I rang up for a well-functioning ambulance to report to DIG CISF before 1.30 PM. My reasoning was that at 2 PM the morning shift of work in the Plant would get over. True to the lax work ethics of India, the workers would go away at about fifteen minutes to 2 PM. The next shift would come in not before 5 minutes past 2 PM. This was the window period available to move in, remove the body when the least number of people would be present without creating a law and order situation, rush technical people to Steel Melting Shop to get production going. We arrived with the force and ambulance near the body. Only one person was sitting on vigil. Seeing us a dozen or so persons at about four hundred meters distance started shouting and coming towards the spot. The ambulance workers were with the stretcher standing paralysed next to the body of the dead worker. The body had decomposed, and the ambulance did not have a sheet to put it beneath the body and lift it up to the stretcher. It was a decisive moment as we had less than a minute to pick up the body and scram; otherwise we would be stopped by the oncoming workers. Without hesitating a moment I took off my new tweed coat and extended it to the ambulance helpers to wrap the body. They did the rest. Barely 100 yards separated us from the rushing workers. We vanished with the body. And by the time striking workers were back at Steel Melting Shop, they were outnumbered; the furnace was roaring. Body gone, cause gone! Tweed coat gone too!

There were as usual many interesting incidents where my involvement helped considerably; but, I shall relate only two more and go on to highlight lessons of GG.

MD called for me and said that the by-product of the Steel Plant-fertiliser was choking the Fertiliser Plant godowns as the Marketing Office of SAIL at Calcutta had failed to procure sufficient orders. I did some practical research, fertiliser was always in short-supply and I knew from my earlier experience that there was profiteering by Fertilizer Dealers. Of course, Urea was more in demand but the fertiliser coming as a by-product from RSP was also in use. I studied the matter with as much knowledge I could gather- farmers, fertiliser dealers, chemical engineers et al. I got approved a marketing policy of discount for bulk-buyers and talked to Govt. of Odisha and Govt. of West Bengal Co-operatives, Within two months, the entire stock was sold and godown floors had to be scraped. All this must have got discussed among the rank and file of the Steel brotherhood. Mr. Krishnamurthy came to visit RSP. Everyone made his presentation; my chance came at the end. In 7 minutes I gave him the gist of our work and high points. He continued to ask for many details; and I was ready with the answers. About half an hour was consumed. He looked at me with approval. Next morning, he took me aside and offered me the job of Director, Commercial of SAIL if I would resign and join. I mumbled that I would have to consult my father. And as usual, it was not to be- both my father and eldest brother turned down the idea. My tenure of deputation ended and I reported back to the State Government.

I must record here the lessons in governance during my tenure in RSP. Gross over-manning is the foremost reason for sickness of PSUs. Rampant trade unionism is the next. We had fine technologists and our PSUs would have been the machines of economic growth. I found the work ethics amongst the senior Management Group exemplary. Decision making was faster except where powerful politicians in charge either directly interfered or though some obliging bureaucrat from the Ministry. Where the Secretary in the Ministry was efficient and supported meritorious performance at Plant level, the PSUs performed well. 'Merit benchmarking' was the crying need for PSUs. Reduction in manpower, mercilessly cutting out the parasites would improve performance of PSUs. If my information is right, RSP is now producing four times more with one-fourth of the manpower. In fact, over-manning is a universal malaise of PSUs all over the world. Another major reason of distortion in performance of the PSUs is the indulgent HR management in PSUs- too many perks apart from over-manning! The unofficial but a standard practice is promoting many officers every four years, Thus there are top heavy management, clogging and distorting flow command to satisfy personal ego. I would rather have a lean and 'Need based structure' where pay scales could be upgraded periodically, but promotion should be entirely need based and open to competition.

10

BHUBANESWAR DEVELOPMENT AUTHORITY

In 1985 when I reported back to the State Government, I was asked to join as Vice Chairman of Bhubaneswar Development Authority. BDA was an example of classic mismanagement. My predecessor was honest and tough; but had no aptitude for Urban Planning or commercial work. In fact, many good IAS colleagues are such, honest and tough-that is all. They are not flexible to mould themselves according to the requirements of the new challenging jobs. BDA came to me with a turnover of about Rs, three and half crores a year with accumulated losses of about thirteen crores. In four years that I stayed as VC BDA, I wiped out all the losses left behind liquidity profit of about Rs. 6 crores in bank accounts, and several BDA owned buildings on rent. I took the annual turn-over to Rs, sixty crores in the last year. All this could happen due to GG and hard work.

Suspense of Suspension

After my posting, I called on the CM, Mr. J. Patnaik. CM knew my work capabilities earlier. But distance in IAS career gives others opportunity to carry bogus tales against you to political bosses. Anyway, I found CM somewhat grave. He started instructing, "Get up early each morning. Go around the city with the Municipality Officer and improve cleanliness." I did not protest or argue that I have no link with the Municipal Officer; he might not even listen to me. My work was different, I was to plan, arrange funds and execute improvements in city infrastructure. I was to do houses; markets etc. for people, with clients' money in an efficient manner so that BDA would make a profit and use it for non-profit but essential infrastructure work. I had this weakness// strength- I disliked the then prevalent practice of bureaucrats getting Politicians to lay Foundation Stone of projects without detailed plans of drawings etc. and the resources required. So, I spent about three months sizing up the situation, the tasks, the resource issues and the quality of HR in BDA. Somehow I bumped into CM in the Secretariat corridor. He indicated to me to follow him to his Chamber. There he burst out, "I had given you some specific instructions. I don't see BDA doing any new work; I am going to suspend you!!" I maintained my poise and said, "Excellency, from your lotus hands I have received two commendations for exceptional work. Why suspend me only? You can dismiss me from Service. I shall never question your decision. But I have just about finished my planning, give me six months. Thereafter each fortnight you will inaugurate a new project; I shall again receive a Commendation from Your Excellency." He looked at me for half a minute, then said "Okay, we shall see", and let me go. After some months the Annual Day celebration of BDA was slated. I went to call on the CM, and showed him the draft of the invitation to citizens where he was the Chief Guest for Inauguration of two new Projects - a market complex, a housing colony. He was mollified and agreed to grace the occasion. Then there was no looking back.

I stayed in BDA close to four years and every two months or so CM would be invited to inaugurate a new project. And all this was done without getting a rupee as budgetary support or loan from the Government. Whatever land was allotted to BDA by the Government, BDA paid for the cost. The only concession was an arrangement to pay the cost in instalments over a period of two years.

Enlightened Political Leader

Once BDA was up and running, it began to be loaded with public civil work projects by different Departments of Government. I became the blue-eyed boy of all seniors and politicians, even Bankers [they found lending to BDA was safe and profitable, BDA never defaulted. On the other hand by the beginning of the third year, BDA had liquid cash and Banks vied with each other to get 'deposits' from BDA.] The Chairman BDA was initially Chief Secretary, Mr. Gyan Chand, an extremely able administrator. Then Mr. D. Ulaka became the Urban Minister as well as the Chairman of BDA. He had a rascal as his Private Secretary who taught him all manners of mischief to the otherwise decent tribal leader. Urban Secretary was most upset. Luckily for both of us the most decent political leader of my life, Mr. B. K. Jena became the Urban Development Minister. Mr Jena was simply brilliant. When I would show him the outline of a project, he would ask me sizes of internal road and size of room and egg me on with words like, "Hota Saheb, we are planning for the Capital City, profit is not everything, let us not cut corners". I was impressed with his aesthetics and with his sense of what is correct and what is not. Once I was invited to his official residence; his wife made much of me and some home-made snacks were served. She couldn't help herself; as Minister and I were about to partake of the repast, she hinted that I should help the Minister who was rather 'simple' to make some money. The turn of events was amazing, the Minister roared at his wife, "You dare insult my guest; I shall go on fast today and not touch any food." I somehow placated the Minister. Sri Jena was as honest as a man in public life in India could be. He used to write some parables like stories and with some hesitation he would read out one or two of them to me. I would give some suggestions as to how to embellish the parable into a story; and he would be gratified.

I launched a very well-designed housing scheme called Palash Palli near the airport. Some colleagues and politicians purchased a few of these houses. I remember that when the scheme was launched initially, about thirty five houses out of 175 remained unsold. Four or five politicians purchased these housing units and took it as my personal favour to them. For many years, off and on this would be suddenly mentioned by someone of them and I would laugh off the topic. But this much I may be permitted to say that, barring one senior colleague, the politicians were more ready to mention in future years of my help- not so much my half a dozen IAS colleagues who bought houses there. Not that I wanted anyone to mention; but, just that it struck me as rather funny. I never, repeat, never approached any of the politicians for any favour nor the IAS colleagues also. A civil servant must have the élan of doing a favour to anyone and forget it the next moment. Otherwise his moral fibre would be gradually corroded.

Results through Attention to Details

I would mention three or four important events of this tenure to show that GG is often not pontificating with Policy Circulars, but it is hands on achievements of goods and services for people. There was a valuable piece of land in the heart of the city. I wanted to leverage it for a sizable profit for BDA. Construction is amenable to the most scientific management if resources and engineering decisions flow simultaneously in time. I had visited Calcutta and had noticed that some six story buildings coming up in 18 months. I arranged for an all India Architectural competition. I had arranged a loan of Rs. three crores from UTI. The tenders were invited. I waited close to two and half months after the last date of tender. Finally, I lost patience, went to Engineer Member's room to know the progress. He explained to me the classical Bhubaneswar State PWD way, about tender, comparative statements, first negotiation, second negotiation et al. I asked him to come ready with his recommendations by afternoon. He came and the gist of his recommendation was that the work would be awarded at 33% above the State Schedule of Rate and would be completed in 37 months. I told him to call all the contractors who had bid to come and meet me the next day at noon. At this he coyly said, "If you meet contractors directly, you may get a bad name in public." I could not help sneering and said, "The doors and windows of my chamber would be open. You will be present along with the Executive Engineer, Finance Member, Land Officer and some others whom I shall ask to come." I requested the Chief Architect of BDA to pin all the drawings of the eight storey Commercial Office project including drawings of the 'grills' in a sequence around the four walls of my chamber. I also called Executive Engineer [Stores] to come to the meeting. At noon the meeting started. All the contractors made a chorus as soon as they had entered my chamber - "Sir, In PWD we quote 36% and in Housing Board 35% above the Schedule. We know you are strict, so that we have quoted only 33%." I requested them to first go round my room, look at the drawings and details as on the walls.

I asked them point-blank if all the detailed drawings were there and their work would not be held up for drawings. They nodded in assent. Then I looked at the E.E. stores and smilingly chided him if he would keep the Stores open each day for twelve hours for issuing cement and rods etc. six days a week and his minions would not demand any 'speed money'; he readily nodded yes. I asked the Finance Member whether we had the money and whether he would be ready make payments every fifteen days [he understood my mood and boldly said he would be in a position to make weekly payments]. I asked the Land Officer whether we had hassle-free land in our possession and water and electricity connections were already available, he assented. The die was cast; the contractors understood the preparation for a unique flow of work and payment. Then I said that the optimum time for completion of the building was 24 months; anyone wanting more time would be loaded adversely at the rate of 1%, anyone who would complete it within a minimum time of 21 months would be given a bonus of 1% per month for the period between 21 to 24 months. I then told the six there would now be a re-tendering limited to the original six contractors and they would quote their considered rates within a week. The work was awarded after 7 days at 3% above the Schedule of Rate and the period quoted- 21 months

Readymade Park in Six Months

The second one relates to building the Indira Gandhi Park on the ground in front of the Secretariat. Indira ji delivered her last public speech on 29th October on this ground; the next morning she was assassinated. CM Odisha decided in a high-level meeting at Secretariat that a memorial park would be established by BDA on this ground [10 acres] with her life-like statue occupying the central vista. A renowned sculptor from Soviet Union was commissioned for the purpose. The moment we came out of CM's Meeting Chamber, Finance Secretary, Mr. R.N. Das grumbled, "Sala[this was just a mannerism for him, not an abuse!], park karega! No money for drinking water and here you have jumped forward to build a park. I shall not give you a penny." I maintained my poise and said, "Sir, you should have said this inside. I have been asked to build the park. I shall start." On 1st May 1985 I was handed over the site. Chief Horticulturist of New Delhi Municipal

Corporation prepared the layout plan; at my insistence, his plan and estimate of Rs. one crore was counter-signed by Secretary, Works Department and Finance Secretary. I allowed my engineers 15 days' time and did not interfere at all. Then on the 16th day I asked for the earth-work tender. The park was on a hard moorum filled ground which was used for decades as the 'Parade Ground' for Republic Day etc. It needed to be contoured with liberal amount of fresh sweet earth so that it can be the ground nurturing a verdant green park. Of course, there were civil engineering elements like the 'flowing' podium, the paths, fountains, boundary wall etc. But the earth dumping and contouring was the main work. BDA had an able Horticulturist, Singh Samant ji. He was desperately waiting for the dumping of fresh earth at site to start. Again the classic practice of PWD Civil Engineers on deputation to BDA with their lugubrious ways vs. Samant and me. They had caught hold of one of my acquaintances who had quoted the lowest- Rs. 230/- per truck load of fresh earth. I stated as usual, shouting that it was too costly, again the drama of BDA getting the lowest rate in comparison to other Government agencies. Again a stroke of luck! I suddenly remembered that to repair the floor of my personal house fifteen days back, I had got a truck load of sand from the river at the outskirts of the town for a mere Rs. 110/-. The EM patiently explained to me that in case of earth the story is totally different; earth would be dug pits and pillars of earth would be measured by the Engineer and entered into MB [Measurement Book}, then the earth will be piled onto the 'dala' of the truck of the contractor, each time 'void' would be calculated for each truck 'dala', the earth would be brought to the site to a nominated place where it would be unloaded and compacted and measured and again entered into the MB. Then Horticulturist would get a chance to engage his labour and spread the earth at the different sites of the park according to his requirements of contour. I lost my cool, asked the horticulturist present, "Do you need all this song and dance or you want earth? I told the young man that he would have to engage the same six trucks whose chassis engine, registration number and the ' dala' size which would have to be the standard 'small size', so that we would pay him for a full truck load of earth at the rate of Rs. 130/-. He would have to take it or leave it. He grumbled but agreed; the horticulturist was elated and agreed to all this arrangement. The park was ready in all details with green lawns, water bodies, cobble path, small decorative plants, Odisha stone statues et-al. Mrs Gandhi's majestic statue [two and half times in size] arrived and was erected on a flowing granite podium.

Raja Festival & Work

But there were one or two anecdotes worth telling. When I went to the site on 1st June giving the engineers, horticulturist and contractors another fifteen days freedom, I found some progress. But true to my nature, I started calculating backward from the zero date of 20th October. After a bit of discussion all officers and contractors agreed that they would have to increase the number of labourers by 20 to 25%. Each contractor agreed and added that he would do it after 'Raja' [a Deej like festival, widely celebrated in Odisha. On my interrogation, all of them said that the 'earth-work labourers were Santal labourers from Mayurbhanj and Keonjhar districts. They would all go home for the Raja festival which would be 13-15 June; and they would come back with more labourers. I immediately calculated that if the workers were to go on leave from 13 June they would stop working from 12th, and most likely they would come back two or three days after 16June. I saw a week's work vanishing. I asked the Contractors to meet me in the evening near the labour jhuggis where they were staying in shanties with their wife and children. A hardy lot! I landed up with a car load of biscuits which I distributed at the hands of the curious contractors to the children. Then I made an announcement to all male/female workers that I have persuaded the contractors to be generous; they would pay double the wages for the entire Raja period. The men would get liquor to drink at evening; the women would be given new sari and the children toys. And labour Sardar would get Rs. one hundred for each new labour he could arrange before 7 June. Everyone picked up the bait; on 13th June work was going on the proposed Indira Park. I was sitting at the office at 10 AM attending to some work. The phone rang; it was Private Secretary to Finance Secretary. "Aare Prasanna, I went to market, I saw something never seen before. There is work going on at your park." I immediately replied, "Sir, I have scared them by taking your name!" He burst out laughing and said he had never seen anyone doing earth work on Raja in Odisha from his childhood. And he said that he was now convinced that I would deliver a proper park in time and that his Under Secretary would come to my office by 10.30 AM the next day with a bank draft of Rs. fifty one lakh. Rabi Das Sir was true to his words, dot on time. The park soon assumed a green verdant shape. We moved some decorative palm trees at night by crane etc. By 22nd October everything looked perfect. PM Rajiv Gandhi ji came by late afternoon on 29 October. I had organised twenty five thousand students with tiranga [tricolour of our National Flag] hats. On the podium, there were only three people-PM, CM and myself. Mr. Patnaik spoke first for a few minutes and requested the PM to inaugurate. PM was shown the switch by me, he pressed and the white buds of tuberose covering the statue slid down to its feet. Just then Indira ji's voice came on for everyone to hear her famous words of her last speech delivered at that very ground- " Desh ki hit me mera katra katra khoon agar bah jaye to mujhe koi abshos nahin.." [If each drop of blood in my body flows down for the benefit of the country, I shall have no regrets.] Rajiv ji was moved; he stood still! He then looked at me, folded his hands to me and to the park full of children and walked down the podium without delivering any speech. Attention to details makes ordinary moments extraordinary. [The credit for this masterpiece of insertion of Indira ji's voice goes to Mr. S.M. Patnaik IAS – junior- who carried the reputation of being honest and gentlemanly in contrast to his name-sake.] And there was a lapse by me too which luckily didn't snowball into a major controversy; but I felt guilty for not having anticipated the possibility. Apparently, when the twenty five thousand students were going out, taking advantage of heavy rush, lack of bright light at exit gates and not having clearly briefed the police for special deployment at the exit points, there was something of a melee and an antisocial touched two girl students inappropriately and escaped in the crowd. We bureaucrats must not think that our responsibilities had ended till the last ordinary guest had left.

Sick Bed to High Court

There were many other dramatic moments of BDA days. I was transferred to the Central Government to join at New Delhi; I tried my utmost to complete the incomplete work. In the process, I had a health break down; my spine went into spasm, I was bandaged from chin to toes lying on a steel bed with weights hanging on my feet for traction at a special Orthopaedic Hospital at Olatpur, midway between Bhubaneswar and Cuttack. My office informed me that a housing scheme which I had launched recently was facing opposition from the local people, and a case had been filed before the 'Vacation Bench' [the Court was on Summer vacation] of the High Court at Cuttack to obtain a 'stay' against the scheme. Now, there was absolutely nothing irregular, it was Government. Land sold to BDA for the scheme. There was a Kali Temple for some decades in the centre of the land; I had planned in the layout to provide for continuance of the existing good looking temple as a high-point of the ambience of the scheme. I was perturbed because I felt that people had trusted me and had already purchased housing units, tenders had been awarded and work had started in full swing. Till that date, in my four years stay in BDA there was never any cost or time overrun in any of my schemes. So I could not let people down and allow matters to drag in Law Courts. I called for my office car, got hold of a pair of scissors and cut off the top layer of my bandage. I went to Cuttack lying supine on the back seat of the car and entered the High Court chamber of the honourable Judge with half of my bandage trailing on the ground in the nick of time. The lawyer from the other side was in full flow-"Your honour, this whole thing is nothing but the ego of an IAS officer, his highhandedness to destroy a beautiful religious structure just to build a couple of houses!" I knew that it was not the correct protocol for me to address the Judge directly. But in that melee of litigants, I thought that it was now or never. I loudly said, "My Lord, this IAS officer has no ego; he has come from the hospital bed to submit himself to the Might of Justice. In the layout I have protected the Temple and have made provisions for a small garden around it to enhance its setting." The Judge, Justice Mahapatra who knew me a bit socially, turned his face away; but he was a just Judge. He said, "I hear some noise from some part of the Court; the BDA person is ensuring fair play. Not only no Stay, but the case is dismissed. Detailed judgement will follow." All the lawyers and litigants present burst out laughing impressed by my dramatic arrival and impassioned plea.

Role Model Seniors

I must pay my debt of gratitude to two Role-Model seniors for my success in BDA; to Mr. M.P. Modi, then the Special Secretary, General Administration, which controlled all land resources and the budget for major projects in Bhubaneswar. After the initial 'stiff upper lip' stance in assessing me, he warmed up to me and guided me for planning and implementing more projects, and loaded BDA with work. Secretary, Works department, an eminent Civil engineer complained to the CM that BDA was being given the works meant for PWD. CM sent for Mr. Modi. Modi ji [affectionately called Lord Modi for his British aristocratic ways] could be sarcastic and back up his sarcasm with data. He went to CM with a host of files, and established that PWD was doing civil works at more than 30% higher cost than the Schedule of Rates and was taking a time of 36 months or more to complete a project; so Modi ji decided to give some work to BDA as it offered to do it at 5-7% higher than Schedule of Rate and within 24 months, and that BDA's drawing and quality of work was better. CM apparently said that G.A, Department could give fifty percent of its works to BDA, PWD had to improve and should also get projects to execute. I was thus the architect and builder of the very popular 'Aamba Bagicha' [near VIP colony] Officers Enclave as I visualized all drawing details from my user's experience of Government quarters and sat with our Architect to explain the requirements.

The other sterling personality was Mr. R. K. Bhujabal, a very dynamic and hard-working IAS officer with a high degree of aesthetics. He was my Boss as Secretary, Urban Development. He was initially fond of me, but soon he became the main adversary. It arose from a silly thing. When he joined U.D. Dept. many of his admirers called on him and said that the urban sector would now improve under him dramatically. Mr. Bhujabal would smile his assent; then a few of them would ask him a favour of allotment of a house to buy. Mr. Bhujabal would then offer a house from the unsold stocks of the State Housing Board at Bhubaneswar. The supplicant without realising that Mr. Bhujbal was also the ex-officio Chairman of the Housing Board would say disparagingly about the Housing Board and request him to put in a word to VC BDA to allot a house constructed by BDA. After a couple of such missives by witless supplicants, Mr. Bhujbal got terribly upset and tried to harass me. But the Chairman ex-officio of BDA was Minister Sri Jena; and true to his great administrative acumen the Minister was playing a balancing role. I was never disrespectful to my IAS Boss but as per habit I was irrepressible. Full credit to Bhujabal Sir; he showed obvious hostile body language but always fought to win through merit and logic. I became more careful in preparing my Board proposal where he was a Member and Minister presided. So the proposals were scrutinised by a microscope by Secretary UD, but always passed the muster. Minister never showed his preference except talking about some aesthetic or design aspect. In one Board meeting in April 1989, I had put up to the Board the latest balance sheet showing the net profit of Rs, 4 crores 56 lakh after wiping out the loss of Rs. 13.50 crore incurred in the period before me. Secretary U.D. said that he would like to check the figures through a special audit and the matter could be up to the next Board. The Minister tried to manage the situation by saying, "Our Secretary is like the Sun and the VC BDA is our Moon." I should have known better, but my urge for making a witty rejoinder got the better of me. I said, "Honourable Minister is absolutely right. Moon can shine only if Sun shines on it. The Moon however, could shine better if Sun were not to shine so much on the other Planets" This was a hint at the Housing Board. Secretary could not say anything; but as we moved out of the meeting, he said, "Okay, Hota Babu, you won today. We shall see." I then realised that Bosses must not be trifled with. One must have a sense of proportion and not try for the 'last word' in a verbal exchange. Boss management is an art. I went down with back spasm the day after the Board meeting.

Minister got to know that I was bed-ridden and came home. He replied to my family when it complained that I had invited my illness by overwork, "No, No! Very few can understand Hota Saheb. He has fallen ill because he has not been allowed to work." To the great credit of generous Bhujabal Saheb, he organised a Board meeting of BDA after a month by which time it had become public that Government of India had asked for my services on deputation. In the meeting, he said that the Special Audit had found out the Balance sheet to be correct.

Minister looked relieved. Bhujabal Saheb further stated that he was moving a special resolution to commend the achievements of Sri Hota as VC BDA. He was generous. Not every time we would meet a large-hearted superior.

Lessons of GG

Now to the lessons of the BDA period about GG: Efficiency, effective work, and hard work round the clock were the usual cornerstone. But additional planks were {Participation] successful seeking involvement of local people to ensure that the schemes were implemented without hitch. Market Survey [eliciting client's choice and capacity] was another input for planning appropriately. Generating institutional finance, [Generating public resources with private participation] engaging Architects for better designed buildings paying them fees as decided by Council of Architects thus bringing in <u>professionalism and quality</u> to civil projects were some other features. Correct Accounting [foundation of Accountability], up to date double entry balance sheet of BDA made it possible for Banks etc. to lend to BDA liberally. BDA started using people's money for projects by making the launch of the schemes attractive and meticulous [above all, delivering all products in time and within the original cost], thus reducing finance cost and increasing profit margins. BDA did not get any budgetary support from the Government during my four years tenure.

Rule of Law was enforced. Most of the people, the poor and the very rich did not know the Act and Rules regarding construction by-laws; the rich thought they were above law. Some exemplary enforcement action against the rich and the powerful [including some senior IAS officers] was undertaken and it created some PR problems; partly through patient personal explanation, partly through wide publicity to the bye laws, the hostility was mitigated to an extent. Some seniors took it very personally, that they were fined for excess construction and complained to my eldest brother; it took quite a bit of doing to convince them that the fine was minimal and their violations were even more.

Transparency in award of works to contractors shielded us from allegations by jealous elements. In fact, right after I was transferred,

Janaki Patnaik ji lost the elections, the other Patnaik - Biju ji came to power. Again the same malcontents instituted an inquiry by an Assembly Committee against Indira Park and me [Politically Janata Dal was opposed to any commemoration of Indira ji's name]. The enquiry was closed down within 48 hours as coastal Irrigation contractors rushed to the Janata MLAs [they were traditionally funded lavishly by these contractors] and informed them that they were being paid at the rate of Rs. 200/- per truck load of earth while BDA paid only Rs.130/- per truck load. If this received wide publicity in the media, there would be a lot of embarrassment. They also told the leading MLAs that Indira Park was completed at a cost of Rs. sixty four lakh only when its sanctioned estimate was Rs. one crore. I really don't know who all helped; but such news reached me at Delhi later in bits and pieces.

The main lesson of GG learnt from tenure in BDA was that, Government and Government 'brands' were still very much acceptable to people provided that there was efficient performance and respect to clients in service and goods delivery. I ensured that all buyers got proper Registered Sale deeds and clear titles. I took pains to clear the dues of the Government for the land and thus was in a position to give marketable titles to buyers. My only failure was that I left about Rs. four crore fifty lakh liquidity behind- I could have put up a good convention centre cum auditorium. The next Minister and VC appointed hundreds of unnecessary persons from the new Minister's constituency in BDA; BDA gradually sank till a reasonable and efficient IAS officer Mr. Rajamoni became VC BDA and improved matters. Much later, a very bright officer Ms. Aparajita Sarangi [now a MP] stole the march over everyone by sprucing up the Bhubaneswar city-scape substantially.

11

Joint Secretary, Ministry of Industry, Government of India

Finally my youngster/junior status in IAS came to an end- I entered the hallowed portal of Secretariat for the first time in my career after twenty years of service, that too direct to Government of India, Ministry of Heavy Industry as a Joint Secretary.

I was quite innocent of careerism. One has to speak to friends and patrons, call on 'powers that be' to get a 'coveted' posting. I had no idea what was coveted and what was not; I had become number two in the IAS list of 1969 batch, so I presumed one would get a posting based on merit. I didn't know that' merit' had been bade goodbye once one entered the service thanks to the UPSC. Thereafter it was all nepotism,

I was initially posted to the Bureau of Public Enterprises [BPE]] as Joint Secretary. I happily joined and started working in the right earnest. Luckily there was a college mate, Mr. Siddharth Behuria, of UP cadre who had worked closely with Mr. G.N. Mehra, Secretary of the Department. Without my having raised the issue with him, he expostulated with Mt. Mehra that he was being unfair to the topper of a batch by posting him to a 'side-lined' job. So I was soon 'rescued'; I was posted to the main Department as Joint Secretary.

First thing one noticed in coming to Delhi was that one was cut down to size so far personal facilities were concerned. One got accustomed to thinking that one was a 24/7 important tool of the Governance in the State, and creature comforts like housing, driver support etc. were small perquisites so that you could devote yourself entirely to work. It was not so in Delhi where there was rampant nepotism in allotment of housing. Officers way junior to us of the 'powerful' cadre particularly were adroit at arranging housing much above their entitlement. The record was beaten by a colleague junior to me- he was not from UP cadre but outshined them by a mile. He managed to move into a C-II ground floor and later wrote a much acclaimed book, 'Integrity- a Way of Life'!!

The work in the Ministry was different from field work. I thanked Fate that I got a chance to be away from Secretariat jobs so long; I had become accustomed to deliver goods and services to people by maximizing resources [or even generating resources in loss making organizations to substantially increase availability of goods and services by the rapidly growing population.]

The Department of Heavy Industry had 47 Public Sector Units to look after. The Secretary had distributed these 47 PSUs amongst 4 Joint Secretaries. I had PSUs like HEC, MAMC, Hindustan Salts, Bharat Ophthalmic Glass, Hindustan Papers and some others like Tyre Corporation of India Ltd. Almost all of them were running on loss and were saddled with unnecessary manpower which dragged these PSUs down. There were CMDs, other functional Directors and the like, but they had very little to show by way of performance. They had old half/unimplemented Order books, eroded working capital, and a lot of unserviceable plants and machinery and stocks lying here and there. I tried my best to restructure them down-size their manpower and improve their productivity succeeding partially. I was also in charge of Planning and General Section of the Department. It took me sometime to fathom the purpose and working of the Department. I may be permitted to relate some stories till I come back to GG.

Delhi ka Laddoo

I was completely out of sorts in Delhi initially. One day loafing during lunch break in Mr. Mansingh's room [he was Joint Secretary, Industry known as the more important segment as gleefully explained by Mansingh ji to neophyte Hota] of the Ministry, in charge of Industrial Policy. Mr. Agarwal-his batch mate- also dropped by and invited him to a party being hosted by Sri Agarwal's relatives in export business. Mr. Mansingh introduced me as his classmate working in Udyog Bhawan. So Agarwal ji insisted that I would come with my wife to this party at Hyatt Regency. We arrived at the party by 8 PM. Neither of us drank. Except Mr. Mansingh and Mr. Agarwal, we knew no one else in that fairly crowded place. Out of boredom we decided to return home. Mr. Mansingh accosted Agarwal ji who said we could not leave without dinner; he then caught hold of the host of the party and introduced us; in turn the hosts said, "Come and meet some important people. And we then were taken to a young person sitting on a large chair being made much of by the hosts. " Hota ji meet our Sir, Addl. collector of Customs. Sir, Hota ji is in IAS." The young man suddenly stood up and asked, "Sir, are you Prasanna Kumar Hota of Jubilee Hall, Delhi University?" I said 'yes'. He then straight fell prostrate and touched my feet. It was a comical sight, the VIP of the party prostrating like that. He stayed supine and said, "Guru Ji, I had vowed that I would pay my obeisance like this if life would give me a chance to meet you. I am a product of the famous Hota's notes which you left behind, which were photocopied and eight batches after you used those notes to qualify for civil service." And as they say- that was that!

I however continued to be in awe of New Delhi ways of working. The quality of drafting, file maintenance and accuracy of paperwork was way better than that I had come across in Odisha.

Public Sector Stories

Back to our main story! I was given additional charge as CMD of Engineering Projects of India Ltd. - one of the PSUs with the Department, pending recruitment of a regular CMD. In six months I turned it around to profit. Basically, I reduced all bogus manpower mercilessly through a VRS scheme, improved Order book and implementation of existing orders, settled a major litigation and collected about Rs. eighteen crores as out of court settlement from Mitsubishi of Japan which helped in the working capital. After six months an insider became the regular CMD chosen by the Public Enterprise Selection Board. The Company started sliding again after three years.

Heavy-weight Made Light

Heavy Engineering Corporation [HEC] Ranchi saw a lot of good times till 1970. Then it started crumbling with its mammoth manpower, elaborate township cost and through rank bad management. Anyway, Sri Mishra, a seasoned technocrat became CMD HEC. I went at him hammers and tongs. The manpower was reduced; I tried to get a policy decision to sell off part of the township. Anyway, reforms/restructuring succeeds when simultaneously there is good momentum of work. Order book was there but the working capital had been totally eroded. State Bank was the principal working capital lender. The local MP sympathetic to HEC got a phone call made from PMO to RBI at Mumbai. Mishra ji and I landed up in Mumbai first at State Bank Headquarters with Dy. MD, Mr. Mahadevan. The AGM assisting Dy. M.D. was polite; Mahadevan ji got rid of us in the midst of my carefully rehearsed spiel about the bright future of a restructured HEC saying, "No point talking here. RBI has to permit any further lending as HEC is a long-standing defaulter." So we went to RBI. Dy. Governor RBI Mr. Amitabh Ghosh assisted by a senior woman colleague met us. I tried my sales pitch as to how the Department and Government were determined to get HEC going again, about reduction of manpower, cost-cutting, order book etc. Before Mr. Ghosh could react, the lady officer effortlessly rolled out all the past promises of the Department which were never followed up; she had every data at her fingertips. She was the worthy adversary - very impressive. Mr. Ghosh looked helplessly at me; obviously the phone from the PM's Office had reached him but not percolated below. I threw a life-line; I said HEC was executing some top strategic defence equipment as part of its order book. Sri Ghosh jumped at it and said, though he entirely agreed with Ms. V-'s analysis, in view of defence security issues, RBI would permit State Bank to extend another Rs. twenty crores a working capital. Ms. V- looked at him in astonishment and disgust and said she would not be a part of any such decision; she just left the meeting. We rushed back to Dy. M.D. SBI's office. It was nearing 5 PM; no food or water all day. Mahadevan ji this time made his intention clear by turning his chair away from us. The poor AGM carried on the dialogue. I said that RBI had agreed to SBI increasing its working capital to HEC by Rs. twenty crores. Dy. MD sitting at a distance pretending to be not listening, could not but join in, "How, how? Who all were there in the meeting?" I said, "Mr. Amitabh Ghosh, Dy. Governor and Miss V-." CMD Mr. Mishra, who had allowed me to talk all the while, spoke up, "Sir, I think she is Mrs. V-." I also stupidly joined issues with him, and said, No, Miss V-." Mishra ji said again, "No Sir! She is Mrs. V-." I would not give up easily and continued - "No! Miss V-". Finally Dy. MD lost his temper and said, "I have been noticing from the morning that you are talking too much! How do you know for sure that she is Miss or Mrs. V-?" At this, I got up, bowed to him and said, "Excellency! I cannot say for sure whether she is Miss or Mrs V-. But my guess is based on the way she argued; it did not appear to me that she ever has had the benefit of saying 'yes' to any man." Mahadevan ji looked at me flabbergasted, folded his hands to me and said. "Please go. We shall give you an additional twenty five crores!" Not a word of this episode is exaggerated!

Four Moghuls: I had the privilege to work in this tenure with four Moghuls of UP; all four Secretaries were from UP cadre and had their inimitable royal style. First and foremost was Mr. G. N. Mehra, a man with a stern exterior but soft heart, quick to appreciate good work. Later he became my life long mentor. The second was Mr. Shiromoni Sharma, a very calm and just boss. The third boss Mr. Surendra Singh impressed me considerably. The fourth Secretary was Mr. Ashok Chandra, a very thorough person in file work and Parliamentary matters. My meticulously prepared reply on a Parliamentary petition forwarded to us for comments on CMD of Maruti Udyog, Mr. R. C. Bhargava revised several times under Mr. Ashok Chandra's penchant for accuracy pleased him. Mr. Surendra Singh was my role-model; he had all the elegance and ability to be a leader in IAS. He never made us do pointless work; he just wanted us to complete it as accurately as possible. But when a reply would go either to the PMO or Supreme Court, he would guide us meticulously. I was once told by him, "Hota, you are very good, no, no, you are outstanding. But you perhaps, have never worked in a Secretariat earlier. You do not know which side of the file to sign when it goes up, and which side of the file you should sign when it comes down." I readily admitted that it was my first posting in a Secretariat job. He laughed and showed me that when a file would go up, I should sign on the right and when it would come down. I should sign on the left margin. Then he taught me how to prepare the answer to a 'Star' question to be answered by the PM. He taught me how, the question should contain maximum in one and half page the gist of the answer called 'At a glance'. Then it should have the full answer in not more than in 3 pages; he taught me how to leave wide margins and give a heading of the paragraph in the left margin if it was page 1, and the heading on the right side margin if it was page 2 so that the VVIP would not be inconvenienced. He told me that contrary to our assumption sometimes, the brain of the VVIP would become razor-sharp under the pressure of responsibility of high office and the VVIP would be thrown off the track by any error. So the 'brief' for the VVIP had to be flawless. He invited all Joint Secretaries to dinner at his home and was as informal as a boss could be. He displayed panache effortlessly. The real problem with the Department was that it got associated with posting of IAS officers earlier in 'powerful' Departments for 'adjustments' to this Department. So brilliant Secretaries just came and bided their time to rebound somewhere else. Willy-nilly, their heart was not in the Department of Heavy Industry.

Case Study for Kellogg School of Management

The other episode worth mentioning in this tenure is the turnaround story of Scooters India Ltd [SIL]. My senior colleague, Mr. Viswanath Anand of UP cadre was looking after SIL. He was its ex officio Chairman. One day I was called to the Secretary's chamber. When I went in, Sri Anand was sitting. Secretary said, "Hota, you are not the Chairman of any PSU. I think it is time that you also become a Chairman. From today, you will be Chairman of Scooters India." I kept quiet and came out with Mr. Anand who said "Hota, sorry! SIL is a lousy Company; it is about to be closed down. Some of the workers are very ill-behaved. There has to be an Annual General Meeting of the Company. The workers could be very nasty; I shall ring up my friend, DG police, who will make all arrangements for your safety." I thanked him and said that I would seek his help if necessary. Then I read up on SIL and read up its last three years balance sheet. I am sorry to mention that many IAS officers lack or neglect this basic training of how to read a balance sheet. My IPICOL/BDA days had honed my ability; I noticed in the balance sheet of the last 3 years of Scooter India that the Company was heading for multi-organ failure; its production in the last three years was Rs. 20 crore, 16 crore and the last financial year it had come down to Rs. 12 crore. It had employee strength of 3129 persons and an annual wage bill of Rs. 15 crores. The employees had no pay revision since the last 7 years or so and they were a demoralised lot. I landed up for the AGM of the Company which was held in the auditorium of the Company. It started at 1PM. I was the only one on the dais as SIL had no Director; the real head was Executive Director[ED] Mr. Sahay who was sitting in the audience. No sooner I picked up the mike to commence the meeting, about ten people from the 50 strong audience rushed up, snatched the microphone from me and started giving vent to their pent up ire; they started abusing me in unparliamentary Bhojpuri Hindi. I was unperturbed and kept looking at them smilingly. After abusing me for an hour or so, they found me sitting calmly and smiling at them and scribbling down some points on a notepad. This got them even angrier and then they rushed to me and started to show clenched fists at my face as if they were going to punch my nose. Dr. Sahay, the ED got very agitated and rushed to my side and whispered whether he should inform the police. I waved him away and continued to smile. This kind of drama went on for three more hours; the handful of agitators-one after one-heaped invectives on me and threatened me physically. I could smell their breath but they never touched me. I gestured to them to hold peace for a minute; and I moved to the front of the dais and took off my shirt partially baring my back. Everyone was bemused as to what I was attempting. I said calmly, "Please make a line, come one by one and slap hard on my back." The commotion stopped and the leader of the agitators said, "Ye pagal kahan se aaya?"[Where has this mad-cap come from?] I laughed and said, "Am I mad or you all? If beating me up will improve the performance of SIL, do beat me. Otherwise keep quiet and listen to me for ten minutes as I have heard you for close to four and half hours." They kept quiet for a minute out of curiosity. I never gave them any speech. I only summarised their points raised in their speech- workers' pay scale should be revised; bogus work should stop, corruption in SIL should end. SIL was a great market brand; it should recover its former position. I asked them whether I have articulated their demands properly. This time the animosity vanished in a trice and all of them vigorously nodded their assent. Then I added that we would all have to do something positive and new to reach the results we desired. They all voiced their support. Thereafter, accompanied by all, I took a tour of the factory. I saw that bits of broken steel parts lying on the lawn and grass growing on one production line. Yet I didn't lose hope. I then asked the bomb-shell question- "I have noticed that in the last 3 years from the Company balance sheet that the production has gone down rapidly; but there is one entry in the balance sheet which is showing growth- Rs. 50 lakh one year, then Rs. 1 crore the next year and this year it is Rs. 2 crore. The chorus of answers said in Bhojpuri Hindi, "Oh Sir. It is a three wheeler called Vikram; it is not our real business; we take some advance from dealers and make these three wheelers." I immediately said that we would make it our exclusive line of business till we would regain profitability. At this the Union leader piped out, "What, Scooter India me scooters nahi banenge? SIL had won Engineering Export Council's award for exporting Rs. 4 crore 50 lakh worth scooters to Turkey last year." I said, "Aap Union leader ho, please go with the Chief of finance and chief of production and come back after you all have worked out the real cost to the Company for having made this export." It was my age old discipline of getting a financial analysis done of most of the issues. The three came back in about twenty minutes and the Union leader sheepishly replied at my prodding that it had cost SIL more than Rs. 6 crores to export scooters worth Rs. 4.5 crores. I immediately shifted to high gear. I used all the abuse in which I was trained by my hostel mates in Delhi University, added some of my own picked up from observations in later years from boozing friends, I let go a volley of unparliamentary abuses on that motley gathering. The small crowd was taken aback at my sudden rough behaviour. I said, "To earn four and half crores, you have spent six crores. I could get all of you arrested right now by the CBI. That is why the Government wants to close down SIL. But, I shall give you a chance provided you accept my condition. In four months I shall turn around your Company, otherwise you can behead me. But till that time, you all have to keep absolutely quiet, maintain complete discipline and work as per my instructions sent through your ED. We shall produce three wheelers only at least for one year." Then they looked at me not with anger but as their leader and saviour; a discussion ensued in much more polite tones. It was apparent that Vikram- the three-wheeler had a larger body than that of a Bajaj three-wheeler. It was quite acceptable to drivers; but, the machinations of the private sector had persuaded all State Transport Authorities STAs barring U.P. and Rajasthan to declare Vikram as not road-worthy due to extra turning radius. I rang up then and there my colleagues in different States and persuaded them to break the nexus at lower levels of the State Transport Authority and declare Vikram to be 'road-fit'. I followed up with a meticulous letter to all States with all technical data and sent teams from SIL to make presentations to STA on the subject. Colleagues in fourteen States permitted Vikram as 'road-fit'. M/S Ferguson engineers were engaged as consultants to advise on manpower; they came back with a figure of 437 persons; I knew it would be impossible for me to reduce the manpower that much, so requested them to rework and come back. In the meantime, I started VRS of Government. Then I talked to ED and asked him to come to Delhi to my office with ten of his best officers. When they came, I locked the door of my room and embraced each one and burst into tears. They were taken aback; I explained to them that the Company could be revived if they showed commitment and love to their Company. I told them that we would have to retain good persons who were productive and indispensable, and let go of the 'useless'. I said the technique would be that each one of them would go and choose his ten best personnel and treat them to some snacks in privacy and embrace each one of them to commit themselves to the company and in turn choose their team best worker and repeat the process. Thus we would have a core productive group of a thousand to sustain SIL.I knew the flip side of thoughtless reduction of manpower through VRS as the good personnel -having a chance of re-employability elsewhere- would be the first to go weakening the Company further. The manpower came down to 1976. Of all the persons, the great Vajpayee ji happened to be the MP from Lucknow and he rang up Secretary Mr. Ashok Chandra [Mr. Surendra Singh had been elevated to the post of Cabinet Secretary] to stop further attrition. Ashok Chandra ji walked into my room; said "Hota, no more VRS in Scooters India. Vajpayee ji has phoned and asked me to request you!" I remonstrated, Mr. Chandra played my trick on me; he came round the table, embraced me and said, "You are brilliant! But I cannot give you the support you deserve. You have done wonders already. Chhod de; tera baap ki property nahi hai!" I replied, "Chhod to dunga; lekin ye mera Baap ki property hai. Aap Department ki Baap ho; ye appki property hai." He sat down in a chair for a couple of minutes silently, looking at the ceiling and then left my room with a sigh. In the remaining part of the year, the production in SIL went up to Rs. 36 crores, the next year Rs. 72 crores and finally up to Rs. 138 crores with a net profit of Rs. 7 crores. It apparently became a case study of 'Turnaround' in Kellogg School of Business as gleefully told to me by Dr. Sahay three years later when I was back in Odisha, but met Dr. Sahay. He had been elevated and was CMD of SIL where he was already ED for seven years by the time I met him in 1993.

I got a grip on the factors that ailed our Public Sector Units during this tenure. The major reason was the unwillingness of the IAS to persuade politicians to take harsh but correct decisions about restructuring PSUs in the interest of the PSUs rather than in the interest of abysmal number of unproductive manpower and too many top level post to fulfil the personal urge of higher officials than for any need of the PSU. Investment and restructuring efforts were made piecemeal manner for some PSUs from time to time but without professional consulting organization's detailed advice. And the electoral illusory gains drove all fiscal discipline out of the window. All across pay-scale rise was announced before 1993 parliamentary elections throwing whatever improvement one had achieved with great difficulty out of gear. The ruling party lost in spite of this gimmick; but the chance of recovery of many PSUs was lost forever.

The skills and lessons of the Joint Secretary period were substantially different than that of the postings under State Government. In interministerial / Departmental meetings, one had to be much more suave and not passionate. If one wanted his proposal to go through a bit of background spade work by way of meeting the important people in the meeting was in order. Networking is an important skill in public affairs. [I realised that I was somewhat deficient in this virtue.] Thoroughness in drafting and presentation of systematic data was appreciated by the bosses and other Departments too. My drafts to Secretaries came back unscathed and accepted in ninety nine percent of the cases in 5 years of my tenure. In the last year of my tenure, Maruti Udyog was put with me. One had to write long and consistent notes to strike a balance between the able persuasions of Mr. R.C.Bhargava, formerly an IAS of UP who wanted all facilities from Central Government but did not want any accountability [Maruti Udyog was a Joint Sector Company where the Government had a substantial equity investment]. Mr. T.R. Prasad who later became Cabinet Secretary once mentioned graciously to me in passing that he had read my long flawless notes and could bargain considerable advantages for the Government of India at time of disinvestment. It was my immense good luck that the four Moghuls of UP cadre gave me glowing assessment remarks and called me to their Chamber to share the remarks with me.

I reported back to the State Government. As my name had been sent for going on a Fellowship to Oxford University from October 1994, I was kept on 'compulsory waiting' for a couple of weeks. Towards the end of September, I was on my way to Oxford.

12

VISITING FELLOW AT OXFORD UNIVERSITY

I had chosen my subject as 'Privatization of Public Sectors of India - in Light of Experience of U.K. I was attached to the Department of Economics of Oxford University as a Visiting Fellow. The habit of scholastic pursuit had been lost; it took a couple of months to realise that one was utilizing one's personal valuable time and it ought not to be wasted just because nobody was supervising my work. Reading the first book took about a month. Immediately, I became conscious that by being a bureaucrat one was exposed to limited and often stultified use of language. I realised that the intellectual world had moved on; the average IAS officer was quite a bit behind in both use of language and data. I tightened my belt and got down to work. Soon I got involved in my subject and researched quite a bit on the subject. One day, I was standing in a famous square of the University area facing a Church; an impressive lady came quietly and stood within touching distance. I just realised that she was the famous Margaret Thatcher; at this juncture a senior police officer came and in a very civil manner requested me to move away. I visited some privatised undertakings including British Steel. My seminar was a great success; there was no standing room left. My college mate and IAS in Karnataka Mr. S. K. das wrote an excellent book on Civil Services across many leading countries. He used to read out some of his findings - those sessions were very insightful. For instance, Singapore paid the best to its Civil Servants, somewhere around US $ 40000.00 per month to its Secretaries. However, the great leader Lee Kuan Yew apparently told his Secretaries that they were 'instruments of the State. If they would ever be found corrupt there would be no inquiry- only a bullet'. The Japanese Civil Service had also great traditions; Secretaries were picked up for the highest post at a comparatively younger age; seniors above them were given placements in the private sector. Thus a Secretary in Japan had a relatively long tenure to accomplish public tasks.

I completed my course of 9 months and benefitted by broadening my intellectual horizon substantially. I got acquainted with computers and their immense capacity. I reported back to Odisha. I do feel the value of sabbaticals for 'Mid-Career Training' in quality institutions IIMs, IITs etc. so that the IAS is challenged in his smugness that creeps onto his personality; and broadens his intellectual horizon. The sabbatical should be limited to 6 months. We may send some IAS abroad to good institutes/universities; a period of 4 month is adequate.]

13

HEALTH SECRETARY, GOVERNMENT OF ODISHA

I reported to the State Government in mid-1995 and was posted as Health Secretary. I accepted and joined without demur. My colleague at Oxford, Mr. Chopra of Rajasthan cadre studied Public Health in Oxford and was posted on return to the Industry Department. Such are the use of 'Specialization". Being Health Secretary of Odisha was not a joyous job. The State had the worst health indices in many areas. The saddest thing was that nobody briefed me about the priorities of this sector to the neophyte bureaucrat who was supposed to be in forefront of making available better health services to common people whose per capita income was one of the lowest in India. I had to thrash around seeking information and knowledge. My limited contacts in the health system were mostly with some doctor friends of Medical Colleges. Dr. Anant Panda was Professor of Gastroenterology in Medical College, Cuttack; Dr. Satpathy a renowned paediatrician was Principal of Berhampur Medical College. Some relatives were doctors in the Directorate of Medical Services and posted away. There was a superiority complex among the tertiary doctors who seldom provided any leadership to the 'periphery' doctors by way of 'Continuing Medical Education and Training. The Director of Health was excellent, so was the Director of Family Welfare. There were two Additional Secretaries both doctors; one was for Medical colleges and the other promoted from periphery cadre. Neither had any interest in any improvement in the Health system and pursued their own private agendas. The Deputy Secretaries were file-pushers; they had no initiative for any qualitative change. I was not the one to give up. I started working from 6.30 AM to 11 PM

I once landed up at the 'Emergency' of the premier Medical College at Cuttack at midnight to observe if services were available and what could be done to improve the facilities. I must say that the experience was moving; the doctors and other staff were trying their best to treat the patients. The demand far outstripped the facilities. I also visited Berhampur and Burla Medical College. I realised that I could not improve the tertiary system very much; reforms need visible budgetary resources to generate enthusiasm.

I hoped to bring about some improvements in the secondary health care. The Chief Secretary had changed and the new Chief Secretary was Mr. R. K. Bhujbal, my old boss. He wanted to visit the Capital Hospital after 4 days. This large hospital with the Health Directorate had about 1200 beds. There were some private nursing homes, but no corporate hospital had come up by then in Bhubaneswar. His visit was a lesson in GG for me. I immediately visited the Capital hospital. The hospital was shabby. I was aghast and blamed myself that sitting in an air-conditioned chamber I was oblivious of the shoddiness pervading the hospital. All government hospitals those days had this acute problem of lack of cleanliness and maintenance. In the 'general ward' of the hospital I found that remains of food eaten by patients and their attendants were strewn all around the floor. In some beds, stray dogs were resting and patients were on the floor. The so-called 'Nursing Home ' section which had single rooms for high officials and the gentry of the town had torn door curtains and bare windows with cobwebs. Everything smelt of criminal negligence and lack of any visibility of ownership. Yet the hospital was overflowing with patients. I got down to details on a war-footing. I was aware that I would not be spared by the Chief Secretary and could be publicly humiliated. That apart, my own conscience troubled me very much. Somehow on the day the Chief Secretary visited, the hospital had been spruced up substantially, and presented a better picture. Mr. Bhujabal came and went around the hospital, every inch of it. Finally, he entered the bathrooms. The bathrooms also looked clean. I was about to breathe a sigh of relief. But Mr. Bhujabal showed why he had acquired his reputation for being a very effective IAS officer. He opened the doors of the toilets; these were full of overflowing night soil. He looked at it and did not utter a word. His silence was like a sword into my heart. I resolved that for an IAS officer, attention to details meant attention to the minutest detail. I threw myself into the details of the Department and its responsibilities.

Only Poor Pay for Medical Care

I spent three Sundays in continuation to visit the Capital Hospital with the Director, Health, Chief Medical Officer of Capital Hospital and others. I went into every inch of the hospital, looked at all the equipment and instruments. On the third visit, I came across the non-working X-Ray machine. It came out that a special bulb costing around Rs. 200/- only was burnt. I asked why it was not replaced since the last three months; the X-Ray in charge told me that he had sent the proposal to the Director for sanction. When I looked at the Director, he looked at the floor and mumbled that he had sent it to my office for 'sanction' of expenditure since two months. I requested him then and there in front of everyone to come up with a proposal of delegation of financial powers for him as well as for the CMO. I added that pending amendment of rules, he would meet me every Monday with the list of pendency; together we would 'clear' the proposals. One journalist, Sri Alloy Mohanty was standing nearby. He said to me that he spent 4 hours each day in the Hospital; he was the Red Cross representative and was there to help the needy from the Red Cross. He asked me that the X-Ray was out of order more than 300 days a year for one small reason or other; he would take the responsibility and pay the cost of keeping the X-Ray working at least 335 days a year provided he on behalf of Red Cross was allowed to charge Rs. thirty per X-Ray. I was told that the Hospital charged Rs. 12/- and in the outside market the charges varied between Rs. 75/- to Rs. 90/- . I immediately agreed to this innovative proposal; there was a chorus of protest from the accompanying doctors who said that it would burden the poor. I showed them the 'log book' of the X-Ray machine; it had worked for only twelve days in the last

365 days. I explained to them the arithmetic- what was beneficial to the poor, whether they should pay Rs. 30/- for 335 days or Rs. 12/- per only 12 days and Rs. 80/- for remaining 323[335-12] days. Then we went to a meeting hall where I wanted everyone to give their suggestions as to how to improve the hospital. I sat on the floor along with 'Safai' workers and made the doctors sit on chairs. The doctors came up with no suggestion. I turned my attention to the Cleaning staff and asked them what were there problems and whether they could work in three shifts as the hospital had to be kept clean, spick and span round the clock. They expressed their resolve to do so provided they had an uninterrupted flow of 'cleaning' materials and props. Then I put forward a hitherto unknown proposal. I said that we should charge Rs. two per OPD visitors and Rs. 4 for day from all indoor patients [per day]. The doctors rose up in a chorus and protested -' how could I tax the poor for health care'! Alloy ji had quietly come into that meeting [the bureaucrat in me was feeling uncomfortable at his presence]. It was nearing 1 PM. Mr. Mohanty got up and spoke without my permission, "Sir, why are you wasting everyone's Sunday? Please go home and let others relax. Nothing will be allowed to be changed. You may try! <u>The only person who pays for health care in this hospital is the poor</u>. The rich and the influential manage their ways with the doctors. And yet please see how the doctors are crying for the poor!" There was pin-drop silence. I said that the funds so collected would remain available to a Doctors Committee to spend it for maintenance and other services. I also said that fifteen percent of the fund collected would be placed separately with Safai workers who could buy cleaning materials and props as per their requirement. An accounts person would sit in the two sets of Committees only to record; he would have no power to object in the meeting. If he so felt aggrieved he would put it up to CMO in writing for future guidance only. Within six months, the collection from patients crossed Rs. fifty lakh; the look of the hospital started changing perceptibly.

Closed Door Meeting

The State health system had a very poor management history. The mismatch was abysmal. The sector was terribly underfunded; but whatever resources were there, these were very poorly managed. The doctors, the main protagonists had no feeling of ownership of the Government assets. From the tertiary to the periphery level most of the doctors were only interested in private practice. And there was no fair system of postings of doctors. Those who could influence the system, mainly the politicians, continued for years at preferred postings at Cuttack Medical College and then at Capital hospital, etc. I had a hilarious close-door meeting with my Health Minister after about three months. Mr. Jagannath Rout was simple in his habits and direct in his approach. He had a close associate Haladhar, who worked as a clerk in the Health Department. When the Minister was not in power Haladhar used to take him around in his scooter to all the way-side snack stalls of Bhubaneswar. After Mr. Rout became the Health Minister, Haladhar became powerful. I had this habit of solving and disposing of administrative matters speedily. Mr. Rout said to me, "Our Secretary is super-brilliant. Everyone praises you for your hard work and quick decisions. Unlike other Secretaries, people have seen you running on the corridors of the Secretariat to speed up work. Haladhar is saying wrong things like what is my gain if I have a super brilliant Secretary. He says that the crowd in my office has thinned because all work is being done fairly and speedily at the level of Secretary. But I am not going to be influenced by mischievous Haladhar. Except that we should have one clear understanding; this Department does not have many tenders or purchases. So, you continue your hard work to improve efficiency; but all transfers and postings will be done by me. Please do not feel sad if any decision of mine is not liked by you." I mumbled some kind of 'thank you' and left his chamber.

Blind Inefficiency

A 'Team' from the Government of India visited. It said that a large World Bank assistance had been extended to Odisha by the Centre for a 'Blindness Control' Programme. Odisha operated on 7000 patients in the first year and 19000 the next year; the agreed target was one lakh patients per year. The Team had come to demand refund of the unspent 80% money. I folded my hands and placated them; called for an emergency strategy meeting late afternoon where I invited them to participate and guide us. I rang up Dr. Padhi, the very competent and very humane Professor of the Eye Department of SCB Medical College to come to the meeting and lead the process. [Later I rang up the Head of Eye Department of Berhampur and Burla Medical college. to get involved in a mass campaign, train eye surgeons of the periphery cadre who had been posted in far-flung places and had lost their skills.] The scheme was discussed threadbare. It turned out that Rs. 200/- per patient was inadequate for follow up, Rs. 300/- was needed. And the State Health Secretary had the power to include areas into the 'difficult' list where Rs. 300/- was admissible. I immediately declared all places of the State except Bhubaneswar as 'difficult area'. Next, there were 54 eye surgeons who had joined Periphery cadre but had never been used for eye surgery. The task was to get them posted to the thirty district hospitals, get them trained in Medical Colleges and give them a 'surgical tool box'. Somehow all this was arranged. The Central Team was impressed with our new commitment and extended the project period by one year. We reached near the magical one lakh figure- 86 thousand against 19000 of the previous year; and I was told that the next year it touched 136000 number of cataract surgeries. The emotional moment of this story was when I went to the Minister, with a file proposing the posting of these 54 eye surgeons to District hospitals. I started with an apology saying that I was breaking my promise to the Honourable Minister not to interfere in postings. Then I put the open file in front of him. He read the long note, got up, came round the table and held me by hand saying, "You think so badly of me! I am not bad, the system is. Here I sign the file. Notify immediately."

Misuse of Power

A small incident occurred which exposed me to my limitations. One retired old man came for redressal of his unsanctioned pension. I called for the Deputy Secretary. The old man started abusing him in unparliamentary language. I lost my temper and called for the police in the Secretariat and had him arrested. Within 20 minutes, I felt very uneasy, stopped all my work, went to the Police post and got the old gentleman released, took his petition and assured him after apologising that I would definitely solve his problem within a week. I felt very ashamed of myself for my lack of humane approach and not having dealt with the situation correctly. Petty power gets to our head instead of the task at hand. GG cannot afford such a mind-set.

Project Report

Chief minister one day sent for me and handed over to me a Project Report prepared by the Himachal Government seeking loan from the World Bank through the Government of India to improve the secondary level of primary health care [the secondary care portion]. By 1995, the capacity in Odisha health system to produce a project report in a coherent manner, get it word-processed submit it to the Government of India and the World Bank was simply non-existent. I created a team with the two Directors and the President of the Doctors Association and involved Xaviers Institute of Management, Bhubaneswar to convert the discussion and data into a coherent Project Report. I am ever so grateful to Director XIMB, Father D'Souza and Dr. S. Roy for helping selflessly in preparing a very well written, logical and persuasive Project Report. Every weekend, we would meet and draw up the Proposal. I found two computers, wrapped in red cloth kept on a shelf of almirahs. No one knew how to use them even for word-processing. With a lot of effort a reluctant young typist was located and pressed into service. He would get up every half an hour and go for tea. I went along and humoured him as I had no choice. Gathering verifiable data on various health indices was a tough task. Drawing up civil engineering plan estimates was tough as there was no such engineer in the Department. However, good people were always there; my old civil engineer friend, Mr. L. N. Barik. In two months, the Project Report requesting the World Bank for Rs. four hundred sixty eight crores was ready, drawn up along the lines of the discipline of the World Bank. I remember that I stood in a private small DTP shop on the road-side on a Sunday in Bhubaneswar to get the required number of copies ready and bound, to be carried by me to Delhi the next day to meet the dateline. There was a stiff competition among all the States, including that by U.P., the home State of the Minister Health, Government of India. Finally, the good news came- the World Bank sanctioned only two more projects from 10 applicant States of India. Odisha was one of the two.

I might leave the story of this period incomplete if I omit to mention a curious matter which partly led to my undoing. When I was made Health Secretary, Basant Biswal ji used his influence and I was also made the Secretary of the Department of Public Relations. I did not mind it initially; in fact, it is almost axiomatic that an IAS officer generally basks in being given the charge of additional 'empires' .But in about four months I found that Department completely against my ilk. I have already mentioned elsewhere that I used to think PR as a skill was dubious and PR guys were dangerous in creating disaffection in any work oriented organization. Here the danger was from outside. I had to bump into Basant Biswal ji now and then in the corridors of the Secretariat. No sooner he would catch a glimpse of me, he would start cribbing loudly even if outsiders were present that there was no gain in making me the Secretary, Department of PR, as his newspaper Samay was not getting more 'advertisements' from PR Department. This was the only work in that department- giving advertisements to publications to publicise Government work, either for propaganda or due to legal notices etc. The Department had already run up a huge backlog for payment and all senior media guys would ring me up to release their dues. So I had generally told my officials in the Department that we would go slow in placing fresh advertisements and first clear the payment already due. These encounters with Biswal ji increased in frequency; I clenched my teeth and somehow restrained myself on all occasions. But I knew that sooner or later I might forget myself and hurl some invectives at him losing my self-control. Then at my repeated insistence, Secretary to CM spoke to the CM and I was relieved of the PR Department. This got the goat of Basant Biswal ji and he thought that I had slighted him by giving up the extra Department he had arranged for me.

A new Blood Bank at Bhubaneswar was inaugurated by the CM Sri J Patnaik. JBP was a sphinx; he would never let others know what his thoughts were. But he made an exception in his speech while inaugurating the Blood Bank- he said that exceptional work was being done in the Health Department. And within fifteen days of that public eulogy, he transferred me to Delhi to the Principal Resident Commissioner's office as a second Resident commissioner. He did this to appease Basant Biswal who had asked me to promote a relatively inexperienced

Gastroenterologist. This doctor spent all his time not in the Medical college but looking after Basant Biswal's co-brother-in-law Dr. Parida's Nursing Home at Cuttack. I was taking my time about the promotion to give it some semblance of public decency. That doctor neither had the eligible years of service nor there was a vacant post. Combined with my action of giving up the charge of the PR Department, this provoked Biswal ji too much. That was that; I went off to Delhi. I spent less than a year as Health Secretary; I did not even had the time to learn that Odisha as well as India's main health issue was improving its Reproductive Child Health indices-IMR, MMR and TFR; rather than setting up tertiary hospitals like AIIMS and the corporate hospitals which were mainly for the rich and politically powerful.

Resident Commissioner at Delhi [1996-1997]

The year was a waste as practically, there was no work. I completed my short story book - but that was personal. Official work or experience wise it was a zero- the only lesson in GG was a negative lesson; how many sinecure posts were there which had no productive work and how poor HR policies of the politicians led to a colossal waste of opportunities of GG. I only remember during my stay in Delhi as Resident Commissioner that I went to meet Mr. Surendra Singh, Cabinet Secretary the day he was retiring after a very distinguished career in IAS. He immediately called me in and said, "Where were you till now? Why have you come today?" I said smilingly that I had come to inspire myself by meeting my Role-Model. He smiled, shook his head in bemusement and I came away. I never knew how to ask for favours my entire working career. It was a short-coming in my personality!

14

SECRETARY, URBAN DEVELOPMENT, GOVERNMENT OF ODISHA

In the latter half of 1997, I was posted as Secretary, Urban Development Department. I came to Bhubaneswar and started working in the right earnest. The Chief Secretary then was Mr. S.B. Mishra a suave and competent officer having the total backing of CM. Basant Biswal ji sought me out [he would lose temper when I would resist a wrong request; then better sense would prevail on him. He would try to lionize me again.] I called on him after joining, he was extremely cordial. I set myself to work from early morning till evening. My Minister was Mr. Pradhan, the nephew of Basant Biswal ji. I committed a big blunder- I did not go to the Minister's office enough to build up a rapport. I showed him due respect only when we met in some meetings; that was not enough. An IAS officer would always do well to spend some strategic time in 'boss management'. I learnt this at great cost to me. I thought that I was working very hard and systematically. A small illustration- the Chief Secretary took a meeting on development projects related to BDA. The VC BDA, otherwise competent, did not put up the draft minutes promptly. I phoned him up [My Motto in my career had been that 'Minutes of Meetings' must be issued within a maximum time of 72 hours. I have noticed with dismay that some otherwise good colleagues sometimes even take a month to issue the 'Minutes'.] He came with the draft full of mistakes. Together we revised the 'draft' meticulously. Then I sent the file to the Chief Secretary. The Minutes were approved with a comment, "I am happy to finally see a draft minutes without a single mistake". It made me sad to realise the casual nature with which others were doing serious office work. I started the practice of going to the desk of the Section Officers of the Department; this enthused the clerical staff very much and I would receive many more number of files each day. I could get on top of these by disposing of each file the same day. Pendency, audit compliance, pension matters, HR grievances, proposals from Urban Bodies all over the State, all started reducing rapidly. I prepared a blueprint for raising of resources by each Municipality and urban body to set up viable commercial projects to generate money for various development works on a long term basis. I engaged the PHD colleagues of whom two Chief Engineers stood out, one Mr. R.M. Patnaik and the other Mr. Samal who prepared plans for augmentation of water supply of 8 major towns and a sewerage plan for Bhubaneswar and Cuttack. A sewerage plan for Puri started getting implemented. I made a grave mistake: there was a Board meeting of Angul Development authority, it was a tiny nascent Urban Body, the Collector, a promoted IAS officer who was BDO with me when I was the Collector, Cuttack and one of my favourites was the Chief Executive Officer of Angul Urban Authority. But he was now the Collector of the Minister's constituency and his confidant. I scolded him a bit on a proposal that came up for discussion as the figures did not tally at all. The Minister was presiding. It did not go down well. I was transferred out of the Department within a week of this. Now one could cite the example of colleagues like Mr. Khemka of Haryana cadre who had apparently been transferred more than a hundred times for being an upright officer. Well, to each, his own! However I feel that a good IAS officer should have a sense of balance and invest time in the art of boss management without indulging or abetting in corruption. Getting transferred frequently is a waste of one's career. I in all earnestness would not say that I was transferred as I resisted Mr. Amar Pradhan's any alleged agenda of corruption. There was no such confrontation or occasion. It was my poor boss management and complacency which affronted the Minister. I just did not spend enough time and got him involved and feel proud of all the new schemes that were on the anvil. If

I were to relieve my career, I would have managed my posting as Urban Development Secretary more adroitly. Quite often, the civil servant is to be blamed for his frequent transfers, though politicians also lack the understanding of a reasonable tenure for the officer to show results. I was posted as Chairman of Odisha State Housing Board. I did not go anywhere to lobby, handed over the charge and went to join the Housing Board.

15

ODISHA STATE HOUSING BOARD

My predecessor, a senior colleague was waiting for me at the Housing Board Office. He promptly handed over the charge adding. "Prasanna, there is no work here. You will have time to write books." I did not comment and joined. I was chastised by my transfer, though the Chief Secretary said over the phone that he was really sorry at my transfer, he tried but could not stop it. He added, "I shall soon arrange better and additional jobs for you." I thanked him and said that it was alright, and that let me try to make a go of the Housing Board-OSHB. OSHB was in a sorry state of affairs. It had unsold stocks of housing and office space in run-down condition as old as 6 years. It had 740 employees and 38 Unions. It was a struggle to pay the salary of the employees each month. It had a gross turnover of a mere Rs. 20 crores the last year. And there were hundreds of cases against it in Consumer Courts. Its major projects had to come to a grinding halt as eight major contractors had moved writ petitions in Odisha High Court and brought 'stay' orders against OSHB.

The first seven days were spent getting acquainted with all these sorry conditions in detail. And every 2 hours each day, some Union or other would barge into my chamber and start giving vent to its demands. Then on the eighth day I got all the unions together and sternly told them not to enter my room for the next four months. I told them to concentrate on work and obey orders. I said that I could turn around OSHB within these four months. If I would fail, they were free to agitate and demand anything. Then, the first thing that I did was to hold a meeting of all senior engineers, Finance Officer, Law Officer etc. also invited the 8 big contractors who had moved the High Court to this meeting. I knew most of them as they had worked with me at Bhubaneswar Development Authority No sooner the meeting started, I requested the Chief Engineer to pour tea into the cups of the contractors. He hesitated. I saw his discomfiture, got up and served tea to the contractors saying, "They are our guests and they have come at our invitation." I added that they were also part of OSHB; they were the 'asset creators', the engineers were only asset creation supervisors Then I turned to the contractors and addressed them with a familiar tone, adding some mild abuse, "How can you spit on the plate on which you are eating? You all have prospered from the time of BDA. Can an outside agency solve our problem? Now that I have come, all problems will be reasonably solved within OSHB. Start stating your grievances. But commit to me that within 72 hours all cases in High Court shall be withdrawn by you." And it happened that way; work resumed with full vigour. But the challenge was to generate capital for completing old work and taking up new work. The only possibility was to raise money by selling the old stocks. And everyone was negative about this in OSHB. "I first looked at a prime housing complex built 5 years back in the central part of Bhubaneswar city. There were 378 flats in four towers and not a single one was sold. I did not believe the story of corruption. I knew that Odisha had good engineering standards; there could not have been such high cost tenders. I visited the housing complex repeatedly to seek a marketing solution. I didn't have much money to spare. I mustered some resources, improved the entry facade of each tower with stone cladding and named each tower with names like Heera, Rupa, Neela, and Moti written with shining bronze in large letters. I drove out all stray cattle and beggars sheltering in its corridors re-established the active possession and presence of OSHB in the complex. Private builders had come up; in my last year of BDA I had thrown open the housing market to the private builders too. Now I invited them and confabulated with them at the site as to how to market these flats. I found out their methods of marketing, their issuance of brochures, and the cost they charged for a square foot of 'super built up area". The pieces immediately fell into position. OSHB had priced the flats announcing its rate per square foot of 'carpet' area while private builders announced their price based on 'super built up area' which was at least 30% plus the carpet area. I quickly reworked the maths, OSHB's rate compared favourably with the market rate. After that the actual challenge of selling the flats came up. I brought out a big advertisement in the local newspapers that OSHB would sell 'fault-free' flats to buyers; any fault found within a year would be rectified by OSHB at once at its own cost. [In Consumer courts cases for a couple of years adding to OSHB' litigation cost and then awards from Rs. ten thousand to twenty thousand in almost all the cases were imposed]. I thought that overall it would be cheaper and better for the 'brand OSHB' to volunteer to rectify faults noticed in the first year at its own cost. I also brought out an advertisement that Chairman OSHB would be personally available at the site to receive prospective buyers and take them round the complex. I spread some moorum at the entry path, put flower pots lining up the entrance road, got double bed cover from home, hired beds and furniture from a 'Tent' house and set up a 'model' flat to show it to prospective customers with flower vase et al. I kept a crate of cold coca cola bottles and sat at the site every Saturday and Sunday morning. Soon the buying started, but not to the desired extent in the desired speed. Then I remembered the advertisements of ORIMARK, an agency of Sri Jitu Mahapatra, an enterprising young man; he would bring out a series of 'To Sell' ads each Saturday and Sunday of private properties in local newspapers. I decided to get him involved paying him 1% commission. He agreed and the flow of Sale started. The Union which had kept quiet till then again rushed into my room and said, "Sir, everything is okay; but now corruption has started". I did not lose patience and asked them to explain. They replied that how could OSHB engage a private property agent and would give him commission? I explained to them OSHB's financial compulsions and the need to generate quick funds. I added that I would permit the Union to sell the flats and pay 2% commission for each flat it sold to a Staff Welfare Fund; and that they were free [three at a time] to go during office time to canvass for sale of flats. To cut the story short, all the flats were sold; the union sold one flat, I sold 134 and ORIMARK sold 243. I did not get any commission, naturally!

I was back to my old habit of working from morning 7 AM till night 10.30 PM. I thought I was on top of the work and OSHB was on the road to recovery. Several new profitable projects were launched. Unsold assets all over the State were liquidated. Some hilarious but instructive events happened.

Administrative Slum

Another day, as usual I was lingering at the office working late and delaying my lunch. I must confess that I had developed a habit of going for lunch to my home [My brother in law, Mr. Senapati, retired Engineer-in- Chief doted on me and insisted that I stay at his home nearby]. One day, around 2.25 PM, I was about to go for lunch. I heard a commotion near the door of my chamber. I came out and found the orderly peon preventing a well-dressed gentleman from entering my room. I escorted the gentleman into my room and made him sit and said, "How can I help you?" he was worked up and said," You have to keep absolutely quiet and listen to me without interruption." I piped in, "Certainly, Sir!" At this interjecture, he lost his temper, "Don't talk at all. I am not going to be impressed with your smooth talk. I want action- and now". He said that he had bought a house from OSHB seven years back in its Shailashree Vihar scheme. He was a Manager in UCO Bank. As OSHB had not given him a proper registered Sale deed, he had availed the concessionary home loan to buy the property. His best friend, another manger in the Bank who was a few months senior to him, had stood as the 'guarantor' of the loan. Now his friend had been promoted to the next level but was not being allowed to join as the Bank said that the guarantor was to produce the Sale Deed. I stopped going for lunch, made him sit and shouted in a loud voice in exasperation; the whole office gathered. I asked about why 'Sale Deed' was not executed for so long. It turned out that OSHB had taken 42 pieces of land from GA Department in Bhubaneswar over the years and OSHB had not completed the process in a single case. I sent the Land Officer of OSHB immediately to Bhubaneswar Development Authority to fetch BDA's Land Officer, Mr. Baliar Singh. He came and at my prodding gave a lecture to all staff of OSHB as to how in my time as VC BDA all transfer of land patches from GA Department were duly completed, and all the purchasers were given Sale Deeds. But at the end he gratuitously added to everyone's merriment, "After Hota Sir left BDA, not a single land transfer further has been completed".

Why do IAS officers complain about politicians? Which politician prevents them from doing their basic work diligently?

I was not the one to give up. I rang up Mr. Priyabrat Patnaik who was Special Secretary of the GA Department. He was very involved with the Bhubaneswar Club and had made it into a vibrant institution by his single-minded devotion. I requested him to arrange a good lunch at the Club for one hundred people to which he, the Director Land, and all the staff. Of the Land section of GA Department numbering 88 were invited, From OSHB there would be 12 including me. I made an impassioned plea about the pending land transfers and how people were suffering because of that and fervently requested them for cooperation. In fifteen days, 22 patches of land were transferred to OSHB completing all paperwork including that of Shailashree Vihar. On the sixteenth day I was transferred out of OSHB. CM JBP was blackmailed by one astute tout about the possibility of a disaffected husband filing a petition in a Court the next day against JBP. Mishra the tout played his cards so well that JBP asked him for the price of hushing up the matter at which, this rogue said, "I understand that OSHB has become functional again. Please make me its Chairman." [There was a very decent Police Inspector attached to JBP for personal security. He had some sense of right and wrong. He used to inform me of the goings on.] A Joint Secretary from the Department suddenly appeared in the OSHB office, showed me the orders and said, "CM wants you to hand over charge now!" In half an hour I gathered some personal belongings a cardboard box and left OSHB.

Young Life Saved

I should mention an instructive incident that took place during my tenure in OSHB, unconnected with official work of OSHB. Basant Biswal ji became the Odisha head of All India Scouts and Guides in January 1998. In January 1999, he arranged an All India Camp of the Scouts. More than 26000 thousand delegates came from all over India. The camp was held in the foothills of Barunei hill, about 30 kilometres from Bhubaneswar. Somehow, he swallowed his animosity and sent words to me to organise and supervise the Campsite and the arrangements. He apparently had become very fond of Sri P.K. Mishra [Mishra Sir was definitely a very competent IAS officer].and put him in overall charge and took daily reports from him. Biswal ji never spoke to me. But everyday P.K. Mishra ji would say that everything was in perfect order and Hota was taking care of all details meticulously. The day of the 'Final' ceremony came; there were speeches and ceremonial rituals; Basant Biswal ji was beaming with satisfaction as the All India Scout officials were praising the excellent arrangements at the camp. I had taken the precaution of involving the local political personage whom I knew from BDA days. Chairman of Khurda Notified Area Council and Dr. Gouri Prasad Singh, Chairman of Jatni NAC were lionised by me to help in receiving the delegates [Khurda Road railway station came under Jatni and the Camp came under Khurda], arranging the Scouts to be sent to the campsite systematically to avoid chaos. After the speeches and ceremony of the final day which got over by 5 PM, the campsite wore the look of a 'deserted banquet hall'. Everybody had got tired; Basant Biswal et al left and forgot the Scouts. Not Prasanna Hota! Dr. G.P Singh! I was nobody for that occasion. But Odisha's name was involved. I got in touch with Dr. Gouri Singh and requested him to keep his team of volunteers active till every scout had boarded the right train. I told him that I would sleep next to the phone; he could ring me up at any time. My anticipation paid dividends; a precious young human life was saved. A young scout of Goa was on a bus from the campsite to the railway station. He chose to ride on the roof of the bus. It was 10 PM at night. The boy suddenly stood up on the roof and his head dashed against a low-hanging branch. Immediately, Dr. Gouri Singh rushed to the spot and phoned me. I told him to take the boy directly to the 'Emergency' of Medical College at Cuttack. I rang up the Medical College. All arrangements were kept ready. Dr. Gouri Singh was in constant touch. Blood was needed early morning. I helped to arrange it, but all the leg work was by Dr. Gouri Singh. The boy would have definitely died for lack of timely treatment. All credit to Dr. Gouri Singh who kept a night long vigil. The parents of the boy wrote Dr. Singh a letter of thanks after fifteen days. Commitment to completion of a task is the bounden duty of the IAS; no argument of being tired! No seeking of any praise too!

16

Principal Resident Commissioner

The rest of 1999 was a blur. JBP must have felt guilty; he posted me as Special Relief Commissioner, Chairman of IPICOL and Chairman of IDC. But I had no tenure; I wanted to get back to Delhi as Additional Secretary. But empanelment was not yet due. There was a big drought in the State; a Central Team came. I with the astute help of Dr. B. P. Das then Engineer in Chief of Irrigation made such a focused and convincing presentation that the Central Team apparently said to CM that it had never seen such a convincing case establishing natural disaster. I was given additional charge of Chairman, IPICOL and also was made the CMD OF IDCOL. However, the charm of working in my home State was over. CM finally sent for me and asked what post I would want. I requested him to post me to Delhi as Principal Resident Commissioner. In the middle of 1999, I was posted to Delhi as Principal Resident Commissioner.

Principal Resident Commissioner

I came to Delhi in a job which was of a limited consequence. Each State had a 'Liaison Office' at Delhi to stay in touch with the Central Government. But with improved communications etcetera, this job had only residual scope to the extent each Department of the State would get it involved. Anyway, soon enough the month of October 1999 came and I got catapulted into hitherto unknown heights.

Larger Than Life

On 26th October, I was asked in the morning to come to the Meeting Room of the Cabinet Secretary-CS. I sat on the third row in a corner away from CS, Mr. Prabhat Kumar. CS announced that there was a dangerous 'low pressure' building up in the Bay of Bengal, and it was likely to hit Odisha with ferocity. So he alerted each key Department to remain prepared with contingency plans. I spoke up about a few pertinent suggestions about topography and vulnerability issues. There was a meeting again on the 26th afternoon. CS knew me a bit and was fond of me. He asked me to take a seat in the first row. I was upgraded-so to say!

On the 27th morning, CS announced that the prediction was that it could be a cyclone beyond wind speed of more than 200 kilometres and asked each Department about its preparedness. I kept on adding, supplementing and correcting the replies of the Agencies. On the 27th afternoon, I was asked to sit next to CS and was directed to state my views without hesitation. On 28th October morning, the Super Cyclone struck Odisha coasts. I rushed to the Meeting Room of CS where everybody was waiting anxiously for my arrival. CS said that it was a Super Cyclone unprecedented in recent times and that the wind speed had reached 300 KMs per hour. Everyone was anxious, and CS gave directions for all-out help to all the Departments and agencies. I rushed back to my tiny office. I tried and luckily I talked to Chief Secretary Mr. S.B. Mishra over phone. He said that I should inform the Cabinet Secretary that all communications with the State would soon be down, and that the Government of Odisha was requesting the Government of India to declare an Emergency and take over the charge of the State. I had the presence of mind to say to him that he should authorise me to incur an expenditure up to Rs. ten crores to initiate relief operations from Delhi, and that I could say about this authorization to CS. The Chief Secretary immediately agreed; and the telephone communications went dead thereafter for the next 96 hours. The next meeting with CS was at 3 PM. I briefed CS about what all the Chief Secretary said. I also mentioned that I was authorized orally by the State Government to incur expenditure up to Rs. ten crores for relief. Then he exhorted all agencies to commence working and said that the next meeting would be on the coming day morning at 10 AM. I emotionally interrupted him and spoke out loudly that, such meetings though important would be of limited value; immediate action was needed. CS instead of chastising me said, "Go ahead! Tell us what you think we can do." I said that a senior Secretary to Government must be designated immediately whom I would assist. A Control Room would be immediately made operative. in his office. I should be permitted to request through him, the Chief Secretaries of all the neighbouring States like Andhra, Madhya Pradesh, Bihar and Bengal to procure relief materials and move towards the State Capital, Bhubaneswar to the extent possible.

Control Room- Night on Secretary's Table

Cabinet Secretary looked at me approvingly; Secretary Agriculture, Mr. Baruah volunteered to host me in his office. We reached the Agriculture Secretary's office. It was Friday evening, the staff had already left. A few were left. I wrote out a long three page handwritten note detailing the relief materials to be procured and taken, the road clearing team, the electricity restoring team, essential medicines listed in detail, water purifying agent and the like. Mr. Bhagat Singh, Central Relief Commissioner transmitted the messages that very night in the name of the Government of India. Mr Baruah went home for an hour, got me dinner from his home and kept me company throughout the night till early morning. He sat in his chair; I slept fitfully on his table. Very early morning, he persuaded me to take a break, go home, freshen up and come to the meeting of CS and that he would also do so. In the meeting taken by CS, it came out that no organization had been able to establish any contact with coastal Odisha. The super-cyclone had stopped moving and was discharging all the water it had accumulated on coastal Odisha. In 24 hours about 24 inches rain fell inundating all the low lying areas and water had submerged most part of coastal Odisha There was also a tidal wave from the sea which came in land 22 kilometres at a height of 22 feet. More than nine thousand persons and about three lakh fifty thousand cattle perished. About five lakh coconut trees got devastated apart from mango and other trees. One lakh fourteen thousand houses were damaged. All this became known much later. On 29th October, I was asked to meet Defence Minister, Mr. George Fernandes who had been made the Chief of Rescue and Relief operations by the Prime Minister, Mr. Vajpayee. He asked me several questions and appeared moved by my commitment and detailed knowledge of the topography. Next day morning, I was taken to the PM where the Defence Minister was also present. Late lamented Ashok Saikia [a college day junior and as per his own admission – a beneficiary of Hota notes] Additional Secretary to PM was there too. PM spent about half an hour with me; he was perceptive to see my inflamed condition, I had kept awake the entire night ringing up Collectors of unaffected districts of Odisha and persuading them to take my words as orders of Government and move relief material and rescue team towards Bhubaneswar. I would stand by them for having committed this expenditure.[Two Collectors particularly stand out in my memory as responsive and action-oriented- Mr. Vijay Arora, Collector Sundargarh and Mr. Vashist, Collector Balasore.] PM looked towards Mr. Fernandes, and said, "Inka jara khayal rakhiye. Feed him some breakfast". Odisha owes a lot to these two great personalities. The Central Government opened its coffers to assist Odisha without any hesitation.

Cabinet Secretary of Stature

Each morning around 10 AM a Coordination meeting used to take place in Shashtri Bhawan; CS used to be present and all agencies including Air Force, Navy and Army were there. I used to ask all the questions and set the agenda for the next day about air-drop, moving army columns, and sending the Navy vessel to Paradeep Port. The Railways and Food Corporation of India were also pressed into service. After a while, CS got up and said, "Agriculture Secretary and Hota will continue the meeting. Everyone should note that Hota's decisions are my decisions. I shall take a report from him later."

In about four days the Rs. ten crores was spent; we had authorised Andhra Pradesh and West Bengal to incur expenditure up to Rs. two crore each, and Bihar and M.P. Rs. one crore each. The remaining Rs. four crores were spent footing the bills of FCI etc. Agriculture Secretary sheepishly told me that Rs. ten crores were exhausted. I felt that under such circumstances my grand posturing each day would be uncalled for.

Nights Under Tent

I never went home at night. Voluntary relief materials were pouring in from all over Delhi and Haryana into the premises of Odisha Bhawan. Their safe-keeping and despatching these through Railways was a big challenge. I pitched a large shamiana type tent, put all the materials there and slept in a chair in the shamiana keeping guard. I did not go to the Coordination meeting. I was there in my tiny office; at about 9 AM, the door to my room opened with a jerk; Mr. Ashok Saikia rushed in and said in his inimitable way, "Sala, phootani dikhata hai!" He caught hold of me by my collar and dragged me unto the road outside. Mr. Prabhat Kumar, the Cabinet Secretary was sitting in the car. Both of them said that the PM had desired that I would lead all relief work and that I was authorised by the Central Government to spend a hundred crores rupees initially and then I could even ask for more. Most interestingly, I accessed only Rs. fifty lakhs from this largesse. I felt proud to belong to the IAS. I was re-charged and behaved almost as a super-man. I was everywhere , from the railway goods shed at Subzi Mandi, at every TV news channel, of course commanding the Coordination meetings and so on. I was careful enough to keep in position a separate Team from my limited staff to concentrate in maintaining detailed accounts of money spent as well as the goods dispatched. I knew from experience when the ship would get into trouble, the rats would be the first to desert the ship; but they would come back once the ship was steadied and attack the lions that steadied the ship at the risk of their lives. All through my career, crises brought out the best in me.

Hope Knocks At The Gate- Beethoven Symphony no. 5

There were some remarkable incidents as the Super-cyclone played out. The first one was when the Prime Minister of Holland flew in and expressed a desire to call on me to commiserate with me the large number of lives lost and the damage to property. The air and other communications were yet to be restored; so, as the Representative of the State of Odisha it was my duty to receive me. I turned the lounge-cum meeting hall of Odisha Bhawan into a proper venue. I produced a CD on the devastation. I chose the background music- a certain portion of

Beethoven's Fifth Symphony. Photographs of the devastation including scenes of burning bodies were pasted around the wall of the lounge. The PM came in a motorcade, entered the meeting hall and greeted me. I gently persuaded him and his Team which included a distinguished looking woman to go round the four corners of the lounge; and then I put on the CD. The music came on- later I learnt that it was famous as "Fate knocks at the Gate'. The Prime Minister was handsome, tall and very impressive; his ears perked up. He said, '' Mr. Hota, I have come to share the sorrow of the people of your State. People of Holland stand with you! I have learnt that you have done outstanding work in providing relief material. The real challenge will come when you go into the reconstruction phase. You will find yourself alone". It provided me the cue. I told him that Odisha could not be alone as such a world leader of stature like Mr. Wim Kok, was a witness to the widespread devastation affecting Odisha. He said that Holland was a small country, what more could it do? I spoke out, "I am an avid reader of human history. Holland may be a small country; but it has brilliant and large-hearted people who have been pioneers in many areas of civilization. I humbly beseech you Excellency to present our case to other civilised nations of Europe; they could respond to your appeal for reconstruction -at least of the 30000 schools, whose roofs have been blown away and the education of about two million children have been interrupted." I added that from these schools about 25 thousand engineers, doctors and scientists were abroad serving European nations and the USA. Mr Kok got up and said, "Madam Minister please note every word of Mr. Hota. I shall follow up. I had come with a donation of $ 5 million. I hereby increase it to 15 million dollars. Mr. Hota, I salute your commitment to your people." Then he left.

Who Is The Future PM?

The Super-cyclone had a series of incidents; I shall narrate the key events. I never slept at home for fifteen days. A few hours on a chair under the tent were my quota of sleep. Luckily, I had a very able deputy, Mr. S.K. Bhargab IAS who stood by me 24/7 and we somehow managed the work and kept detailed accounts. After 10 days or so, my role started reducing with the State Government becoming functional and communications being restored. One day an envelope came from Andhra Government; it said that Andhra was given two crores of rupees and it had spent Rs. 6 crores 56 lakh asking for the remaining Rs. four crore fifty six lakh.. By that time the newspapers were full of the heroic leadership of Mr. Chandra Babu Naidu in organising relief operations for Odisha. Some papers even started saying that he was the next Prime Minister material. As I was looking at the demand sent by Andhra, Mr. K.P. Singhdeo then an MP of Congress party entered my room and started shouting that no work was being done; it would be better if Mr. Chandra Babu Naidu was also made the CM of Odisha.. [During those days everyone was extra emotional and talked in high pitch blaming somebody or the other. I calmed him down, and pushed the letter of Andhra Government towards him. He read the letter and was thoroughly puzzled. I explained to him that he was a MP in Opposition; he did not have any power to get Odisha a rupee; but, if he were to follow my suggestion carefully he could get Odisha money and get a lot of publicity for himself. His ears perked up. I told him to go to the Lok Sabha that day early and wait. Sooner or later, the Telugu Desam MPs would eulogise Mr. Naidu. The speaker was from Telugu Desam; he was bound to permit the 'Mention' beyond normal work of the day. I told Singhdeo Sir that as soon as this 'tamasha' would begin, he would get up and raise a 'Point of Order' and simply mention "On Payment"! And lo and behold, it exactly happened the very same way. Two MPs got up and started praising Mr. Naidu [as per rule only one Member should speak at one time, but obviously the Speaker was indulgent] as a great leader fit to be the future PM of India. Singhdeo ji got up and raised a point of order. Everyone looked at him curiously. He said, "Great work, but on payment!" Hell broke loose! All Telugu Desam MPs got up and shouted at him and moved a 'Privilege Motion' against him for misleading the House which was immediately accepted by the Speaker and was scheduled by him to be discussed at 1 PM. K.P ji rushed back to my office. He was all flustered and accused me of landing him in soup. I then started searching for Andhra's letter which I had photo-copied. The original and the copy were somewhere lost in the pile of papers cluttering my table. KP ji lost his temper and caught hold of my collars. Luckily at the very moment I found the precious papers and showed those to him. He regained his composure and said that he was in a hurry to reach Lok Sabha and I should hand over the letter to him. I reasoned with him, "Sir, this is your golden chance. Please take the photocopy but don't table it. Instead, get up and apologise to the house." KP ji interrupted me and started losing his temper again saying that I was making him apologise. I explained to him that he was actually setting a trap for Mr. Naidu. He would say in his apology that he was withdrawing his remark if Andhra government never demanded any payment and would not demand payment in future. Then later, Mr. Singhdeo could call a small press conference and reveal the letter from Andhra. KP ji left happily and followed my advice. His apology was formally recorded by the loyal Speaker and conveyed to Mr. Naidu immediately. The Press came to know of Andhra's demand for money and it was front page news in most of the newspapers. Mr. KP Singhdeo got the publicity in the papers for revealing the doings of Andhra. Mr. Naidu had scheduled a visit to Bhubaneswar the next day; he could not back out. He landed in Bhubaneswar and a mob of Press Reporters accosted him about the demand for payment. He had to say that all that was without his knowledge; and that no sooner he came to know of it he had waived all demands. In fact, promptly a letter came from the Resident Commissioner, Andhra stating that the demand for Rs. four crore fifty six lakh stood withdrawn and should be considered as Andhra's contribution to the people of Odisha. However, there was another fax message from the Government of West Bengal stating that it had spent Rs. 6 crore 13 lakh and it would be happy if I would arrange to pay Rs.4 crore 13 lakh. Coincidentally, at this very moment, there was a phone call from Bhubaneswar, "Dada [brother], I am Bhattacharjee from The Telegraph paper speaking from Bhubaneswar. I questioned Mr. Naidu; he replied that he stopped all demand for payment no sooner he knew of it. What is the truth?" I got my chance. I told him to forget about Mr. Naidu; I added that the Odias traditionally considered the Bengalis as their older brother and the Telugus as their younger brother. Why should one berate the younger brother when the elder brother had sent a bill for Rs. 4 crore 13 lakh. Dearest Bhattacharji ji perhaps had a beer or two at the Bhubaneswar Club from where he was ringing up. He got into high gear immediately. 'Beta der eto dimag! Dekhun aami ki korechi! [It meant that he would set right all highhandedness of the Bengal Government in a day.]' It was a Shakespearian comedy. Next day, The Telegraph carried front page news with the photographs of Mr. Naidu and Mr. Jyoti Basu side by side and asked the question. "Who is the future Prime Minister material of India- Is it Mr. Naidu who waived all demand no sooner than he learnt of it or Mr. Basu who promised Rs. ten crores help, but had sent a bill for Rs. 4.13 crore to Odisha?'" The rhetoric hit the Bull's Eye. I got a call from the Special Relief Commissioner of West Bengal. He said that all of them had got a dressing down from honourable Sri Jyoti Basu, and that the entire Rs. 6 crore 13 lakhs was to be treated as a gift of people of Bengal to Odisha. Funnily, the story did not end there. After fifteen days, some smart bureaucrat wrote from Andhra that the amount waived was Rs. 4 crore 56 lakh; so, I should arrange to pay the Rs. two crore to Andhra. You have to believe the element of luck that is often pivotal in a man's life. My phone rang; on the line was my lovable friend, Sri Bhattacharjee, the ace journalist who I had not met till then. He said that he had come to Delhi for some training. I promptly invited him to a lunch of fish and rice in Odisha Niwas canteen. He came and after he had food, I brought him to my office and placed the letter of Andhra Government before him. The Bengali in him got him choleric, and he said I should watch the fun the next day. Again front-page news came up in The Telegraph- 'Is this the future Prime Minister of India who renegades for a mere Rs. two crore?' and below was the full story. Next day by 11 AM there was a thick envelope from Resident Commissioner, Andhra; It contained a letter saying that Rs. two crore would no more be demanded. There was also a Bank Draft for Rs. 5 crore with a short note that CM Andhra had collected this money for Odisha; he wanted it to be spent for relief at my discretion. Of course, I promptly sent the money to my State Government. I never consulted or sought approval of anyone, and acted on my wit and initiative entirely

Dukhesu Anudbignamana Sukhesu Bigataspruha

The third episode was sordid. Some polythene to be used as temporary roofing for shelter was procured at the urgent direction of the new

Chief Minister, Mr. Gomango [God's good man; but the aftermath of the Super cyclone was too much for him to handle]. I knew the pit falls; I assembled a quality control team of the Directorate General of Supply and Disposals and the Army DGQ. But there was an emergency and very little time; people in large numbers were under the open sky. 769.6 quintals of polythene was dispatched by train in a sealed goods van. In the same train, Catholic Relief Everywhere and some other donors also sent their polythene material in other vans. 43 rake loads of different materials were sent by me through the help of Railways; most of the officers at Bhubaneswar ran home each day early evening as there was no electricity and they felt that their families would be unsafe. The best and hardworking officers had been sent to Ersama Block where more than nine thousand people had perished in the tidal wave. So, there was utter mismanagement at the railway station. There was a great failure by and large of the bureaucracy at Bhubaneswar. There was utter chaos in receiving the goods at Bhubaneswar Railway station. All materials got mixed up. On top of it some of the lawyers filed a PIL at the High Court that bungling had taken place in the purchase of polythene. At Bhubaneswar, the office of State Relief Commissioner bought polythene at Rs. 78/- per kilo while we bought it at Rs. 54- at Delhi. We claimed to have sent 769.6 quintals. The Relief Commissioner's office claimed to have received 454 quintals; so they claimed some kind of crazy arithmetic that Rs. 54/- was a fiction; we at Delhi had spent about 41 lakh of rupees for 454 quintals of material; thus the purchase by Relief Commissioner was at cheaper rate. My colleague Mr. Sunil Bhargav never admitted defeat. Armed with all the wagon numbers and other details he went to Bhubaneswar and traced every ounce of the material and our dispatch of 769.6 quintals was accounted for to the dot. It took him some time to trace and establish all the details. I was called by the High Court in the meantime to appear. Honourable Justice Patra was in Chair. As the proceedings started some lawyers sitting idle in the Court started asking some unfounded offensive questions. Justice Patra whom I didn't know at all, sternly said, "All must behave with decorum. If anyone has any specific evidence he can put it up. No insulting question is permitted without specific evidence." The lawyers thereafter asked some routine questions and the matter got closed. Thus where I was expecting a Padmashree, I had to face a judicial proceeding. Ungrateful leaders, ungrateful people and ungrateful system! I know that I am contradicting myself- after all, I am a weak man. An IAS Officer has to be a true Karmayogi; he should have no other expectations than producing results for the people. He has to be above rewards and insults!

17

ADDITIONAL SECRETARY COMMERCE IN GOVERNMENT OF INDIA

I was posted as Home Secretary, government of Odisha. I could not join as simultaneously my empanelment took place to the rank of Additional Secretary, in the Government of India. And I moved out from the Odisha Government. Then I saw naked politics among batch mates to lobby for 'coveted' postings beyond their inter-se rank and competence. I did not even go to Mr. Ashok Saikia or Mr. Prabhat Kumar who had become very fond of me. In Odia, there is a proverb-'The sleeping son gets no share'! It has been the story of my life. But over all, no regrets! From unknown quarters good work and accolades kept showering on me throughout my career.

I was initially posted as Additional Secretary, Defence; but, before I could join some astute junior in the batch grabbed it. I was posted as the Additional Secretary and F.A.in the Department of Commerce as well as the Department of Textiles. As per my usual habit, I immersed myself in work. I had to work with two tough Secretaries; the Commerce Secretary was Mr. P. Sengupta. The Textile Secretary, Mr. Anil Kumar was equally tough. Both of them however, were civil with me, I was always prepared and never gave them any occasion. But both of them were often very severe with other colleagues in 'Review' meetings. The Budget discussion with the Planning Commission was on the anvil. Surprisingly I found neither of the Secretaries getting much involved with preparation and presentation of their respective budgets. I always thought the Budget gave any Department the chance to organise its annual plan of program and work; it should be taken very seriously. The Economic Advisors in the Departments were in charge. I forced myself in and took meetings of both the Department's top officials. I found that both the Economic Advisors had limited appreciation of the two Departments programs and requirement of funds. They had simply added 10% to each item of the last Budget and prepared the 'budgets' without any special argument. I reviewed each program with senior officials and prepared a budget asking for 30% more for each of the Departments justifying the demand in light of achievements last year and the continuing and new programs this year. The 'Budget' files went up to respective Secretaries and promptly came back as approved. Thereafter, I proceeded to rehearse our 'Demands' with each senior program officer who would speak and answer in the meeting with the Planning Commission. EA Commerce played along; EA Textiles showed some discomfort and apparently went to Secretary, Textile to complain. She got a dressing down from the Secretary and behaved better after that. The appointed day arrived for the meeting. I had also planned the sitting order of our group. I had also planned the menu of the lunch [it was a day-long meeting] and procured the lunch [I had done some sleuthing] from the favourite restaurant of the Planning Commission Officers. We were ready and all of us as a Team were spot on in the discussions. That year of my two Departments got a budgetary increase of 25% each. I had hardly spent four months and just was getting into my stride when I was posted as Vice Chairman Delhi Development Authority DDA. I balked and did not rush there to join. The matter hung in balance for 15 days. Finally, I was prevailed upon to join. I smelt some mischief behind my change in posting; someone in illusory competition might have thought that DDA then being a difficult organization, I would fall flat on my face during the DDA tenure as VC either by succumbing to corruption or would fail to improve its working thus tarnishing my own reputation. I was the so-called' 'topper of the batch' as the person above me in the list had gone to the USA for good. Funnily, though due to some machinations his name continued for many years to be shown in the top of 1969 batch perhaps, only to prevent leaders noticing my name first.

18

Vice Chairman, Delhi Development Authority

I joined the job a good fifteen days after the notification. I kept my mind open to new learning and launched myself into work. DDA was a mammoth challenge, a balking horse under a new rider. It took me about two months to come to grip with some basic tasks which were at the roots of innumerable litigation against the DDA [22000 cases in lower Courts, and 7000 cases in the High Court.]. Every Wednesday was earmarked as Grievance Redressal Day in my Chamber; that was the only time the common man could get access to the VC. At 9 AM I used to be in my chair, by 9.30 AM there were crowds of visitors sometimes in excess of five hundred at one time. There was jostling and impatience on part of the visitors to get my attention first. There used to be near chaos initially, but in 6 weeks, the rush started reducing gradually. The first week or second week hearing was something like my experience in the first AGM of Scooters India- extremely aggressive and foul words were used by many. I kept my nerves, kept a smiling countenance and first heard the Women with children, aged persons, women and then men. The chaos started settling down. I adopted extraordinary speed in disposing of the matters in a positive manner. The good word spread, and people behaved much better gradually. I kept a group of chosen officers according to my estimation of their ability and not routinely as per rank. All grievance references were noted in the register systematically, later put into computer lists etc. I found to my consternation that the basics had been neglected in DDA for a long time and no one had bothered to look at the basic functioning of the work of the office like the despatch of a letter and receipt of a letter. Many of the grievances related to simple matters like- 'we did not receive DDA's reply' or 'our replies are missing in DDA files'. There were innumerable grievances about refund of 'Application Money' to 'unsuccessful applicants'. And then there were 1lakh 56 thousand cases pending with DDA four years or more after the applicants paid all 'conversion fees' to get their property converted from 'lease' to 'freehold'.

Turning The Neglected Beast Into A Beauty

I assembled my team, and increased delegation of powers up to a hundred rupees [many cases were kept pending for lack of original land revenue payment [to DDA] as far back as 1975 and so. The land revenue due could be as low as ,say twenty rupees, and in 2000 when I was in DDA a property worth a few crores where the applicant would have paid a few lakhs as fees would be kept hanging in 'suspense' account. Perhaps, only DDA's banks were benefiting by keeping these money without paying interest or paying a nominal interest. I remember with gratitude colleagues like Mr. Laxman Rao, the Finance Member, Mr. D.B. Gupta [later Chief Secretary of Rajasthan], Mr. Parimal Rai [later Chief Secretary of Goa] and innumerable other colleagues like Mrs. Asma Manzar and Mr. J. Chandra who willingly came forward, increased their working hours, accepted my suggestions for simplifying the procedures and methods after discussion, debate, and amendments. In six months the backlog in conversion came down to 5%. The System of dispatch and receipt of letters etc. from applicants was overhauled. I introduced the system of asking for 'Applications for Allotments' through nominated public sector Banks with their several branches in and around Delhi. The unsuccessful applicant would get the credit of his application money the day the results were out and were shared with the Banks promptly. The artificial rush at DDA started reducing. I must mention with gratitude two sterling personalities who were my bosses in this phase, Mr. Jagmohan. The Urban Development Minister and Mr. Vijay Kapur IAS [retired] the Lt. Governor of Delhi. DDA had a troublesome structure; the real day to day boss was the Lt. Governor; but, the Minister Urban Development and even Secretary Urban Development could call for the Vice chairman and issue him written or oral instructions. Chief Minister, Delhi was not in line of command but would send her request. Mrs. Sheila Dixit was the chief Minister. She was a competent and astute personality; Chief Secretary Delhi Mrs. Shailaja. Chandra was her able officer. When after a year or so CS Delhi at prodding of CM asked me whether we could review pending requests of Delhi Government for allotment of land for various public purposes I sent her a list of 45 pieces of land allotment done to Delhi Government in my time [without anyone having to remind me] in contrasts to less than five per year in the earlier years. Mrs. Chandra said that she would brief CM about this initiative by me. Thereafter, in any public function if CM Delhi would sight me she would call for me and greet me. She never rang me up or spoke for any private matter.

The problem for VC DDA was to maintain a balance between his subordination to Lt. Governor and the Urban Development Minister. Both had formidable reputations as achievers. And it sometimes happens that a situation where two brilliant persons cross each other's path often, leads to discomfort for juniors. I managed to maintain a balance reasonably except I failed in one big matter for not having briefed L.G. first. I thought of a brilliant idea while the late lamented Sriyukta Sahib Singh Verma ji M.P. from Outer Delhi constituency was sitting in my chamber about various public issues of Dwarka, part of his constituency. He was requesting something about some unreasonable demand of the villagers of that area. To divert him from putting pressure on me, I started discussing my idea and it unfolded beautifully. I said we should realise that DDA should not be bogged down in details 24/7. I drew his attention to the fact that all the four symbolic shots of Delhi's great architecture which were used as the backdrop for introducing the great architectural tradition and monuments of Delhi are all 'foreign' architecture- the Qutub Minar, the Red Fort, the India Gate and the Lotus Temple. It was time that DDA was woken up to its role of being the Lord Viswakarma of Delhi. DDA should do something on the scale of the Rajpath starting from Rashtrapati Bhawan to India Gate and beyond to the National Sports Club which consisted of a landmass of 364 acres. It was designed as a sovereign vista. There was such a patch of land with DDA in Sector 19 of Dwarka of 365 acres which was in the 'flying tunnel' zone of the airport. No high-rise buildings were permitted. By that time DDA had started making very good profit from its assets and projects. Dr. Verma was down to earth, close to all categories of people and had his eyes and ears open to what all was going on anywhere in Delhi including DDA. So I told him in my office chamber about the concept of Bharat Vandana- a National Heritage park with a Central Vista called Bharat Marg starting from a massive green round 'mela [fair]' ground, the Bharat Marg adorned on both sides by low-rise replicas of grand ancient monuments of each State of India set in green shrubs and fountains. Each State would easily spend ten to twenty crores to showcase its glory to attract international tourists often starting their India tour from Delhi. The Bharat Vandana Marg would come and end into a semi-shrunken round building like our Parliament and this building would house all 'Lalit Kala'- paintings, sculpture, murals etc. and 'Performing Kala' like dance, music theatre etc. round the clock. Dr. Verma took me to Mr. Jagmohan at once without any prior appointment. Mr. Jagmohan heard from Dr. Verma the concept, asked me some questions and then expressed the desire to lay the 'Foundation Stone' of this project the next day in the morning. I erred terribly on such a scale the first time in my life- it was against my principle - planning in detail, first, working out all the drawings and estimates and only then launching a project. I could not resist the tide of political enthusiasm. I should have first got the concept cleared from Lt. Governor who was my Role -Model for his hard work, clear-cut decision making process. He had never overturned any of my suggestions or decisions earlier. The UD Minister went ahead with his Foundation Stone ceremony; the Lt. Governor did not figure in the function and the 'Dream Project' of my life perished in face of subsequent opposition in a subtle manner from Mr. Kapur. Mr. Jagmohan was shifted from Urban Development Dr. S.S. Verma was on back foot.

But I am getting ahead with a story at the expense of a recount of the solid work done in DDA to improve GG.

No Delay Reduced Corruption

The first principle of GG was learnt in the course of facing the challenge of the massive backlog of work piled up in DDA. I have described the matter of pending conversion of lease deeds into freehold. But this was only a tip of the iceberg. Anyway, the first principle of GG practised was the disposal of a file the same day that it came into my office room. I would work there till 8 PM; and then resume working on the files from 9 Pm till at least midnight. I would feel sleepy and drained out; but I would urge myself on and complete the disposal. Delay caused corruption. There was a perceptible improvement in DDA gradually. All colleagues drew strength from my practice of speedy disposal, and pendency reduced dramatically, evident in the dramatic drop in litigation against DDA. Our Legal Advisor and I reviewed together the whole legal interface of DDA - the panel of lawyers, their briefing by our officials led by the Legal Branch, their fees, the arrangements at the Legal Office DDA had at the High Court. Everywhere the capacity was carefully augmented after holding repeated meetings with the panel of lawyers. I took a bold decision; we doubled the rate of fees paid to the lawyers. DDA's legal bills were above Rs. two crores per year. And believe it or not, DDA's litigation reduced by 75%, and the annual legal fee bill at double the rate remained around one crore fifty lakh rupees. We had illustrious lawyers in our panel. Justice Sanjay K. Kaul was from DDA's panel and had just been elevated to Judgeship in Delhi High Court. Justice Gita Mittal ji was then a lawyer and one of the leading lights of our legal panel. She sometimes dropped in at the office and guided me about the improvements needed in our legal arrangements. These inputs were of great value. Another legal personality was a District Judge Smt. Pratibha Rani. She was very kind to occasionally offer suggestions for improvements of our procedures, never about any private case. She was elevated later to Delhi High Court. An IAS officer these days does not operate in isolation; he cannot be smug by managing political leaders only. Judiciary now plays a significant role sometimes in administrative matters. The litigation in his organization should be carefully looked into by the IAS to avoid judicial and legal embarrassments.

I also attended to the most important responsibilities of DDA - creation of housing, infrastructure, maintenance of the DDA 'Greens'.

Gradually, my pro- engineer stance became evident; I attended all their 'Celebrations' and 'Meetings'. I roamed as much as humanly possible the work-sites and looked for opportunities to point out any good work done by the engineering staff. Positive approach paid much better dividends. We increased the number of new civil engineering projects substantially; where DDA was doing on the average five thousand new housing each year, I launched a plan to increase it to 25000 per year.

Sports Complexes - Headache to Profit

Now to the gardens and sports complexes of DDA! DDA had twenty six Sport Complexes, the Siri Fort Sports complex being the show piece. And soon I started receiving phone calls from distinguished colleagues and personalities of Delhi, complaining about different short-comings in different Sports complexes. Sometimes it could be about a torn net or a missing T.T., a stinking bathroom etc. I got fed up; neither I could retort to the known personalities nor could I close my ears. I then thought of a strategy. We quickly recruited twenty six retired Colonels, Majors and Captains as managers of these complexes. They were clearly told that they were to manage their respective Centres as Profit Centres. DDA however would foot the bill for the first six months. The turn-around was dramatic; Complaints vanished within a fortnight and I received phones and requests thereafter for membership.

Vigorous and productive management of the public assets entrusted with an IAS officer is the first requirement of GG. Losses and under-performance arise in Public Institutions mostly due to slipshod and indifferent management.

Dwarka Dwara

The opening up of Dwarka was a major challenge. The assets created there by DDA were remaining unsold. The auction of commercial plots did not even fetch the 'reserve' price. The major roads planned for Dwarka were too few and were not wide enough. Under guidance of Lt. Governor Mr. Kapur I prepared a bold initiative and created four new major openings to Dwarka including the Palam Fly-over. I remember particularly the meeting with Air Force and Army land authorities in a common meeting as the flyover was to go through their land and all together 17 acres of military land was needed. The negotiation could have gone on for months. I asked them about the compensation; they came up with a figure of 34 acres. I said to them that they were the defenders of the whole country; so the entire country belonged to them. DDA would give Army and Air force forty acres provided the Minutes of the Meeting would be immediately drawn up and signed as the 'final' operative decision of both sides and the DDA would get possession of 'Defence' land within 7 days of its allotting and handing over possession of the promised forty acres. Every Defence official burst into good cheers and the Palam flyover was constructed in a record time by L&T. Those were better days; Secretaries to the Government of India were not being kept in prison without conviction. Lt. Governor encouraged me and without batting an eyelid I signed a hundred crore contract with L&T. Of Course, from my super-cyclone experience I knew the importance of following the correct financial procedures; but I did not dither and waste time. The entire procedure was completed in a week and the work was awarded. DDA made thousands of crores from Dwarka assets as soon as all major roads started being implemented in the field and progressed rapidly and became visible every day.

In today's atmosphere very dynamic colleagues have also started playing safe and decision making has become tardy. With an unsympathetic judiciary, and enforcement agencies without 'development work experience' and without supervisory links to the IAS playing an autonomous role, have started taking the upper hand. These agencies do not have interdisciplinary experience or composition and are sometimes alleged to play partisan roles. In the recent past, the two top officials of a premier agency engaged in prolonged public spat bringing governance in the country to ridicule even during the time of a 'strong' Prime Minister.

I took the initiative to turn my 'Grievance Day' into a system. DDA had a patriarchal reputation; it was infamous for misbehaving with visitors coming to DDA to get their work done. I changed this perception; we organised the 'Reception' area like airport counters. Fourteen mid-level colleagues with their name clip and 'May I Help

You' tag manned the Reception area and received the visitors and worked as a problem solver. It was possible to give them 'incentive' allowance motivating them to get involved. Every three months, fifty percent of these personnel were changed to keep up their 'freshness'. Clean cool drinking water and tea was served free of cost. The Finance Member rushed into my room and said that 'free' tea might invite an audit objection. I requested him to put up his note; when he did that I wrote below that, DDA owed its financial prosperity to 'clients' and servicing them well would increase revenue of DDA. However, if there would be a shortfall, the deficit could be recovered from my pay. FM vanished with that file, it did not surface again. The next day, as my habit was, I started looking at the last three 'Balance Sheets' of DDA. I noted the curious jump of 'medical reimbursement to employees' in the balance sheet to the tune of Rs. six crores last year. I immediately convened a meeting of the top officials including the Finance Member and Commissioner Personnel Mr. Sunil Sharma- a brilliant officer of the Railway Personnel Service on deputation with DDA. and asked them to look into this and report. The skeleton tumbled out of the cupboard by late afternoon. Six private hospitals- each had suddenly billed one crore of rupees extra in the last year. To cut the story short, these were black-listed; the practice of 'cash free' transactions was abolished making the employee check and pay for his bill first and then get reimbursed. I looked at the Finance Member and said mischievously that here was the savings available for serving free tea to the clients of DDA.

Unknown Brilliant Colleague

A curious incident may be permitted to be mentioned. The Cabinet Secretary, Mr. T. R. Prasad took a meeting on DDA. The Urban Secretary was also present. Cabinet Secretary expressed unhappiness that a lot of grievances were there against DDA addressed to his Office. I briefly explained the systemic reforms and the drop in litigation by people against DDA and submitted that things were not perfect but more than fifty percent improvements had already occurred. Cabinet Secretaries were generally very busy personalities, so the best of them could be impatient sometimes. He looked at my request to glance at the data in his office. Against about twelve hundred complaints to his office against

DDA each of the past several years, there was a sharp decline- only about 350 complaints were registered in his office against DDA in the previous year. He would not give up easily; he said it could also mean that people had registered less number of complaints as they were not having hopes of redressal. I should have been more tactful in reply; but I said, "Sir, with utmost submission may I point out that these are reductions in petitions to the Cabinet Secretariat. Sir, you could not be meaning that they are losing faith in the highest forum." I quickly added to moderate my bravado, "DDA has improved. You may perhaps, kindly consider asking Secretary Coordination to carry out a special inspection of DDA." CS was gracious; he said "Keep at it. You are a doer; just keep at it, things must improve. I shall keep a watch!" And then he asked me to go with Secretary Coordination to his room. I did so. Mr. Vijay Goel, then an emerging leader of BJP in Delhi was sitting there. He started his lamentation-"DDA is full of corruption!" I took up the challenge immediately and demanded to know of a specific instance. He was also combative, said, "Phone pe DDAwale paise mangte hain!" I lost my head and said "Let Secretary Coordination choose a number, let the 'speaker phone' be on. Let Mr. Goel talk, concealing his identity." So the drama started- at Mr. Goel's prodding, a number of 'Land Allotment section" was connected. Mr. Goel enquired about getting a piece of land for some institutional purpose. The officer at the other point patiently explained to him the procedure and the criteria. Then Mr. Goel dropped a hint, "Oopar se kitna aur lagega?" the officer replied with civility but with firmness, "No more of this nonsense. You must have patience, come and get your work done provided you are qualified. Offering money is in bad taste; money cannot get your work done. My advice is, do not engage any middleman also. If you deserve an allotment, submit your case properly. Decisions will be on merit." I did not know the excellent colleague on the phone who stood his ground, enhanced the reputation of DDA and made my day.

All Duty No Date

I may be pardoned for recounting an anecdote about 'decision-making' challenges in DDA. One day near the lunch hours, I heard a muffled crying of a woman at the door of my chamber. I went up and opened my door; there was an aristocratic looking but dishevelled young woman standing there with a tear-stained face sobbing away. I ushered her in and asked her what her problem was. She explained that her father was dead and she lived with her mother. They had their main asset- one large house in the New Friends Colony put on rent to Essar Motors to for the residential purpose of the company's executives. Essar motors had put a signboard on the building reading -Guest House' It was actually used as a 'transit' guest house for Essar's own executives on tour. DDA had suddenly sent her a demand of Rs. seventy two lakh as 'misuse' charge alleging 'commercial' use of the residential property. I postponed my lunch and immediately got her file. I studied it carefully, I studied the rules on the subject and came to the conclusion that it was a clear case of tyranny by DDA officials who had over-interpreted the law and levied charges where no such proof of commercial use was there. A mere signboard by the tenant company to help its touring officers to identify the building easily could not be stretched to levy 'misuse' charges. I wrote in the file- "Misinterpretation of rules! No commercial use/misuse is established. Issue the applicant a letter immediately that no charges were payable to DDA." Within five minutes, FM came into and said that my powers for waiver were limited to Rs. eight lakh only in a single case; this order of mine had to be taken to the 'full meeting of DDA'. I took the file from his hand and wrote further- "FM to calculate the financial implications of the wastage of management time caused by errant officials by raising bogus demands and to please send back the file to me fixing responsibility for recovery of cost for initiating and then continuing a wasteful activity." FM went away with the file; within twenty minutes the person sitting now with my Private Secretary and waiting, got her letter of 'No Demand'. Next day the person concerned- this time elegantly dressed- appeared again in my chamber. She invited me to go out to dinner with her. I refused politely stating that I did not eat out. She looked at me for some moments and said, "You are the first man to refuse my invitation" And she left!

Madan Khurana, prominent BJP leader wanted me out because he wanted a particular officer to succeed me to organise his campaign for the coming elections. I did not resist though I had started enjoying the challenges of DDA. There was some inauguration -perhaps, the Vijay Veer Awas. The Prime Minister came as the Chief Guest. I knew my transfer order was ready; I avoided fawning around PM lest he would think that I was seeking any favour. He, however, was perceptive. As he was returning to his car after the function, he detached himself from the VVIP group, came to where I was standing at a distance and shook my hands warmly. My DDA days ended! I was posted as Additional Secretary, Urban Development Department of Government of India

19

ADDITIONAL SECRETARY, URBAN DEVELOPMENT, GOVERNMENT OF INDIA

I left DDA without regret [except for my failure to pilot Bharat Vandana]. I joined my office at Nirman Bhawan and without feeling the slightest demotivation threw myself back to work. Somehow, the two Urban Development Secretaries under whom I worked had great faith in me and loaded me with all the important work. Generally, in many Departments of Government of India, the Additional Secretaries cool their heels without much work. It was different in my case. I was asked to look after CPWD and the Directorate of Estates.

Central Public Works Department - CPWD:

My love affair with civil engineers continued throughout my career. It reached its pinnacle when I became the Additional Secretary, Urban Development. I quickly realised that CPWD consisted of the best civil engineering personnel of the country. Many of them were from IITs; they had been recruited through a tough Competitive examination by UPSC. Yet I was observant enough to notice a curious lack of excitement about work in the group. I understood the demotivation soon enough. For one reason or another, there were 765 cases many of which were registered against most of the top engineers of CPWD; and these were pending with the Central vigilance Commission. I quietly got all the connected papers of each case and studied them thoroughly. I took a month to get everything ready. Then I called on CVC and some known colleagues in CVC at important levels and discussed with them my analyses and documents. The net result was that about 500 cases were outright closed; a hundred or so were closed with 'Censure' or similar minor punishment.

My next step was to become the 'Marketing' Executive of CPWD. I parleyed with several Departments and Ministries and restored Central Government's different civil engineering work with different Ministries back to CPWD. The Parliament House Library and Media complex was the most prestigious one. I remember to have argued vehemently with my indulgent Secretary Urban Development, Mr. Khanna when he made some negative remark about the work culture in CPWD. To his gracious credit, my Secretary only smiled disbelievingly but let me have my way seeing my boundless enthusiasm. Incomplete, slow-moving government Housing projects in Delhi and elsewhere were fast-tracked; CPWD seniors did not mind my going from site to site and solving problems including getting the 'Fire Office Clearance' within seven days of completion of each project [this used to take close to a year, the newly made housing assets would deteriorate waiting for 'Fire clearance' for one year or so. Then the documents would go to the Directorate of Estate where another inspection would be carried out pointing out needs for small repairs and easily another three to six months would be wasted before 'allottees' would get their allotment and occupy the 'old' new houses/flats. I moved indefatigably and planned in a manner that within 15 days of completion, the housing assets got occupied. It saved CPWD a lot of money on unnecessary watch and ward and repairing charges. However, I never interfered in their technical matters or tenders.

Then I noticed a peculiar occurrence happening in front of Nirman Bhawan on a daily basis. Around lunch time every day, a group of about 30 to 40 persons would gather in front of the Nirman Bhawan and start raising slogans of- "Hai, Hai!! Down, Down!!" My immediate office staff smiled sardonically and informed me that this was going on for innumerable years; the group of disaffected persons were actually Junior

Engineers [Diploma holders] of CPWD who gathered there to ventilate their grievances against Degree Engineers of CPWD who occupied the higher echelons of CPWD. One day I decided to take things into my hand. While returning from somewhere, I requested Driver ji to stop the car near the demonstrators. I caught hold of about five leader types by their hand and asked them to come with me to my office. I would think that they did not know who I was. But my confident demeanour made them follow my asking instinctively. They came with me to my office. I phoned Director General [DG] CPWD through my mobile to please come to my room with three senior-most Additional DGs Soon my room was crowded with the adversaries. I had asked my staff to keep 'tea & biscuits ready. And I launched myself onto a high moral ground tinged with emotional appeal. I said to the seniors that they should have been feeling very uncomfortable when their younger brothers were suffering every day in the sun; then I turned to the JE group and said that they ought to feel ashamed as they were washing their mother institution CPWD's linens in public and making CPWD look dirty unnecessarily. The JE group burst out into lamentation that they had to resort to this tactic as the seniors never gave them a hearing and their grievances remained unsolved over years. I addressed DG Saheb and said he was the father-figure of the CPWD family. He would have to promise me that he would sit with JEs and look into their complaints and find solutions. If anything would not be doable, DG and I would meet and find some solution. I would assist him in this, come to his chamber once a week. Believe it or not, the one and half years I stayed as Additional Secretary, Urban Development no further demonstration took place. My Secretary boss must have been watching from the sidelines, but never interfered. And the most touching incident of my career then took place.

If Only My Father Were Alive to Know!

Rumours were doing the rounds that our batch had been empanelled for Secretary-positions. The natural expectation was that I would be the first one to become a Secretary to the Government of India from my batch as I was on the top of the list. At this juncture, one day at about 3 PM the door to my room opened and the three senior most

Additional Director Generals of CPWD trouped in. I was happy to see them as CPWD had become vibrant again. They looked at one another, and finally one of them said, "Sir, Our DG is retiring at the end of this month." I promptly shared with them that I had taken the necessary administrative steps to prepare the panel of three eligible seniors in order of merit -cum -seniority and though there was an initial delay in putting up the proposal to ACC [Appoint committee of Cabinet], now the papers had reached the PMO after Home Minister had concurred. Orders were expected any day. I also told them that I would not hesitate to share that they were the three whose names had been recommended for the position. At this all three of them said simultaneously, "No, No! We have not come for that. We want to tell you that we have heard that you are likely to be promoted to become a Secretary to the Government of India. The post of our Director General is also considered as equivalent to Secretary to the Government of India. We have come to request you to agree to become our DG." I was speechless; my eyes became misty - in front of me were three noblest souls who were willing to sacrifice their prized post for an outsider! I was truly moved- it was the highest honour a bureaucrat would receive in his career. Frankly, when the Ambassador of Norway rang up many years later conveying that the Government of Norway had decided to confer 'Knighthood' on me in recognition of my work for health of women and children of the world, I was happy but never so touched.

20

SECRETARY FAMILY WELFARE & HEALTH, GOVERNMENT OF INDIA

A week had passed thereafter; my posting as the Secretary, Family Welfare in the Ministry of Health was notified. In those days, there used to be two Secretaries in the Ministry of Health and Family Welfare. By convention, the more senior person used to be posted as Secretary Health and the newer colleague used to be the Secretary, Family Welfare. Secretary Family Welfare looked after primary health care, mother and child health, Immunization and population issues. The Health Secretary looked after everything else. As a Secretary to the Government of India, I entered the same Nirman Bhawan, this time from Gate no. 6 instead of Gate no. 1. Only after spending a couple of months in Health Ministry, I learnt that a posting in Health Ministry that too as the Secretary, Family Welfare was not considered a posting befitting for a 'topper'; such postings were for the goody-goody ones in a batch. I did not get demotivated and started working with the right earnest.

Darkness Under The Lamp

Reviewing the work of the past and strategies adopted to achieve the goals of the Department in RCH, I found gradually the disquieting evidence that India was entirely dependent on Western multilateral agencies for evolving its strategies. There had been no dynamism infused into an important segment of the country's development agenda. Initially, there was court paid to me by these Western agencies. I started attending seminars morning and afternoon, mostly organised by these bi-lateral or multilateral agencies. Lighting the lamp to declare the seminar open generally in some five star hotel, listening to a bunch of public health data about infant mortality-IMR, maternal mortality-MMR and fertility ratios-TFR without any road-map emerging out of these seminars/workshops for a well-argued set of actions was the merry occupation of the Agencies, the officials in the Ministries, the members of the favoured NGOs. The ambience used to be pleasant and the lunch/tea sumptuous. It pains me to call names; but, for sake of enumerating what is GG and what is sheer skulduggery, I have to use an extreme word. A nincompoop atmosphere had pervaded the Family Welfare Department. One of the previous Secretaries very fond of 'lamp-lighting' and addressing seminars arranged every week by Western agencies in five-star venues had fallen into the trap and had publicly declared and adopted 'target-free approach' for all the important work of the Department. There was a definite lobby to keep India where it was - close to Sub-Saharan countries in health indices particularly in IMR, MMR, and TFR - while shedding crocodile tears about India's health condition. In the name of some stray abuse of 'human rights' during the Central and State governments' efforts to reduce TFR, all emphasis on accountability and performance in the field was given the go-by under the 'target free approach' era. Mercifully, the system draws a line somewhere; the nincompoop was by-passed, his junior became Health Secretary; but the damage to mothers and children health was incalculable as the non-performer continued his lamp lighting activities in RCH sector while health indices of OBIMARU States remained in darkness.

It was not my contention that Western Agencies were to be shown the door. These agencies were windows to learning; but, while learning one must not surrender or suspend the faculty of thinking to the 'educator'. My gradual realisation was that India had to think for itself if it had to improve its health indices.

Immunization coverage was around 40%. The two southern States like Kerala and Tamil Nadu had coverage of about 90 percent while States like Bihar, Uttar Pradesh had coverage around 30%. There would be survey based data researches galore showing this fact in many dramatic ways; but, none of the 'surveys' laid down any road-map of improving coverage, The 'study' or seminar would come to pious conclusions like the level of women's education being the highest in Kerala, the states' performance in immunization was the best. I realised to my dismay that the nincompoop era of 'target free approach' had completely corroded any managerial approach to study the tasks of the Family Welfare Department and find solutions to bring about improvements.

Inimitable Dr, APJ Kalam

The Health Minister Mrs. Sushma Swaraj was a very gracious personage and was considered one of the best public speakers of India. A curious incident happened. Dr. APJ Kalam adorned the position of President of India. Some get elevated to a high position; some adorn a position coveted by many but add nothing. Kalam Saheb was one who made the Chair of the President of India proud by agreeing to accept the position. Smt. Swaraj sent for me soon after Kalam Saheb's swearing in. She said that the President had asked her to meet him. She knew that Dr. Kalam was interested in 'Population' issues. She wanted me to remain ready with all population related data and to accompany her along with my senior colleague the Health Secretary, Mr. Rao. On the appointed time we went to Rashtrapati Bhawan led by Mrs. Swaraj. We took our seats in the office chamber and waited for the arrival of the President. Dr. Kalam came in and greeted us in his very civil manner; he immediately said to Mrs. Swaraj, "Minister, we should do something about our rapid population increase." At this, Sushma ji looked at me from the corner of her eyes with an 'I told you' glint and launched forth, "President Sir, this is a historic moment for our country. We should be able to solve the population issue by sheer example. I am your Health Minister and I have only one child that too a daughter. Our Vice President has also one child only and that to a daughter. [By that time, the gender imbalance in India's population was acutely visible in the North Western states like Punjab, Haryana, Delhi, Gujarat and even in Tamil Nadu and Andhra. Female foeticide was rampant through clandestine unethical medical practice leading to sex selection.] And

President Sir, our Prime Minister is a bachelor and so is our President." Mrs. Swaraj was halted in her mid-speech. Dr. Kalam got up half way from his chair with a look of horror on his august countenance and remonstrated, "No, no, Minister! I am a Brahmachari." Obviously, he did not want to be bracketed with Mr. Vajpayee. The Health Minister, Health Secretary and I - all three displayed exemplary OLQ- officer like qualities and maintained our composure without a single wrinkle changing on our face. The discussion thereafter did not proceed long. We all came back and never referred to the Presidential clarification and its imports.

It was my good luck that I was first posted as the Secretary, Family Welfare in the Health Ministry. Even as the Health Secretary of Odisha I could not gather a snap-shot of this vast socially important Sector. Like many, I thought of Health as setting up big hospitals, filling them with new equipment and instruments. Becoming Secretary FW compelled me to look at the real issues of the Health Sector. Reproductive Child Health was the foundation of Health of a country like India which had still very poor health indices by 2003 when I became the Secretary FW. Most of the educated including doctors in India had no clue [including myself who had been the Health Secretary of a State] that India had a pregnancy cohort of about three crores a year. Of the about 2.8 crore babies born per year, about 11 lakh used to die within 28 days of their birth and about 22 lakh in all. About one lakh fifty thousand mothers used to die because of 'delivery' complications. These figures were annual national average- Kerala had IMR of 10 while Madhya Pradesh had IMR of 71. Tamil Nadu had MMR of 150 while UP had about 700 per one lakh. And Tamil Nadu had TFR [which determines the population growth, a TFR of 2 is considered ideal as a correct replacement factor leading to population stabilization] of 1.8 while Bihar had TFR of 3.3.The regional State -wide disparities were huge. And a good RCH was the foundation of all other health issues. So age of marriage of a woman, antenatal care, safe delivery, early and exclusive breastfeeding, complete immunization starting with zero dose, nutrition of mother and baby, avoidance of quick second pregnancy [through availability of Family Planning products and access to it, particularly by the woman], eradication of diseases like polio, measles, diarrhoea mostly through good hygiene and safe drinking water] etc. were of great importance. If these all could be ensured later years' morbidity and mortality would also reduce substantially. However, these were issues of Public Health, and unfortunately the cream of the medical profession- the doctors- were interested in curative care. Public Health was boring to them- it did not contribute to their practice. There were some eminent Public Health doctors. But they were mostly besotted with the Western Agencies' paradigm on public health and never tried to evolve a discourse suitable to India. The most eminent ones often got their 'grants' and financial support from one or the other Western agencies and were under their intellectual hegemony. Very few of the doctors were Public health managers or even doctor leaders in the institutions they worked in barring persons like Dr. Shakti Gupta of AIIMS. I felt overwhelmed at the lack of managerial skill at all levels of the Central and State government Health system. As an IAS officer one had to work in several sectors and face different challenges. The challenge in the Health Sector appeared overwhelming as there were very few managerial structures in this sector. Public Health was the core of the Government Health system; however, tertiary care seemed to have occupied the central space. Somehow one chartered Accountant, Mr. Sanjay Saxena had come into my Department ostensibly to keep accounts of the 'donors' fund for India's large polio eradication programme. I searched him out within a month and started using his expertise in many areas. The requirement of GG is not only to have 'skill-balance' in the HR needed for a particular sector; it also requires vigorous management of this HR to get optimal results. An example of poor work culture in the 'Target free' era- Mr. Saxena had never been called by Secretary FW for any discussion except in large inconsequential meetings where his expertise was never used. The financial mismanagement was colossal. The Secretary of the nincompoop era was known for personal integrity. However it never occurred to him that his Department was 'surrendering' without being able to spend close to one thousand five hundred crore about 30% each year of the total budget of Rs. 5 thousand crore allocated to FW Department as its annual budget. Yet the very same person must have participated [as I initially did] in seminars crying hoarse that the Government of India must increase its budgetary allocation of 1% of

GDP for Health to at least 2.5%. Intellectual dishonesty, not realising the tasks expected of an officer, non-utilization of the Budget, wasting disproportionate time in futile seminars as Chief Guest is in my humble opinion also a form of insidious corruption. I have noticed with great regret that quite a number of colleagues do not understand that the IAS was created as an all India Service to work hard in a purposeful manner to attain public tasks set before it. Many are happy writing a stiff opposing note to politician's wish, or pointing out flaws in any initiative taken by any work-minded colleague without suggesting constructive alternatives. Back to Mr. Sanjay!

UNI-SAFE Brought To Book

I started asking Sanjay ji to tell me how much 'donor fund' was committed for the polio eradication programme and how much we had billed this fund with account statements. The skeleton jumped out of the cupboard- bills had not been submitted systematically in the last three years, there was unreimbursed bills from the soft credit at 2.5% or so by World Bank lying in the Ministry to the tune of more than seven hundred crores of rupees as the program officials and the Secretary had not bothered. I had read somewhere that the cost of funds to the Government of India was above 7% those days. And this was a precious foreign exchange waiting to flow into Government of India coffers. In three days, the bills were raised and the reimbursement came. The Health Ministry had no concept of its larger role for the sector, particularly its promotional role for boosting manufacture of health products used in the country. My brief background in Commerce Ministry helped. I had noted there various Councils set up on PPP mode to boost exports in different sectors. These Councils also helped monitor 'dumping' by countries like China and levying countervailing duties to protect domestic manufacturers. I looked at the different components of the Polio Eradication programme. About twelve hundred crore of rupees were each year in this one single programme. Of this the cost of the vaccine alone was more than seven hundred crores of rupees. True to my work habit, I looked at the method of procurement. There were four Indian manufacturers - two public sectors and two private sectors - and several European manufacturers. UNICEF had been appointed as the procuring agency. It was the eighth year of procurement by the time I became the Secretary FW. i analysed the steps involved in the procurement. It was a repetitive set of steps each year after the first couple of years of procurement. And UNICEF was charging a horrendously high fee of 8% year after year. I called all the Indian manufacturers for some brain-storming. It turned out that Indian manufacturers always quoted the lowest price; UNICEF awarded them 60% of the order. The rest 40% was distributed to European manufacturers at their higher quoted price on the plea of 'global vaccine security' meaning that more suppliers had to be nurtured for the World Polio Eradication Programme. I wrote a long detailed letter to UNICEF saying that it could not load other manufacturers such a large quantity that too at their higher quoted costs. At best it could place twenty percent of the order for vaccine security plea of theirs provided the European/ other manufacturers agreed to supply at the L1 price. UNICEF, accustomed to the cosy nincompoop era, tried to hit back saying that their tender and order placement was a secret process and they were thinking of causing an inquiry against me for 'invading' the sanctity of their process. I was not intimidated and wrote back that I would expect a Delegation of suitably senior officials of their procurement branch to come immediately and apologise to me ; otherwise I would write to Secretary General of United Nations as a member Sovereign country about unethical practices of UNICEF and their misbehaviour towards a Member country. The bullet hit the mark; UNICEF senior delegation came, apologised, agreed to my suggestions and I reduced their procurement fee to 2%. We saved at least a hundred fifty crore of rupees each year thereafter and Indian manufacturers got a boost. I briefed my Minister [a Congress coalition had come to power in Centre, Dr. Ramadoss was the Health minister.]; he was visibly happy as for some reasons in the past he disliked UNICEF.

Basic Finance

I have gone ahead with my story. Other noteworthy events occurred in the time of Smt. Swaraj as Health Minister. First of all, I went flat out to probe and solve the causes of poor ability of the FW Department to commit expenditure and surrender 30% of its budget year after year. It turned out that the States did not send 'utilization certificates' [UCs] and so a lot of money under Centrally sponsored Schemes could not be released to them. The Southern States like Tamil Nadu and Kerala somehow utilised every rupee and sent the necessary documents in time. [Interacting with these two Southern States, I later found out that each of them had a chartered accountant working in the Health Department and was in charge of accounts.] It was the group of OBIMARU States which clogged the process. I tried to recollect my days as the Health Secretary of Odisha and Health Department's interface with the FW Department of India. There was hardly any interaction between the Centre and the State. Each year some cheque/draft would come from the Centre, generally after October and quite a few in February and March asking the State to utilise it by 31st March and send back UC. The bank drafts would be in an envelope accompanied by a single paper mentioning a scheme's number but not even the 'title' or any other details. I got into the tedious details; apparently, the 'Scheme' Section would send its recommendation to the Financial Adviser and the Finance Wing would prepare the drafts and put the scheme number and post it to the States. Some details of the 'Scheme' might have been communicated to the States in the first quarter of the year without specifying the exact quantum of Central Assistance; but no follow up would be made to keep the States prepared. The release of funds would be by fits and starts towards the third and fourth quarter - a substantial amount in March itself-; and again the Scheme section would not follow up and link the release of funds to a particular scheme. Most of the States with poor governance records would be all at sea. The bank draft would either remain un-cashed by the State or if credited to the State account would still remain unspent as the Finance Department of the State would not permit expenditure without schematic details. This rigmarole was going on for years; states like Bihar and Assam were holding on to funds for three years or more without committing expenditure. I prodded the FA, I recruited through WHO's assistance on deputation a brilliant officer of Indian Civil Accounts Service, Mr. Rajesh Kumar - constituted two sets of teams under his leadership and made these teams go from State to State Within three months ninety percent of the backlog of funds lying with states were traced and expenditure began in right earnest and by six months all the UCs were on Centre's table. The Health Administration during the nincompoop era of target free approach had reached its nadir and had to be lifted by catching hold of the shoe laces. I saw that Budget Management was the most important tool to get the States on board and also energise my own colleagues in the Department. I involved rank and file in preparation of the Budget. Every officer knew the details of his scheme; I made the programme officials crunch the numbers State-wise and scheme -wise and made the FA tally up the Budget. We had pre-budget discussions with the Planning Commission and Department of Expenditure. By January, our Department was ready with a detailed Budget mounted on an e-platform. When the Budget document was sent to the Finance Ministry, I sent emails to all the Health Secretaries and Finance Secretaries and Planning Commissioners of the States that the Health budget support for the particular State was likely to be long the line of the e-budget communicated to them and that they should start preparing plans for implementation. I also told them that as soon as the Budget would be introduced in the Parliament I would confirm the headings and the amounts again. The day the Budget was introduced in the Parliament, I came to learn of our proposed allocation. I again called all scheme officials and briefed them that they would prepare 'action Plan' and 'Fund Release Plan' and put up to me. I wrote to states that the allocation as conveyed to them stood firm subject to Parliamentary sovereignty to approve the Budget; I would confirm to them the schemes and amounts finally the day the Budget was passed in the Parliament. Thus in 2004-05 Finance Year, the schemes were well-known to the States by March; the allocation was conveyed at the beginning of the FY and funds started flowing from May. the expenditure and performance showed remarkable improvement. Not to mention that each Bank Draft released carried an accompanying explanation of the scheme and other procedures. Rajesh Kumar and Sanjay Saxena were able supporters to FA and I; and we started an e-MIS for monitoring the Budget. I apologise for burdening the readers with details; but, often GG consists in looking at minute details to improve vital processes. SOPs all across all Departments of Government of India and States need rebooting, particularly the financial processes.

A senior IAS officer's first duty is Budget Management; the second duty is to ensure that there is skill-balance available for implementation of policies and programmes. Existing HR has to be gingered up, and sometimes it has to be augmented with right expertise through recruitment of some key personnel.

National Rural Health Mission

The Congress coalition Government headed by Dr. Manmohan Singh did accord some priority to the Health sector unlike many other past governments. Dr. Ramadoss was asked to meet the PM. My Minister came back and said that the Prime Minister wanted a vigorous primary health care system; Dr. Singh apparently as a child suffered from a small eye problem; no doctor was available nearby his village. It could not be taken care of. He suffered lifelong problems with his eyesight. The PM expressed a desire to launch a National Rural Health Mission. Additional Secretary to PM, Mr. Gopalakrishnan landed up in my office and started helping me to unroll the concept. I owe this brilliant Officer a great deal of gratitude. After a couple of meetings, we understood each other well- he had a humane view of the NRHM; I had a strong managerial approach. We sometimes shared my frugal lunch brought from my home and argued incessantly but constructively. For instance, Mr. Gopalakrishnan came up with the ingenious idea that we should send Rs. twenty thousand to each of the ANM centres [about one lakh fifty thousand in the country] giving some broad guidelines. ANM could spend the money as she liked within the guidelines and get it vetted by the Sarpanch where her Centre was located. It did have a dramatic effect. NRHM was launched in 2005. Till that time I had spent more than a year's time trying my best to hold meetings at different state headquarters of ANMs and encouraging them to speak up about their problems and give suggestions about improving Mother and Child Health. I never could elicit any satisfactory participation from them in these long meetings. They simply would not speak, shake their heads and would sit down. I even got ANMs to come from Tamil Nadu to speak to ANMs conferences of some of the Northern States- yet the involvement of ANMs of Northern States did not improve. However, after we released the Rs. twenty thousand lump-sum grant, there was a remarkable change. The ANMs became vociferous in all the meetings and gave many useful suggestions.

Initially, ours was a small team. One benefitted from the work discipline of DDA days - working hours from 6. 30 AM to night 11.30 PM. Our main challenge was to reach every village; the ANM was already overburdened. So we thought of a 'voluntary worker'- a married resident woman in each village. ASHA- Accredited Social Health Activist [HOPE], a coinage of Mr. J. S. Kang. Her income would not be through salaries, but through work related incentives. In a couple of years about a million ASHAs were recruited starting with the OBiMARU States- Odisha, Bihar, MP, Assam, Rajasthan and Uttar Pradesh. The personnel gap and skill imbalance in the Government health sector was very large. We recruited more than a hundred twenty thousand personnel, including about 10 thousand MBAs, 10 thousand accountants, Chartered Accountants and cost Accountants and a large number of persons qualified in Masters of Social Works. We recruited on a contract basis several doctors, nurses and paramedics. Computers and computer operators were sent to each Block.

NRHM taught me that leaders would always be in a hurry; large scale policies/programmes would be announced by them. People at large would expect the benefits from these policies to flow immediately. The challenge for the IAS was to design and implement these policies on a continuous dynamic basis learning on the go, looking at fundamental issues of HR [including their morale and motivation], infrastructure, skill balance[the core technical /medical personnel and the support services like management of various processes including interface with common people-HR, Finance, day to day maintenance needed for vigorous sustainable implementation, training, remain alert to nut and bolt issues like logistic chain, maintenance, local ownership through participation and generating resources from users as much for supplementing revenue cost as much for improving service delivery through accountability, and above all ultimately a transparent publicly announced health delivery system where there was no discrimination. Services had to be made available respecting the privacy and dignity of the patient Two false slogans had dogged health sector over years- the first was a promise of 'free' health care to all, and the second that the doctors and medical personnel were expected to be 'godly' in their action and behaviour while the fact was that they were like other professions and human beings having their strength and weakness. I was also sucked into these assumptions; it took me a few years to get out of these false notions and design better processes and systems for NRHM. One of the banes of IAS these days is the extremely short tenure many IAS Secretaries spend as Secretary of one Department. Jockeying for more glamorous positions and political fragility/preference combine to make some colleagues spend not even a year in any particular Department. Luckily for me, I continued in the same Ministry all through my Secretary days. Health was a very complex sector, the variables were many, the service delivery was way below par, and too much backlog of unattended public health services had piled up. There was no tradition of determined action. It needed time to understand all the interconnected and inter-sectorial issues to create sustainable design of implementation. I am grateful to my Team of many colleagues who stood by me and tolerated my mania for revising proposal notes several times to put in position practical implementation structures. I also unhesitatingly express gratitude to my Health Minister Dr. Ramadoss, Prime Minister, Dr. Manmohan Singh and Smt. Sonia Gandhi [notwithstanding the fact that the latter two fell into a nepotism trap set by their trusted bureaucrat and denied me later my apex post] who stood by me against onslaught of personalities like Mr. Chidambaram and Dr. Montek Ahluwalia- for once, both of them saw eye to eye and opposed my policy presentation on NRHM tooth and nail because they were entirely sceptical -from their deep experience- that the States might not come on board and State leaders like Mr. Mulayam Singh Yadav would hardly be bothered to follow my managerial model, they would go on transferring doctors at the drop of a hat- and the whole NRHM with its carefully designed edifice with ASHAs at the bottom of the pyramid would get mired in misadministration of the State political leaders. In fact, the first Presentation of the policy and design of NRHM took nearly two hours- I was defending throughout against the continuous attack and scepticism of Chidambaram ji and Dr. Ahluwalia with Member Health of Planning Commission lending them support calling the design based on the principles of vigorous management as a way of denial of 'human rights'[the whole health sector had many pious 'parasites' who had carved out niches of spokesperson-ship on different segments of health, they never had dirtied their lily hands with any actual service delivery work, but were great critics of any positive action on the pretext that these field service deliveries sometimes resulted in callus treatment of people by the doctors. Their particular target was the 'family planning-fertility reduction'- programmes by the Government. They loved the 'target free' approach; it gave them continuous fodder for their seminars/researches]. Mr. P. Sainath had published a book titled 'Everybody Loves a Good Drought'. It could also be a title for the health system of the country - 'Everybody Profits From Bad Health and Inefficient Health Care in India'. At the end of two hours of acrimonious debate in which the PM remained a mute witness, finally everyone looked at Dr. Singh for a decision. PM ji looked at FM and Chairman, Planning commission, and said, "Aap oonko kooch karne denge to woh karenge na!" Then he looked at me and said, "You please start!" and he left the chamber. After that, in spite of his busy schedules, PM held coordination meetings with the Health Ministry for 6 months to ensure that we were not derailed. In these meetings he was always supportive; if he had anything to say it was always constructive. Mrs. Gandhi also took up NRHM as one of her priorities and held bi-monthly meetings and lent constant support. NRHM could take shape and matured quickly because of the unstinted support of these two leaders. Dr. Ramadoss permitted me to work unfettered. He never interfered negatively with NRHM. He was the best Health Minister for unfurling reforms in the health system. In fact, I never knew him; many of my colleagues in other Ministries including the top bureaucratic boss warned me that I would be put under pressure by his coterie to facilitate money making. I never came across any such pressure. On the other hand, he became my supporter seeing my incessant hard work and innovative solutions.

Health Minister's Pressure

Health Minister kept on raising the bar of our goals of Public Health. After three months of his becoming the Health Minister, I met Dr. N. K. Arora who used to be Professor Paediatrics of AIIMS, Delhi who explained the most distressing facts about our immunization programme. Dr. Arora's large survey showed that due to careless practice at the field level, 65% of the injections being administered for immunization were unsafe. The ANMS of Odisha, Bihar, MP, Rajasthan, and UP - OBIMARU States were not boiling the syringes properly; often they did not have clean water/ vessels and ran out of spirit etc. I became alarmed and briefed my Minister. The solution was in use of 'auto-destructive syringes', i.e. after one use the syringe could not be used again. I was worried about the cost of universal use of this syringe in the entire immunization programme. Dr. Ramadoss got after me; I was still hemming and hawing to accommodate the apparent large cost within our Budget. Entire credit to Dr. Ramadoss; without my knowledge he 'engineered' a question in Lok Sabha about 'Injection safety' in immunization programme, and answered making a commitment that Government of India would switch to Auto-destructive syringes within 4 months. He returned from the Parliament and triumphantly told me that he had given a commitment in Parliament and so I would have just to do it ASAP. And it was done; with large scale procurement, the costs fell down dramatically. The entire immunization coverage got a boost as wasteful, time consuming and unsafe practices got abolished. Later I came across a combined United Nations Resolution of 2001 which called upon all member states to switch over to AD syringes. The nincompoops even did not do this small bit of work while they were surrendering Rs. 1500 crores or more each year. Nor did any Western agency draw my attention to this very vital intervention.

Bridge with Mr. Bill Gates

An interesting aside! NRHM soon attracted the attention of the 'health community' of the world. Western agencies started lending support and stopped their domineering seminar approach. Mr. Bill Gates and Mrs. Belinda Gates announced their Gates Foundation with billions of dollars of funds for ameliorating health conditions of the developing countries. They came to India and expressed their desire to meet our Health Minister in his office. The time and date got fixed. Mr. Dhanavel- one of the most agreeable and able IAS officers of Tamil Nadu and Private Secretary to the Minister- came to my room and suggested that we both should go down and receive the Gate couple at the entry to Nirman Bhawan. I readily agreed and we both went and waited. Soon the Gate couple arrived. Mr. Bill Gates shook hands with us and we ushered in their group through the lift to our minister's chamber on the third floor. As soon as we entered the chamber, I was alert enough to notice that my young Minister was yet to arrive. Heavens fell on my head; it was a terrible breach of protocol - having given a time to a world personality and not being present for the meeting! The situation had to be handled with tact, discretion and aplomb. As I was in the front of the 'Delegation', I quickly maneuvered their entry in a manner that they would not be able to sight Minister's chair. Then I made them sit on the sofa with their back to the Minister's chair. Without wasting a second I burst forth into my diversionary tactics, and said addressing elegant Mr. Belinda Gates, "Ma'am, your husband is admired all over the world for his many qualities of the head and heart. However, I admire him for one more reason; I am impressed that amidst his extremely busy schedule, he finds time to play the game of Bridge." Hearing these words, Mr. Gates smiled and said out of politeness, "Oh! Do you also play Bridge?" I grabbed my chance and said, "Excellency, would you like to know how I got my membership of Oxfordshire Bridge Club?" He had to nod positively again out of politeness. I said, "I was on a Fellowship for about a year in Oxford University. Like a drunk smelling out the nearest pub, I soon found out the nearest Bridge Club- the Oxfordshire Bridge club. I started going there two to three times a week to play. After about a month, the Secretary of the club- a proper British officious type accosted me and said, "Mr. Hota, I understand that you are a visiting Fellow at our university. You have to apply for a temporary membership of our club to the Board of Governors and appear for an interview. The application was made and the time was fixed for 7 PM on Saturday. I have this very poor habit of being unpunctual, so I made it a point to arrive by 6.30 PM. I had time to kill, so I started leafing through the newspaper lying on the table in the lobby where I was waiting. The news caught my attention- it said that Laura had divorced Mr. Donald Trump. I inadvertently smiled. It was about 6.50 PM. the Secretary sauntered in from the Committee Room and spotted me. He growled, "Mr. Hota! Aren't you waiting for your interview? What makes you smile?" I said, "Sir, the newspaper reported that Laura has divorced Trump." The Secretary was truculent and said, "What's that to do with your interview?" I maintained my composure and said, "I see it like this.

Laura met Donald in a Club; he gave her a diamond; she gave him her heart; but, soon she called spade a spade and it was No Trump!" The Secretary looked at me bemused and requested me to wait. He went into the Committee Room, reappeared after five minutes and said, "No further interview, Sir. You are admitted." Mrs Gates started laughing and Bill ji said 'Please repeat, it is a good one let me take it down." Five to seven minutes were consumed without anyone noticing it. My minister breezed in, came from behind saying, ``Welcome, Welcome!" The moment was saved!

Performance Begets Trust

There were several small and big dramatic moments during Health Ministry days. Mr. Gopalakrishnan, Additional Secretary to the PM persuaded me to merge the vertical stand-alone programmes in the Health system under a common District Health management Group. Monitoring and implementation gathered pace. I was made the single Health Secretary of the Ministry when my senior retired in 2005. It was announced to me by Dr. Ramadoss; I thanked him saying that it was his graciousness which made it possible. He was decent enough to say immediately, "You deserve it. I have noted from the first month that in all meetings you do not read from any paper; but, your words are always to the point and the data you use are most convincing."

It was work, work and work round the clock in the Health Ministry-from early morning till late night. And beyond the Delhi durbar, the real health was to unfold in the States. My target was the 'Low performing States like Rajasthan, Odisha, Bihar, Madhya Pradesh and UP. As UP just did not bother, I concentrated on the rest. I kept on trying to persuade my IAS colleagues in the States that we must increase the managerial content in all our health programmes and create process reforms to increase the velocity of money in our multi-layered health system which we had started calling under a new coinage- Continuum of Care. We also emphasized to the States the virtues of local management structures for hospital call Rogi Kalyan Samiti and persuaded them to levy a small amount of 'user charges' to generate flexi-fund for local emergency needs. I requested States to involve the Panchayati Raj structure into the Rogi Kalyan Samitis for popular support and emergency help from Panchayti Raj functionaries in the field. I went across to the Secretary, Woman and Child Development Department of the Government of India and issued a jointly signed letter to integrate ASHAs with the Anganwadi system.

The Public Sector Undertakings got a boost as I was always a pro-public sector person my entire career. I used to be bemused at the general behaviour of Babudom towards the PSUs. I openly said to my officials that the PSUs were special purpose vehicles of the Ministry; their employees were as much a Government servant as we were. All of us would do well to support and respect our senior PSU officials. It was a pleasure to see that the PSUs all increased their turnover manifold during my time earning profit.

We planned AIIMS in many States. Only a few could be grounded as my senior colleagues whom I entrusted the task of awarding work got mired in hesitation and raising objections to all proposals; so very few could make progress. IAS officers must have the courage to take decisions and not feel satisfied that they have done their job by pointing out deficiencies and shooting down proposals. Fortunately, my successor was a brilliant person and he also had a reasonable tenure. So many of the AIIMS are there by now [though many of them have severe manpower shortages due to bureaucratic inefficient management, all these should have been put under an autonomous Public Sector structure- Hospital corporation of India. I shall expound this point in the concluding chapters of my book.]

'Don' Quixote of Health Education

It was not all smooth sailing or all achievements either. In the field of Medical Education, I could make little impact. The Medical council of India had become the private property of an able organizer like 'Dr. Don' [he was called so by his followers]. When I became the unified Health Secretary, I initially tried; then quickly I understood the political forces belonging to all Parties and even elements in top Judiciary lending Dr. Don their strength. I realised that either I would concentrate on the doable tasks in the Ministry or could face a sudden transfer via the machinations of Dr. Don and his coterie. And then the tasks which I had started as Secretary FW and the dream initiative of NRHM would falter badly. I briefed my Minster and requested him to tackle and control Medical Education through any officer he would choose; I frankly told him that I had decided not to be involved as I was very upset with the mischief that was going on and would lose my sense of perspective while tackling it. Dr. Ramadoss heard me through, smiled and agreed with my assessment of the situation.

Great Regrets

There were other regrets also; I could not restructure nursing education and Continuing Medical Education of nurses in light of the rapid development of specialized nursing emerging in the health sector. The ANM Training schools were shabby; these needed special attention to improve their capacity. Many more medicines should have come under the 'over the counter' category to improve access of the common man to quick affordable care for ordinary ailments. Health being a State subject, much more partnership with Health managers of each state including the top brass like Health Secretary, Directors was needed. We should have held workshops in each state headquarters requesting the Health Secretary of the respective State to lead the discussion and make a presentation on what reforms in systems they proposed, Securing the involvement of the State Health system was of utmost importance. Most of the 'low performing States' continued to be tardy in their implementation because the quality of their administration across all sectors was poor. And the Ministry could not provide systematic ethical support to manufacturers of health goods in the country. Even today, too much of the consumables are being imported. The procurement process should have been standardized and made much more efficient. Possibly all this can happen if my submissions on the proposed Hospital Corporation of India at Annexure-I is seriously considered and implemented.

My personal relationship with the officials of Western agencies was cordial; but, soon enough I started refusing their invitations to unproductive 'seminars' even if some of these gave me chances for trips abroad and enjoy five star ambience. I kept on asking them for specific suggestions for actions on public health and started gently chiding them that they had neglected a vital task of forecasting the future need of balanced manpower for the first changing Medical sector. WHO responded and called for a Regional Conference on 'Future Manpower Need of the Medical Sector'. It was held in Dhaka, all the Health Ministers of SAARC countries attended along with Thailand and Myanmar. My Minister nominated me to attend. The meeting started with an opening address by Additional Director General of WHO, he talked of this as a major new initiative by WHO and said that WHO was committed to the task of forecasting the manpower needed for Health in all Member countries. Then one after another, the honourable Health Ministers of different countries spoke. My turn as a bureaucrat representing a Member country came last. This gave me the advantage to have the perspective of different viewpoints on the subject. But instead of delivering an erudite speech, I deliberately assumed a posture. I sought permission of the Chair that before speaking anything I might be permitted to raise a Point of Order. The Health Minister of Bangladesh was presiding and he consented. I asked that if WHO was serious about its task to do manpower forecasting, I would be privileged if in the meeting chamber there was at least one person who had a degree in HR from any recognised management institution and if such a person would raise his hand for a minute. This question brought the house down- the Health Minister of Maldives could not contain his mirth when no hands went up to my question. He got up interrupting me while laughing and said, "This is the way we have been discussing serious public health issues all our life. We accept and wake up at your words." I thereafter implored all to see the need of introducing a skill balance in the Health Sector- apart from medical personnel who were the most important personnel. We needed MBAs CAs, Engineers and such other skills for all round vigorous management of health assets throughout the world. Addl. DG of WHO when he summarized the day's proceedings sportively acknowledged that Indian representative had pointed out a major shortcoming in the way a serious agenda had been approached and that he would go back and discuss in Headquarters with all his colleagues about the need of 'skill balance' as pointed out by me.

Coffee at Midnight

I had an interesting episode with my Minister. Once, it so happened that all important files going to him for his approval remained pending with him for three weeks. The work in the Ministry came almost to a standstill position. One evening I thought of a stratagem. I had great faith in the integrity and sagacity of Mr. Dhanavel the IAS private Secretary to Minister. He was staying alone in a room in Tamil Nadu Bhawan in Chanakyapuri, New Delhi. I went to him and requested him to just humour me in whatever I was going to do that night. He also had immense faith in me and readily agreed. I arranged one more car; and we drove with all the files pending in the Minister's office in the dicky of the cars to the Minister's residence. We reached around 9.45 PM. We sat in the drawing room and soon our Minister came from the interior of the house and asked me what had brought me to him at this late hour. I quickly thought of an excuse and said that I was missing my grandchild, and I had come to play with his youngest daughter who was a cute charmer, very well behaved for a three year old. By then, Mrs. Ramadoss had joined us. She was grace and nobility personified. One respected her naturally in spite of her relatively young age. Soon her youngest daughter came in; and also coffee and snacks. I started playing a game of 'hide and seek' with the child. The Minster was not to be fooled; he again asked, "Now, Mr. Hota, please tell me the purpose of your visit". I was not to be outdone readily. I picked up his youngest daughter by my two hands and hoisted her up towards my head and said, "See Sir, when she grows to be as tall as this she would be so proud about you! She would tell all her college friends that her father as Health Minister of India changed mothers' health in India for the better dramatically. I cannot let my youngest friend down and permit anyone to talk a single bad word about her father." My Minister kept looking at me quizzically. I put the child down and said, "Sir, you are the Minister; you are my Boss. I am proud to work under you. However, of late, there are murmurs in the Ministry that files for more than twenty days have piled up in the Honourable Minister's office. You are the final authority, you may agree, say yes, or you may reject the proposal in any file. Or you may also seek any clarification or further information. But the files remaining in limbo are getting us unwanted attention." Dr. Ramadoss looked at Mr. Dhanavel and asked, "Are there so many files pending for so long?" Mr. Dhanavel nodded assent. Dr. Ramadoss said that he would dispose of the files in a day or two. I said that the coffee in his home was excellent and I was in no hurry to go. The files were there in the cars that have accompanied us. If the Minister would kindly permit, it would be a great idea for me and Mr. Dhanavel to put up the files and to explain these to him on that undisturbed night. So the Minister continued to sit on the sofa; I sat on the carpet, Mr. Dhanavel gave to me one after another file. I put it up to my Minister. Mrs. Ramadoss brought in more coffee and biscuits. By 3 AM all the files were disposed of!! In today's time of fake videos someone could have made a video of my shenanigans of carrying the Minister's child and my sitting on the carpet and showing files to the Minister and that would have been that. However, eternal credit to Dr. Ramadoss; he could have brushed me off and could have shown me the door; but, he was noble- his wife and children were watching- all of them behaved so gracefully-what they say in Old English, 'Noblesse Oblige'!

The other embarrassment occurred when the policy of 'reservation' for OBCs was announced for medical education. AIIMS Delhi's students were at the forefront of the agitation against this policy. My Minister belonged to OBC; he came to know that Director AIIMS Dr. Venugopal was indirectly instigating the students to agitate. The rift between Dr. Ramadoss and Dr. Venugopal widened rapidly; my counselling to both fell on deaf ears. I told my Minster within closed doors that Dr. Venugopal had sympathisers in the PM's house as well as in the Supreme Court. A battle with him would be unproductive and attract adverse publicity. My Minister who was generally responsive to me did not budge. So also Dr. Venugopal whom I told that in a democracy, the political leader is above any functionary even if the functionary was brilliant. I quietly told him about my having arranged a much larger budget and staff to assist him in his vision of a well-provided AIIMS. Nothing worked; their spat became the centre of media controversy; and both of them misunderstood me as being partisan. And both lost face in public, wasted their energy in egoistic posturing.

Mothers Invade Hospitals

Now to the positive work in the Ministry. Maternal mortality ratio MMR was very high in India and so was Infant mortality. The National Maternity Benefit scheme was announced by late lamented Mr. Vajpayee from the Red fort in 1995. The scheme promised a help of Rs. five hundred for each mother of 'Below Poverty Level BPL' who had given birth. It was initially administered by the Rural Development Ministry, then by Panchayati Raj and finally it came to the Health Ministry. The total disbursement per annum was Rs. twenty crores. This is unbelievable, but this is an indicator of the indifference of bureaucracy busy in seminars and inaugurations and 'foreign travels'. The BPL mothers constituted about 30% of the total, more pregnancies occurred in the poorer population due to lack of access to family planning, and thus on a conservative estimate about one crore births took place and one crore BPL mothers should have benefitted with an outgo of around five hundred crores of rupees per year. I looked at the financial processes and took several steps to make the States aware of the benefits that should flow to mothers of poor sections. The figure jumped to ninety crore of rupees and started climbing. However, it was far below from my expectations. I benefited from all the data crunching, and realised that the scheme itself had some barriers like the mother had to belong to BPL category and she should be mother of two. Some population stabilization enthusiasts must have thought that it was a way of discouraging many children in BPL families. The real need of good motherhood in India had to be centred around 'Safe Delivery'. There were some excellent officers of Indian Statistical Service on deputation with the Health Ministry. With a little pep talk they rose to the occasion and put forward real time data. I particularly remember Sri Maiti who helped me recast the National Maternity benefit Scheme to the new vibrant and immensely successful Janani Suraskhya Yojana-JSY. In fact, the renaming was done by Sushma Swaraj ji, but the content underwent dramatic changes only on the last day of my tenure, i.e. on the day of my retirement. The key to safe delivery was increasing 'institutional delivery', that meant the mother had to give birth in a health facility so that if any complication arose, the three Ds could be avoided- Delay in diagnosis of a complication in delivery, Delay in coming to a health institution and finally, the Delay in commencement of treatment. But the ground realities were abysmal. There were about 28000 public hospitals under Central and the State Governments. Only about 9000 were functional. The rest would open at best for a couple of hours in the late morning and then would close down for the day. We took bold decisions. We sent twenty five thousand rupees per year to each small hospital, fifty thousand to Block Hospital and a lakh of rupees to District hospitals. They could spend the money as per their local priorities but the expenditure had to be pre-approved in the Hospital Management Committee and detailed accounts had to be rendered to States who in turn would have to certify to us the summary and appropriateness of the expenditure.

So Many Useless Ones Like Me

I revised the entire JSY program. Two days before I was to retire, I could get the matter approved from my Minister as Chairman of the Empowered Group [A coup permitted by PM whereby the powers of the Cabinet were delegated to this Group of Ministers]. I got the concurrence of 'Finance' and approval of Dr. Ramadoss on a three page long handwritten note where I submitted that the prevalent BPL category was a fallacy in maternal delivery. Generally girls in our society would not marry boys in the same village; they would get out of the BPL list of the parental home; by the time their name could get incorporated into BPL list of the In-Laws family, many years could pass, and the married girl could have become mother of many children. I further argued that the facility available in the general/maternity wards of our public hospitals for delivering mothers was the barest minimum and thus fit only for BPL. I used the flexibility of English language to propose that any woman going for delivery to a general ward of a public hospital, if she would certify that she was in BPL, self-certification would be accepted. I further argued that I belonged to a family of eight siblings and had friends who had 14 siblings. I said that if our mothers would have had a chance to go to a hospital for delivery, their entire life would not have been wasted in child bearing and child rearing as they would have come to learn about family planning methods and products;

and then they would not have been saddled with 'so many useless ones like me'. [Reading these lines both the Finance Advisor and Minister became misty-eyed]. I proposed a package of Rs. two thousand for mothers in Low Performing States and about eight hundred rupees or so for well performing States. Out of two thousand rupees for each delivery, six hundred rupees would be with ASHA to enable her to visit the home of the expectant mother, coax her and her guardians that when the expected date of delivery would draw near, the mother to be would be escorted by ASHA to the nearby Government hospital where the mother would be cared for and would be given a further sum of one thousand four hundred rupees to cover her incidental expenses. [In fact, some Indian researchers said that the cost of a delivery was a minimum of Rs. three thousand and two thousand was not enough. What the revised JSY did was to make the mothers overcome the fear of a hostile, unwelcome' hospital atmosphere. The money was incidental. JSY created an entitlement for the ordinary mother.] In 2006 before the revision in JSY, a mere five lakh women belonging to poorer homes went to a health institution. After the revised JSY was announced, one crore five lakh women went to public hospitals for delivery within a year. It was an unprecedented flood of patients and even an inefficient hospital had to pull up its socks and keep its basic amenities going. Electricity and water became available with the 'flexi - fund that had been released to each hospital. The conditions were far from satisfactory in many hospitals; but the journey to improvement began steadfastly. And most interestingly, other types of patients -when they saw a lighted hospital at night- also started coming to the hospital round the clock. So a 'demand driven' change compelled these non-functional and semi-functional hospitals to improve their performance willy-nilly. The revised JSY programme also had financial provisions and guidelines for referral of complicated deliveries from less equipped hospitals to better equipped hospitals - for the travel cost, medicine, C-section etc.; but this part took time to become operative. Notwithstanding all the shortcomings that dogged the public hospitals, maternal mortality drastically came down. In a year or so, the MMR fell from 520 per one lakh mother to 279 and then fell below two hundred. Similarly, a major attempt was undertaken to save infant lives. Special New Born Care Units were planned for each district of the country. Dr. Arun Singh of West Bengal was our friend, philosopher and guide. UNICEF tried its best to steal the credit. Whatever the case might have been, with ASHAs at the base, improvement in early and exclusive breastfeeding and improved immunization and pregnancy spacing, the infant mortality ratio was halved. These were public health records and drew worldwide attention. My last act as the Health Secretary of India was to sign the letters to the Chief Secretaries, Health Secretaries and Finance Secretaries of all the States and Union Territories of India. Then I walked into the meeting room where my farewell party had been organised. Thus my tenure in the Health Ministry which lasted for three years and eight months, and my career as an IAS officer of about 38 years concluded.

Night-Long Vigil

Two small but specific incidents stand out in my memory of my Health Secretary days. The first related to the horrendous terrorist blast that took place in Sarojini Nagar Market of New Delhi which killed more than a hundred fifty persons and injured several hundred more from burns. It occurred in the late afternoon. I rushed to Safdarjung Hospital immediately. I found a huge crowd desperately either seeking information about their missing friend/relatives or having brought in an injured person, they were even more keen to know the condition of the patient. Somehow, I made my way through the surging crowd and went in. The doctors recognised me and made a request that they were doing their best; supplies of medicines etc. were there. All that they needed was security- no outsider should be allowed to enter the burn wards and contaminate the sterile atmosphere so important to give a burn victim some chance of recovery. I came out and found the crowd swelling by minutes. I immediately thought of a way; I requested some friends in the TV media to rush their live coverage team to my residence. I went live on TV channels and made an appeal to people of Delhi not to breach hospital barriers and never to go to the Burn Wards. I assured them that I would personally go from hospital to hospital and ensure proper treatment was being given round the clock. I further said that I stood committed to my promise of vigil on the hospitals on their behalf throughout the night. I announced my mobile and landline numbers on the TV and said that anyone was welcome to call me up throughout the night as I would not sleep and keep going round the hospitals; but none should go himself to any hospital to get in and inquire. The mob subsided in Safdarjung and RML hospitals. My phone kept ringing throughout the night. At about 2.30 AM there was a call- "Are you the Health Secretary, Hota ji speaking?" I replied in the affirmative. Then the voice said, "I am speaking from 10 Janpath. Smt. Sonia Gandhi ji wanted to know if you have been going to the hospitals." I replied that every hour I touched base by visiting the two hospitals and inquiring from doctors what support if any, they needed. And in both RML and Safdarjung the doctors were awake and on active duty trying their best. All political leaders are not bad all the time as some bureaucrats smugly think.

Japanese Encephalitis

The other matter was related to a sudden spurt in Japanese Encephalitis- JE- in the Gorakhpur region of UP. This dreaded disease was something like a brain fever, attacked children from 5 to 15 years. As usual the UP Government was hardly bothered. Anyway a Central Team went and reported that more than 3000 were dead, about 4000 children were maimed and about twenty thousand children were admitted to various health institutions of the region. The disease was merciless in targeting the children of poorer families- might be an issue with nutrition and immunity. Dr. Ramadoss[I must admit he was the best Health Minister India had who understood public health and was always for pro poor/ common man initiatives.] got hold of me and asked me to find a solution and not leave it to the routine of Central and State doctors. I immediately sought out all experts and their views. The answer was -mass immunization. It meant immunizing about 1 crore 11 lakh children of UP, Bihar and parts of West Bengal. The available capacity of vaccine in the country was about only ten lakh dose that too which could be produced over a period of 6 months. And each dose manufactured in some small vaccine producing PSU would cost Rs. 150 per dose and a booster dose also had to be administered on completion of three months of the first dose. That meant India simply did not have the capacity. I consulted far and wide; the Indian country head of WHO was a fine colleague. He went all out to support us. We located 10 million doses of this vaccine with Japan which wanted to donate the vaccine free of cost. But the story was that this batch had one or two contamination so Japan did not use the vaccine itself. So we could not take the risk; the media in India was like a bloodhound, if you could manage to save ten thousand lives it was all right; but, if one child died hell would break loose in the media. Then we found out that China produced the vaccine in huge quantities; but, the catch was that the Chinese vaccine had not undergone 'human trial' in India. Following the trial protocol would mean costs and time of at least one year. Then I found out that this Chinese vaccine had been tested on humans in Nepal. I prepared a note at my level stating that Nepalese and Indians were neighbours and had similar physiognomy; my DG Health -the neurotic neurologist- was hemming and hawing, so I excluded him from the process. I requested our WHO colleague to sign the note as jointly prepared. He told me that the Chinese vaccine was efficient; it needed one dose of administration only; but, adverse reactions were not documented, so the child who would be inoculated would have to stay near a health facility for 5 days after inoculation. I remonstrated with him and said, "Dr. Habayeb, this is not possible in the field conditions of India. If the children are to be saved we have to broaden our shoulders and take responsibilities." He came back to my room in an hour and signed the note. Then the Managing Director of the Chinese vaccine manufacturing company flew in. She and I were alone in my chamber. She nodded in the affirmative to my question as to whether she would be able to supply 12 million doses of vaccine in one go. Then the all-important question of cost tumbled out of my mouth. [I was nervous about the costs as the Indian vaccine cost as a measurement would mean that we would have to spend about Rs. 300 crore or so. I had no choice; if she asked for 300 rupees per dose I would have had to agree.] The MD said that it would cost eight rupees per dose. I could not believe my ears, I was about to hug her in gratitude but refrained as she was a personable woman. So in ten crore of rupees we immunized 11 million children within a period of 7 days. JE vanished for about six years. Then as usual, Indian Health bureaucracy was busy hobnobbing with Western agencies and inaugurations- the immunization programme was neglected and JE reappeared.

Challenges of Implementation

NRHM taught me that leaders would always be in a hurry; large scale policies/programmes would be announced by them. People at large would expect the benefits from these policies to flow immediately. The challenge for the IAS was to design and implement these policies on a continuous dynamic basis learning on the go, looking at fundamental issues of HR [including their morale and motivation], infrastructure, skill balance[the core technical /medical personnel and the support services like management of various processes including interface with common people-HR, Finance, day to day maintenance needed for vigorous sustainable implementation, training, remain alert to nut and bolt issues like logistic chain, maintenance, local ownership through participation and generating resources from users as much for supplementing revenue cost as much for improving service delivery through accountability, and above all ultimately a transparent publicly announced health delivery system where there was no discrimination. Services had to be made available respecting the privacy and dignity of the patient.

False Promises and Ground Reality

Two false slogans had dogged health sector over years- the first was a promise of 'free' health care to all, and the second that the doctors and medical personnel were expected to be 'godly' in their action and behaviour while the fact was that they were like other professions and human beings having their strength and weakness. I was also sucked into these assumptions; it took me a few years to get out of these false notions and design better processes and systems for NRHM. One of the banes of IAS these days is the extremely short tenure many IAS Secretaries spend as Secretary of one Department. Jockeying for more glamorous positions and political fragility/preference combine to make some colleagues spend not even a year in any particular Department. Luckily for me, I continued in the same Ministry all through my Secretary-ship.

The Latin Aristocrat

I was sent a message four months before my retirement on behalf of the Prime Minister, Norway to come and visit him ASAP. True to my habits I was reluctant. But some more calls by the Principal Secretary to PM Norway aroused my curiosity. I went to Norway accompanied by my colleague, Dr. Haldar dealing with Immunization as the PM of Norway wanted to discuss issues of immunization coverage. I arrived at Bergen, Norway's second largest city. Immediately, a closed door meeting started. The Norwegian group consisted of about ten, and we were two Indians. I explained to them all that we were doing in India-about relieving the ANM from the task of collecting vaccine from the Block hospital cold chain and arranging finance for an alternative person to deliver vaccine to the immunization site, the universal use of AD syringes thus relieving the ANM from the tedium from carrying heavy pan, kerosene etc. for sterilising syringes, the reduction in size of BCG packs from 8 to 4 for more rational use of the vaccine in spite of slightly higher financial implication, the mobilization of mothers and babies one to two days before to come for immunization, the use of Anganwadi and Anganwadi worker as the local senior of ASHA in coordinating all important ingredients to motivate larger turn out of mothers and babies, the purchase of additional cold chain equipment and overhauling the existing ones to keep them working to the correct technical specifications and ensuring release of vaccine in time from Block hospital early in the morning to enable a full working day being available for immunization, considering some flex-fund with Anganwadi Centre to provide transport support for babies coming from a distance, holding a second session in the afternoon in the hamlet which is part of a village but situated at a distance- and so on. The Norwegian side had a very distinguished looking person with royal Latin American features. He would attack every initiative described by me mercilessly. Throughout the day for about six hours it was a loud acrimonious debate. I did not know him from Adam and nor did I bother. In the evening there was dinner in a restaurant and I found him sitting next to me. He offered to pour me some champagne; I politely told him that I did not drink. Gradually over food, fellowship developed and I found him to be a perfect gentleman. Next day morning, the presentation and cross-examination continued but the opposition to my 'managerial model' subsided. The Latin gentleman then continued questioning but in a more constructive way and tested me whether I knew the entire picture in terms of data and costs. Perhaps, he got satisfied with my answers and sincerity of purpose; by lunchtime he had become practically our spokesperson. Any questions raised by the Norway Team were answered by him rather than by me. After lunch the Prime Minister flew in from Oslo and there was an 'open session' where the PM, Norway spoke to an audience of about three hundred about Norway's commitment to improving Mother and Child Health throughout the world. That meeting lasted for an hour. Then we retired to a 'closed room' meeting where only six people apart from the PM and his Principal Secretary were present. The Latin aristocrat was also there. PM, Norway addressed him first and said, "Excellency, what is your opinion on Mr. Hota's proposal?" I perked up- the Latin gentleman with whom I debated bitterly could be no ordinary person! He addressed the PM and said, "Prime Minister, I have been for six years Executive Director at WHO. I am the longest serving Health Minister of a major country- Mexico. I have seldom come across such a well-conceived and sincerely presented programme to improve immunization in India. Mr. Hota must be supported." Then the three other Norwegians spoke in detail about various aspects of the immunization issue, and my presentation. A lot of data and micro details were spoken of. I noticed that the PM was getting tired of focusing on so much data. He finally turned to me and said, "Mr. Hota, why do you need our money?" I replied with alacrity, "Excellency, Indian health budget is about 3 billion US dollars per year. So a hundred million dollar or so over five years from Norway is not about money. This money may help as a catalytic element. What is needed more than the money is to carry the message of love and concern of children of Norway to the children of India- Prime Minister may kindly choose for the project a 'brand mascot'- a quicksilver problem solving impish Norwegian child-hero about whom I had read in Norwegian folk tales in my childhood." I immediately saw that I had registered in his head and heart. He said that initially a sum of a hundred million dollars stood sanctioned for a special child immunization project by Norway through a United Nations agency to be implemented in India. He also said that he would speak to the Prime Minister of India for a 'Joint Declaration' on the subject. Then he looked at me and dropped the bombshell- he said that he understood that I would be retiring soon from Government of India;

he was counting on my heading and leading the programme in India by joining the selected United Nations Agency. I came back to India from Norway avoiding an answer.

Reaching India, I was sent for by Mr. Pulak Chatterji who represented Mrs. Gandhi in day to day matters in the PMO. He said to me that Mrs. Gandhi thought well of my abilities and she would like me to head Prashar Bharati. I briefed him about the Norwegian proposal and asked him for his advice. He said as much as I was considered a performer, my continuance in the Health Sector would generate better value for the country. So I should join the United Nations. In retrospect, I now feel that I should have stayed aligned with a Government organization. IAS officers like me cannot get their satisfaction from money; they get their satisfaction from influencing public service with positive leadership backed by the authority of the Government. Several times after retirement, I attended some discussions etc. in Doordarshan. a couple of times some senior staff of Doordarshan accosted me in the corridors of the Studios and lamented that I did not join Prashar Bharati. So did I, not once but several times. Earning money is secondary; self-esteem and job satisfaction should be the primary consideration for an IAS officer. Many colleagues vie for foreign postings or deputation to UNICEF etc. even within India for higher salaries; most of these jobs have little content.

21

DIRECTOR UNITED NATIONS OFFICE FOR PROJECTS AND SERVICES [UNOPS]

I joined UNOPS as a Director to head their 'Norway-India Partnership Initiative Child Health 'programme known by the acronym - NIPI. The whole office had to be set up from scratch; the different elements of the program unfolded in intense discussion with the Embassy, Oslo, and UNOPS. We should take up three districts representing average child health indices of the State of each of five low performing States- Rajasthan, Madhya Pradesh, Odisha, Bihar and Uttar Pradesh. The last- UP never came on board. You cannot make an impact in a State with politicians and bureaucrats having no idea of the need of public health.

I initially got a free hand to roll out the programme of NIPI and child health. We adopted a strategy that at the State level, the Health Secretary of the State would head the NIPI-State Coordination meetings. And the expenditure for the extra initiatives agreed to in this joint meeting would be provided into the State Health budget to commit the expenditure. In each State, NIPI set up a State level small office.

Yashoda

We introduced an important additional voluntary health worker called 'yashoda' [the legendary mythical mother figure who brought up Lord

Krishna in his infancy with love and care even if she was only the foster mother. When i had thought of ASHA, i did not realise how quickly she would be overloaded with health work at her village level. For her to come with the expectant mother to a health institution was enough of a task for her. To stay with the mother in the ward and look after her was next to impossible. Say a maternity ward of a District hospital had 20 beds; 20 different ASHAs coming form 20 different villages would have been themselves a burden on the District Hospital. Yet the mothers staying for a minimum of 48 hours in hospital was important, both for the safety of the delivery and the new born. We noticed that in many hospitals mothers left within hours of delivery often even without the 'birth dose' of immunization having been administered. So we introduced a 'Yashoda', a woman volunteer worker living nearby the hospital. The Yashodas were to work in maternity ward and in shifts- one Yashoda looking after 5 mothers at a time. The Yashodas were to motivate and arrange zero dose immunization, early and exclusive breast feeding and the general comforts and monitoring of the mother's condition after delivery and alert nurses/doctors about emergencies. They were also trained to educate the mother for child care at home including follow up immunization. They were to teach mothers to avoid immediate bathing of the new-born. And Yashodas were to explain and inform mothers about family planning products to avoid the next unplanned pregnancy. The history of Public Health in India is dotted with incomplete programmes and ejection of good result yielding initiatives by egoistic bureaucrats. The ASHAs have survived, so has the Janani Surakshya Yojana JSY. But the Yashoda scheme has survived in two or three States only. Health care for the common man never factors in affection and dignity needed by the care seeker. And so we still have a health delivery system skewed towards private practice and indifference to the common man. The present PM increased the entitlement of motherhood from Rs. 2000/- to 6000/- on a selected number of districts [perhaps, 57] under Pradhan Mantri Matru Vandana Yojana. In my humble opinion, it should have been a universal increase from Rs. 2000/- fixed in 2006 to at least Rs. 3500/- for all common mothers under JSY.

We also trained and incentivised ASHAs for more number of follow up visits of the new-born at the home. This improved both MMR and

NMR. Yet, away from the real authority of Government I came across good indifferent and bad performance by colleagues in the Health Sector. Quite a few disliked their post in the Health sector thinking they were meant for greater laurels. The adhocism in recruitment and non-retention of managers in NRHM was disquieting. The post I created with so much thought that of District Maternity & Child Health Manger petered out in a few years. RCH, the most important segment of public health, started floundering in terms of the quality of care delivered. The special new-born care units often had the trained paediatrician or MBBS doctor posted away at the drop of a hat by whimsical politicians. Good assets began to be managed indifferently. There were stray incidents of fire in a couple of new-born care units out of about 800 Units put up across the country leading to public demand for inquiries to establish culpability. Nobody spoke of detailed vigorous management as the required preventive step.

Ekalavya & the Eye of the Needle

Yet the NIPI programme contributed in the key areas. A small example should suffice. Bharatpur is a comparatively backward district of Rajasthan, It was a NIPI program district where yashoda were recruited, trained and put to work in the District Hospital maternity ward. The foreign funded programmes have a protocol of conducting a 'baseline' survey to establish the benchmarks at the beginning of a programme. To my horror, the survey established that the birth dose immunization coverage of immunization of new born in the district hospital was a mere 40%. Just if one would think about it- the babies were born in the hospital; it being a District Hospital there could be no shortage of vaccine materials[the cold chain, the injections, the vaccines and the trained nurse to give the vaccine,]- yet the coverage was a mere 40%. Anyway, our Yashodas were enjoined to persuade and try for getting the babies to be administered the 'zero dose' after their birth in the hospital. In a matter of three months, our Yashodas could make an impact and the coverage figure went up to 65%. My colleague in NIPI, Dr. Pappu who had extensive hands-on field level child health care delivery experience in West Bengal rushed into my room all excited; he said that we should write a special letter to headquarters of UNOPS and Norwegian authorities that in a mere three months' time we had achieved more than a fifty percent jump over the baseline figure. I requested him that I had no objection; he could write such a letter. However, I urged him to consider that the coverage should be at least 90% as it was a District Hospital setting. He agreed and mumbled something about software of WHO to track babies for immunization. I said to him that he was free to do so; but, as far as I was concerned he would help me by sending the programme manager of Rajasthan NIPI office to go to Bharatpur District hospital. Pradeep ji [the programme manager] reached and asked me for instructions. I told him that he would just supervise the Yashodas for five days, monitor the immunization sessions and report to me every evening. In four days, the cat was out of the bag. Apparently, the immunization session was conducted by a nurse every morning. The official time was from 9.30 AM to 12 noon. But the nurse would amble along by 10 AM, immunise a few babies and by 11 AM she would close the counter. There were no immunization sessions in the evening. There were none on all weekends and holidays. Dr. M. L. Jain was one of the most able and pragmatic medical leaders I met in my life. He was Director RCH in Rajasthan Government. When I brought all these to his notice, he immediately issued Government Orders to all Government hospitals for holding immunization sessions twice a day, 365 days a year with 'roaster' arrangements etc. The next month onwards, immunization coverage in all the Government hospitals of Rajasthan rose to 90%. Our NIPI programme generated a lot of excitement in the Child Health sector. UNICEF was alarmed; it tried its best to sabotage our program, but could not succeed.

The Prime Minister of Norway, Honourable Jen Stoltenberg came on an official visit to India, met our PM- there was a Joint Declaration. Then the PM of Norway went to the field to assess the work done and its impact. He went beyond the beaten path [I and NIPI officials were asked not to accompany him and stay back on the main road] into two villages randomly selected by him off the road. I was told that he interacted through his own interpreter with the villagers extensively. He spent nearly three hours by himself. He did not exchange too many words with me thereafter and returned to Norway. I was a bit perturbed about the impressions he might have gathered. Then about fifteen days passed; the Ambassador of Norway rang me up one afternoon and conveyed to me the news that the King of Norway had bestowed Knighthood on me with the title - 'Knight Kommander' [equivalent to India's Padma Bhushan]. God and Devil rule the world in equal proportion - there are no definite rules of rewards and punishment in spite of all religious pronouncements. I was deprived of the post of Cabinet Secretary; it was said that a Machiavellian but suave personage of PMO had to compensate for his peccadillo; this Knighthood was some compensation.

I left NIPI when Mr. Jen Stoltenberg lost the election in 2013; I found the changed behaviour of the bureaucracy at the Embassy with limited knowledge but unlimited powers to interfere stifling.

22

BACK TO GOOD GOVERNANCE

I shall now attempt to draw out lessons from my work life and try to match it to the theory of Good Governance. I also would try to suggest some new but vital governance structures and processes which could make an impact on a scale in our country. I hasten to assure that I do not claim infallibility or monopoly of all knowledge of GG. My goal in this book is to stimulate thinking by colleagues and leaders and centre-stage a nation-wide movement for GG for a more prosperous India to emerge. However, before summarizing my suggestion on GG, I seek indulgence of all on three major ideas which I have developed with a lot of research and thought over last 7 years, These three are ideas of scale; if they could be picked up by government of the day, I dare say that there should be a sizeable impact on certain areas of GG. However, the horizon of GG is much more than my ideas. My suggestions are context-specific. My ideas and my stories are incidental. The purpose of this book is to put GG centre-stage as the main discourse of Indian Administrative system through continuous participation of rank and file and people of all walks of life. The IAS becomes relevant if it comes out of its self-centeredness and facilitates the process.

The first relates to the overhauling of the present Departmental structures of Central and State Governments to make these more efficient through systematic reforms based on wide participation of officers of a Department and engagement of Consultants from the Private Sector.

The second is about the Health care delivery expansion- a chain of new modern District [eventually about 1500 in number] and Block hospitals [about 12000] through a proposed Hospital Corporation of India to provide 'Standard Health Care at Standard Cost.

The third is about setting up a chain [about ten thousand] of 'Saathi Centres' in each Block Headquarters-an e-based additional structure to the currently overloaded District Administration.

Leadership of the country may kindly appreciate that social sector projects announced in India by whichever Govt. have failed to deliver the intended benefits to the common man due to inadequate designing of service delivery issues. Learn as you go along; let us launch the programme immediately in the field as it the core idea is good for people; we have a time limit in terms of tenure [whether as Govt.s or as bureaucrats], so let us take the credit for revolutionary social sector programme immediately- all this and similar approach of the past will lead us to haphazard implementation. Then the blame game will start - how could Govt. start a new PSU on health, or a slew of other well-meaning social sector schemes inadequately designed and poorly implemented, wasting the country's resources. I have taken pains to put as an annexure to this book a methodology of designing the concept of Hospital Corporation of India. It would show the complexity and the patience and time needed to present the country with a quality healthcare scheme.

Basic Elements of Good Governance

Before one writes highfalutin treatise on Good Governance, an IAS officer has first to be an excellent productive civil servant. In spite of some injustice one may meet now and then, I strongly affirm that a hardworking, extremely productive, honest, 'civil' civil servant carries a great premium for the people and most of the leaders. And even if he is not in a nepotistic chain, he is bound to have a reasonable career and public recognition at the end.

In the narrative of my career, I have avoided jargons. I assert that Good Governance for an average officer at any stage of his career is still based on first principles like common sense, hard work, simplicity, planning, team work, financial analysis, sound human resource policies and constant flexibility to acquire new knowledge and methods to achieve the public goods and services goals entrusted to him by vigorous management of the resources available/accessible to him. Taking utmost pride in the assigned work, and working with steadfast determination to succeed in delivering a larger volume of goods and services should be the hallmark of an IAS officer, Determination to succeed in one's career has only to be a by-product, Whether one succeeds in careerism or not, sooner or later colleagues will look at such an officer with some derision. The negative list of first principles are equally important: an able administrator must avoid public display of ego; must avoid the opprobrium that he is high-handed, should avoid indulgences, should not seek publicity for himself, should not set standards for his subordinates/Team which he himself does not follow. He must avoid procrastination and realise that the fundamental quality of an outstanding civil servant is quick and final disposal of the matter before him. He must develop respect for all branches of the State; he must accept that today's civil servant is more than ever has to be civil and has also to give out an image that he is a servant of the people- not the rich and powerful only but also the common people. He must not unwittingly steal the limelight from his political bosses and senior colleagues for the well-done work/project even where his hard work could be the cornerstone of the job. As far as possible he must not contradict or show his boss or the political leader in poor light in public or official discussions even if he is sure of his facts.

The e-technologies provide both a challenge and an opportunity for achieving higher efficiency and reach. However, even here in use of e-technology the ability and felicity of the client is to be kept uppermost in mind while designing E-Systems. I unequivocally agree and support introduction of e-facilitation of access to governance and its promises for common man and to increase the accountability of public officials at all levels. Visualization of the common citizen's convenience through a 'bottom-up' approach is likely to have more user-friendly and pragmatic e-platforms for governance. My proposal at Annexure-II about setting up 10,000 Saathi [E-Facilitation] Centres should be seen in this perspective.

I submit after considerable introspection that in the IAS, many officers are equal to each other in talent. I am only one of the many. However, what distinguishes a good officer from an average one is the determination to produce results for common people by stretching oneself beyond the routine. Dedication to results will eventually lead to analytical planned hard work and stretching oneself beyond the call of ordinary duty to achieve. New technology tools offer greater chance for Good Governance but old attitude will yield uneven results. I also say that only a generous at heart person will make a good IAS officer. Andre Agassi said that he studied the videos of 15 matches he lost to Borg to identify how to read the direction of the service of Borg. That is both the attitude and the dedication worth emulating by an IAS Officer who wants to focus on being an outstanding contributor to public service.

23

COMPLEXITIES OF GOOD GOVERNANCE

The eight other elements of Good Governance enunciated by the Western multilaterals and UN Agencies have now to be seen in their overall context. They are not wrong when they enumerate all the ideal goals as well as prerequisites of GG. It is not a tautology to say that GG is both the prerequisite and the goal of GG. And this tautology acquires meaning when 'Efficiency and Effectiveness' imbue all the elements described by the World Bank. For instance, emphasis on Rule of Law becomes hollow when cases drag on in Courts for years. The first touchstone for judicial independence is its accountability; and accountability starts with speedy disposal of cases.

The higher judiciary is mostly an assemblage of ex-lawyers only. The definition of the World Bank falls short of a key phrase when it describes GG as "the manner in which power is exercised in the management of a country's economic and social resources for development". After the word 'development', the key phrase should be 'of a larger volume of goods and services for its people.' One can even add a word more-goods and services and 'happiness'. The tenure in the Health Ministry finally opened my eyes to the false narration of my country's social sector strategies - social goods will be provided free of cost by the Maa-Baap Raj Government, Centre or State. In school days senior cousins would borrow; when asked to return they would glibly say- 'Payable when able'. So also is the history of our social sector pretensions of our governance from 1950 till date. Particularly in Health, in the name of service to the poor, Government of all hues have constantly doled out a poor service. Common Indians now want 'Standard Services at Standard Cost.' Our village Government school with two teachers and capacity for eighty has now only ten students. All families including SC families send their children to an English medium private school at Block headquarters.

Co-participation of the people is a must cost wise and membership in Hospital Management Committees at Block and district level through Panchayti Raj institutions.

The complexity of designing large systems for GG is best explained in the document at the Annexure- I: Hospital Corporation of India. It will show the meticulous pain-staking complex juxtaposition of details that are needed to design for a sustainable GG framework in a vital social sector. The first six elements of the elucidation on GG by the World Bank [excluding the point b) on Rule of Law] appear repetitive: Participation, Equity, Consensus-building and Responsiveness are four facets of the same square. Transparency is an important issue and it can be conjoined with Accountability. Efficiency - Effectiveness and Vision are part of the same continuum; they lend credence and content to all other elements of GG.

We have to now seek solutions within our country's resources and governance realities solutions to increasing the efficiency and effectiveness of our Ministries and State Departments. I have attempted an analytical tool [which can always be improved on as it is a set of dynamic concepts] for senior IAS officers to use in improving governance in their respective charges.

I have said already that GG by IAS would yield many benefits but other pillars of democracy have also to come forward. The disposal in Courts must improve immediately. I dare mention two very simple steps to reduce litigations in two areas immediately- Civil and Matrimonial matters. In both sets of cases, the process drags on for years. In Civil, filing of Interim Applications- IA- ad nauseum by a party interested in frustrating a decision can easily be handled by taking up the consideration of the main suit simultaneously on each 'date'. Then the main case will get decided soon enough and the obstructive IAs will be infructuous. In matrimonial matters, the law should be amended to make it mandatory for the Courts to grant the plea of 'divorce' within one year of filing the case. This one year could be utilised for counselling, mediation etc. After that all pending disputes like maintenance, custody of children etc. could continue as 'civil' litigation, but 'divorce' would be pronounced. The matrimonial cases have crossed the million marks. The Act prohibits lawyers; lawyers are to be allowed only in special cases with permission of the Court stating the reasons in writing. But if you go to a Family court, you will find the Courtroom full of lawyers only. Cases drag on for years. It is a mockery of the law.

Focus on Simplicity

Often there are very simple and direct solutions to many apparently complex issues; vested interests of professionals and self-serving groups prevent their adoption. **Democracy and good governance are ultimately to be tested on the touch-stone of common man's interest. No group or process is sacrosanct; no privileges of the elite of all branches of society are relevant, if these corrode the rights of the citizen and impede the benefits of GG to people. GG delivered with efficiency and effectiveness should determine all matters. All titles like Parliamentary privileges, judicial independence, and security of service of civil servants and so on are otherwise hollow and self-serving.**

A Suggestion of a Framework for Professional Implementation of Large Social Sector Programmes / Social Goods Delivery Institutions:

It is true that Governance is a vast subject and details have to be addressed. Serving IAS colleagues at senior level are requested to go through this with proactive thinking. They could always make the suggested framework better and more contexts-specific.

Designing and Implementation Challenges:

More often than not, important social sector programmes are announced in a 'political' hurry without prior implementation analyses and or detailed design. At least three to six months must be spent in detailing and designing to avoid major breakdowns and wastages even in the most well intentioned programmes before the programmes are rolled out to field. This is not often possible, as the political class is impatient and wants immediate announcement and implementation. Even a sincere bureaucrat could be misunderstood, if he would not commence action on the announced program immediately. The Civil Servant has to be astute in handling this sensitive interim period; he must make positive statements about the policy and its benefits and show that he is working round the clock for implementation. He could even create politically affirmative atmosphere and buy time for designing the program efficiently by engaging the political leader with tasks of IEC and publicity about the key elements of the policy and helping the political class to take the program to the people, in the sense of advocacy and garnering popular support, support of the States, Media, Opinion Leaders and the like.

The ingredients of the framework are

- A hard look at the Core Program/subprogram/Major Tasks – Content and distribution analysis. Political Class. For that matter the overreaching Judiciary these days, announce social/ environmental or any such goals with pompous authority and often put unrealistic timelines for delivery. Detailing of the goals, the sub goals leading to the main goal have to be very clearly analysed and tasks and sub-tasks and owners of these tasks as policy starts travelling down and becomes action /deliverables and ultimately actual delivery to the a real time client on day to day [often minute to minute basis] basis

- The flaw creeps into the detailing by top groups of bureaucrats/ technocrats often for their lack of complete knowledge of entire and varying field realities. So top brass engaged in detailing should always try to invite in some 'junior/field level functionary, and seek his participation and opinion in planning of tasks and implementation.

- I must recount here a hilarious but absolutely truthful account of an actual ostrich-administration attitude [Ostriches apparently close their eyes when they charge at any danger.] In 1989 I got posted to Delhi from Odisha where I had acquired some reputation in project implementation and handling emergencies like huge floods etc. The quality of office work at Delhi offices was certainly better and I was initially a bit intimidated in the nonchalant bureaucratic corridors of Central Ministries. In any case, till then I was never posted in my 20 years career inside a Secretariat. So I landed up at Delhi as a Joint Secretary in the Ministry of Heavy Industry which handled motley of manufacturing PSUs – MAMC, Durgapur which manufactured heavy material handling equipment, particularly for coal, power and steel sector was with me. A meeting was called by the C-Secretary where the Additional Secretary P- was present. It was about the delay in commissioning a 'washery' -very vital for better power production. It was an era of acute power shortage and this huge plant at Madhuban was badly delayed. My Secretary asked me to attend with CMD MAMC, Mr. Roy. We lesser minions were seated earlier; I was barely a month old and every bit a callow neophyte- my first exposure to the might of Central Govt. and its astute bureaucrats with huge designations. The C- Secretary and Additional Secretary, P- breezed into the meeting together. The meeting started with an opening salvo by Addl. Secy. P-, who in his best Ox-bridge diction warned us that PM himself was monitoring power production and he would be very disappointed at the tardy progress of this important Washery. The C- Secretary looked around; suddenly his eyes got focused on me, and he blurted out 'Hota is here; he will handle everything now, otherwise heads will roll.' Gratified at being recognized by a super boss in a crowded room, frightened like Alice in the wonderland of Delhi- Heads will roll- I squirmed and tried to look properly serious. The Review progressed; mostly the Secretary and the Addl. Secretary spoke; I kept my own counsel and some interrupted replies were attempted by different agencies about the delay.

♦ The C- Secretary again focused on me and said 'Hota, what nonsense is this; you are supposed to be a doer, why the delay of 1 year, why has your PSU not delivered the material handling equipment? Anyway, all take note, now Hota is in charge, in 3 months everything has to be completed. Otherwise heads will roll'. Mr. Roy whispered, 'Sir, say- 6 months because HSCL of Steel Ministry has to do the civil foundation before our large equipment can be brought to site and affixed.' I mustered courage, got up and said six months in the minimum would be needed as civil foundation was not yet done. At this the C- Secretary gave the Joint Secretary, Steel a dressing down, During all this going on between the top brass -all in suits as winter had commenced, - a gentleman with a large load of files clutched to his chest –in bush shirt- was trying to get up and say something; each time some senior sitting next to him would pull him down and he would collapse with his load of files onto his chair. I noticed this happening 3 times. The meeting ended in 20 minutes and everyone trooped out led according to seniority. I lingered on. The bush shirt clad man was all alone gathering his sheaf of files and looking totally bewildered; I sidled up to him and asked, 'Who are you Sir, and what were you trying to say?' He looked relieved that finally he got his chance; in chaste Bhojpuri Hindi he said in his sing-song voice 'I am the Civil Engineer of HSCL at the site at Madhuban- the land is yet to be acquired by State Govt. and handed over to us!' So much for the high level review meeting which must have cost thousands of rupees in logistics and management time. The Lesson: please always permit the grass-root levels to speak of the ground reality. Glossing over would simply not do!!

♦ Such was more often than not the quality of quite a few review meetings until the 1990s throughout the country. Our feudal mind-set of Governance prevented us from listening to grass root working levels. Colossal non-performance was often the result. **And believe me, it gives me absolutely no pleasure to call names of IAS officers; I was an IAS officer and whatever in life I achieved was through the IAS. However, GG demands that we open up, do soul searching and improve our performance substantially.** The liberalisation after the early 1990s came due to below par performance of the Indian bureaucracy, particularly the IAS which lacked the esprit de core to meet the challenges of development administration.

♦ HR- Analyses of skill balance required for the program through analysis of existing HR and road map for additional HR. Must ensure modern skill balance input through a core of professionally qualified HR, FINANCE [Chartered Accountants], other professionals like engineers, procurement specialists and IT Unit.

♦ Financial Advisors in Ministries are mostly IAS officers with short tenures and no training in modern finance. They are important as Coordinators and linking programs to multi-Ministries etc. However, it is not often ensured that each FA Unit has at least one or two Chartered Accountants who are IT savvy and can assist the FA and the Secretary with Financial analysis serving as vital management information systems.

♦ I have already discussed about budget preparation and e-communication and e-monitoring of budgets in the chapter of Health Ministry. Suffice to say that this is a vital process.

♦ Procurement capacity and process; Contract needs and contract management process and manpower.

♦ Physical Space needs analysis: Engineering/Maintenance support team [civil infrastructure, equipment and instrument maintenance back-up]; [Govt. space often suffers from poor maintenance and inadequate provision for visiting public; periodic review of facility upkeep, housekeeping and waste management is a must.

♦ Training- Load analysis, Existing Capacity, new capacities and process needed

♦ **IT processes** as a crosscutting issue, manpower and capacity. [Very important, the sooner the better].

♦ Analysis and structuring of regular Administrative/management processes, and providing for in-built arrangement for periodic updating.

- Monitoring and Evaluation Process and Capacity- arranging for it through IT based financial monitoring at least once in two months. Annual stocktaking of HR, organizational structure and skill balance is a must. Currently, there is an instruction for a Secretary of the Department to sign such an annual Assessment Report. The Ministry of Personnel does not insist on getting and scrutinizing any due diligence undertaken by the concerned Department as and when the Report is submitted to it. Unfortunately, there is no HR exercise undertaken before either preparing or signing the Report.

- Annual / periodic look at improving 'process management', by embedding impulse for evaluation and reforms [recognizing and rewarding all worthwhile suggestions] at multiple levels and making conscious arrangements for field level feedback.

- Governance set-up and democratic accountability- Grass-root level and multi-layered popular participation [This may appear irksome, but is helpful in the long run for IEC, feedback and mid-course corrections].

- IEC/ Client servicing features

- Gender and disadvantaged groups special need analysis and provisioning.

- Sui generis issues requiring special attention of the Specific program /Institution. Hospitals for instance, need tremendous input for waste-management/visitor management and high-grade daily maintenance. [Most Govt. hospitals present a shabby atmosphere-awful bathrooms, no arrangement for drinking water, inadequate signage, increasing chances of cross-infection and client-revulsion]

- **Annual Report** [Often tokenistic, but better than no Report. If formatted properly, over a period it documents the progress and the lessons. It must mandatorily contain a chapter on 'Listing of Major Assets and their Management' followed by a chapter on Input and Output Analyses, and a chapter on 'Failures and Lessons'. The draft report must be put to the Public Domain inviting grievances and suggestions through an e-process, which could then become 'people's part' of the Report. It can then be followed by a 'chapter' - on Proposed Reforms.

- Benefitting from Consultancy knowledge available in the market: The corporate private sector is efficient; part of its efficiency lays in its ability and willingness to access current market knowledge through engagement of highly skilled Consultancy organizations.

- Govt. Departments plod through and seldom subject themselves to systematic outside efficiency audits. Agencies like the World Bank [WHO, UNICEF in Health] bring out some 'situation analysis' report on different sectors. These reports are partially useful to start a discussion on problems of a particular sector; but, true to their 'diplomatic' style and need to sound profound, the reports contain no efficiency analyses or bold solutions and jargonize the issues obfuscating assimilation by lower level of bureaucracy. Often, these reports are prepared without invitation by the Department; so, there is no internal participation from different levels from within giving a report a lack of authenticity or relevance in Indian context.

- Traditionally, this activity of Report preparation is dominated by Economists; and economists by habit avoid accountability for their pronouncements. So, these reports while do serve a good purpose do not serve a great purpose.

- It is submitted that **Indians must now overthrow 'thought' colonialism** [I am not a leftist'; I am deliberately being provocative to stimulate a debate]. We look too much Westward to seek answers to Indian problems. The Indian intellectual Diaspora has to learn group dynamics and find 'Indian' solutions to Indian problems albeit benefitting from open min to world best practice.

- Rhetoric apart, I plead for liberal engagement of **top-notch consultancy firms to study our Departments under active leadership and involvement of the departmental bureaucracy**

at different levels to re-engineer our structures/process/ manpower of the departments for achieving much higher efficiency. Participation in the efficiency restructuring exercise by consultants must involve wide participation of all levels of the Officials of the Department. Involvement of only the Secretary level may result ultimately in a Report which does not generate wide enthusiasm during implementation.

♦ Ministries and Departments at Centre cannot rest subjecting themselves to efficiency audit through consultancy. **Similar process has to start with the corresponding Departments of the States.** It is important for each Department to look at PSUs with it, redefine and increase their role and efficiency. At least, in Health and Education there is immediate need for starting new PSUs; too much space has been conceded to private sector; the lower middle class and upper poor constituting the largest band of population has been deprived of its substantial savings[even incurring debt] to access private sector health care and education.

Some Personal Thoughts on GG:

♦ We may immediately consider the creation of the post of a Special Cabinet Secretary to coordinate and lead social sector Ministries.

♦ To take the country rapidly forward, GG attempted by IAS is not enough by itself. We urgently need electoral reforms and judicial reforms.

♦ We need greater acknowledgement of the need of cooperative federalism for carrying forward the agenda of GG. **The National Development Council must be made to play a much more active role in setting up the agenda for a dynamic GG.**

♦ Too many Ministries and Departments-Government must be lean and purposive.

♦ Not more than sixty percent of the civil servants should reach the level of Secretary to Government of India. There must be a pressure to perform throughout the career of a civil servant.

♦ The pay etc. of a Secretary to Govt. of India should be substantially more. It is to be seen as a reward for a life-long hard and productive work maintaining complete integrity.

♦ A system of seeking collaboration with reputed institutions like IITs and IIMs etc. should be attempted based on reciprocity.

♦ We urgently need a supplementation to the traditional District Administration structure. We need an e-enabled support system like 'Saathi Centres' to provide a second spine to the administrative system at Block level. The National Informatics Centre has done a splendid job; the stage is now to bring in the Saathi Centres- one in each Block to provide -e access to common people and improve accountability of field organizations at the Block, Tehsil and District levels.

♦ A vibrant country like India is not frozen in misgovernance. There have been several excellent initiatives in improving the quality and quantity of governance which are very well chronicled in Mr. Amitabh Kant's book of 2019-Incredible India 2.0.Governemnt of India has now put up a Good Governance Centre to focus on issues of Governance. However, the important job of Secretary Administrative Reforms [AR] is viewed by incumbents traditionally as a non-job. I met one Secretary AR out of my personal volition to learn and suggest a few tips about commencing a country-wide process of GG. Mr. E- used to be a personal friend at some stage of my career. He spent half an hour with me. However, most of that half an hour, he was sighing with sorrow that he had been posted to a non-job. The Department of ARPG should be bifurcated immediately. The Department of Pension and Grievances should be back with the Secretary, Personnel. The Department of AR must be with Secretary Coordination in Cabinet Secretariat re-designated as Secretary Coordination and Administrative Reforms working as the main support to the Cabinet Secretary so that AR gets the necessary attention. And abolition of one post of a non-performing Secretary could be a small step forward towards commencing GG.

24

THE ISSUE OF CORRUPTION

Many eminent colleagues have written books on their experience and have deliberated at length on the very disturbing and real issue of corruption pervading many walks of governance. Corruption corrodes GG and dissipates its energy from serving people efficiently - there is no doubt about it. There are many books on the subject; I mention only three, namely Mr. Madhav Godbole's book on Good Governance, Mr. Sovan Kanungo's 'A Bureaucrat Speaks' and Mr. Anil Swarup's 'Not Just A Civil Servant'. I may be permitted not to repeat the many of the right lamentations about corruption and the many suggestions as to how to contain it. I have some out of box suggestions.

Firstly, the best answer to combat corruption is increasing transactional speed of governance through adoption of e-processes as quickly as possible. Pending conversion to appropriate e-process, the speed of disposal must be the 'mantra' of Good Governance- as much for the IAS as more so for the Judiciary. **Delay is the root of corruption.** I must be pardoned for recording here a disquieting incident. In my boy-scout enthusiasm, I called on some select Secretaries now and then to discuss my ideas on GG, particularly about reforms and some new structures to increase service delivery/governance capacity. A Secretary who had worked with me earlier and I considered him as the best of my juniors spared the time to meet me. He was full of courtesies. But to my horror, I found that his office chamber was full of files in every nook and corner. Ninety nine percent of the files coming to a Secretary must go out of his chamber within 12 to 18 hours or earlier; otherwise GG gets clogged notwithstanding all good reputations and intentions. In Judiciary, one has come across instances of judgments being held in reserve for sometimes as much as a year. There could be some valid reason like heavy workload; but unwittingly it is an invitation to middlemen and fixers to pollute the process.

Secondly, the CBI must be converted into an agency having multidisciplinary personnel drawn from different Services for it to be able to appreciate the bona-fide or malafide behind a set of decisions.

Thirdly, the definition of corruption must include the activities or rather the non-activities of quite a number of IAS officers who seldom take responsibility and or work in any productive manner. Drawing salary and perks without doing any work and setting 'target free approach' for work in the Department, not utilising substantial part of the Departmental Budget is also corruption. Some friends have made lame excuses for such officers saying, 'But he is an honest officer". I would beg pardon to raise the question that being honest is axiomatic for a civil servant; he cannot be anything else. However, this does not absolve him/her from not delivering the work in the post which he is occupying.

And then there are some colleagues who are so obsessed with the issue of corruption in their organizations where they have been posted that they create imbalance and the main purposes of the organization get side-tracked. A small example- there was a colleague who was known for her annoyance with the corrupt. In course of her career, unfortunately she was by-passed at the last stage of her career. Luckily, in a review, she was promoted and was posted to a Scientific Organization in the rank of Additional Secretary. We had worked together for a brief while. We met by chance after her promotion in a social gathering. I congratulated her and in order to encourage her I said that the Scientific Organization had an important role to play for the country and she should see it as an opportunity for her to spend the remaining year of her career in supporting the technical people for better systems. She said, "Sir, you do not know. This place is full of thieves; the drivers were all stealing petrol from the office cars. When I caught them, they went on a strike. And the Technical people did not come out in my support." An Additional Secretary should have a better perspective of her important position to contribute to an organization rather than start with catching drivers.

In essence, I submit that corruption is rampant and is a real issue, Electoral costs and judicial clogging have to be addressed through simple but fundamental reforms if corruption is to be tackled systemically. I have experienced personally widespread corruption at Tax offices, Tehsils [described in shocking detail in Saathi Centre Annexure], Electricity office etc. Where the e-system is in effective vogue and or the top officer has grip over his work and colleagues, corruption is considerably less. My Saathi Centre suggestion in the Annexure II is a e-method to create an alternative spine at Block level to challenge the monopoly of existing lower level Government staff who invariably enjoy harassing people, People have to be empowered to fight corruption through an alternative officially accredited route to get their legitimate work done. It is bound to reduce corruption.

25

CONCLUSIONS

I always held Ekalavya- the great archery warrior of Mahabharata as my ideal. Guru Drona took his disciples to a leafy tree and asked all to look at the tree intently and describe to him what they saw. Many said many things; Duryodhan said that he saw a bird hiding, Yudhisthira- the head of the bird and. Arjuna - the eye of the bird. If Ekalavya would have been asked even without his being there, he would have seen the retina of the eye of the bird through sheer introspection and vision! Many times in my career, I found the way to GG best secured by cutting through the jargons- the distractions- and focusing on the retina. I regret and apologise that in the process sometimes I was impatient with mediocrity, and the rituals of lugubrious speech making after lighting of lamps etc. This was in excess in the public health sector. After elaborately crunching public health data, the public health experts took no responsibility for suggesting specific action. The only departure was my meeting Dr. Arora and the adoption of AD syringes in our Immunization programme in 2005. It could be because the technical experts might have met with misbehaviour or indifference of a sub-par performing bureaucracy over the years when their suggestions met with indifference. Alternatively, the public health discourse was full of analyses leading to paralysis. My recipe for Good Governance in India in one sentence: Improve designing ability, skill balance particularly in e-based finance and HR, speed of disposal of matters, sensitivity to the need and ability of the common man to participate in services meant for him. The best way to Good Governance is simplicity, consistency and determined action to attain efficiency.

In India, of late a lot of governance space is now occupied by the Judiciary. I have no quarrels with it as I feel that it has happened because of executive and political failures. We need a strong and independent judiciary. However, this also has to be tested on the touch-stone of people's interest. No sham 'Public Interest Litigation', but real and timely service of people's interest! The basic requirement is a system NOT of the lawyers for the lawyers and by the lawyers - but a speedy system of dispensation of justice not kowtowing to the pecuniary interests of lawyers' brotherhood. In fact, we must have an All India Judicial Service through a Union Judicial Service Commission. Advocacy and judgeship must be separated at an early stage as these are different skills. The present system suffers from many infirmities and opaqueness concerning recruitment to higher judiciary. **In effect, real judicial independence will be better secured once Judgeship is separated from lawyers and given a proper merit based professional status through public examination based recruitment.**

Each pillar of Government must have a sense of balance for the composite pluralism of India to yield rich dividends. I recount here some wise words of a very good humane and efficient Minster of Odisha. He was Revenue Minister when I was Collector. He lost the election. We met in a social gathering. I went up to him and greeted him politely. He suddenly made an uncharacteristic remark- "So, Hota ji, how are things? A lot of compromises?" I replied, "The same as in your time, Sir." He should have let it rest; but he persisted- "You don't admit; but, I know." This got my goat. I asked his permission to ask him what I said was my long cherished question. He asked me to go ahead. I said "Sir, we join the IAS hoping from the first day a good life. Leaders say that they seek vote as they are idealists and want to serve the people. But afterwards, we are asked to be idealistic and leaders want the good life." I thought that I had him. But Mr. Mohanty did not lose his composure. He said after a pause- "Hota Ji, remember that society consists of many groups. Every group must have a sense of proportion, perform the tasks which are primary to it, respect the other groups; and all groups must respect one another and permit each group to function well." I was won over by his astute comment. Good governance to be effective must seek from the political and judicial leaders, administrative space for a well-functioning bureaucracy to design and implement policies. Intimidated bureaucracy or a slothful group seeking advancement based on non-merit skills like nepotism and PR will create imbalance.

Some say that Democracy and Efficiency are incompatible. Democracy needs consensus building, it also means limited tenures for political governments; they are not for long term goals. Many goals of GG need detailed planning and investment of time before jumping into the public arena with slogans of achievements. China shows GG and its benefits to its people challenging the Western Agencies' emphasis on participation of all elements of people and groups of civil societies. China does not provide for the elaborate judicial system emphasised by the Western agencies. India has embarked on a 'No Return' journey of an imitation of Western liberal democracies. The only experiment with Centralism was when Emergency was declared in 1975. It initially yielded some benefits of discipline like trains running in time, law and order improving all around. However, soon it deteriorated into unpopular and insensitive implementation of apparently good plans like the vasectomy programme. The bureaucracy became tyrannical. Moral hazards started. Mrs. Gandhi herself lifted the Emergency even if there was no real large-scale revolutionary challenge to her authority. And thereafter, for bad or for good, our country is wedded to our version of 'cancelling' democracy'; we elect a government sometimes with a clear mandate, but, the very next morning we start ensuring through a determined 'Opposition' to prevent the elected government from effectively functioning. And as Paul H. Appleby said a long time back-'India is extremely federal.' These days often a substantial number of States have Governments elected to power belonging to Parties opposing the Party in power at the Centre. So achieving GG in India will need a charismatic approach of Cooperative Federalism where there has to be a national patriotic agenda for developing our country beyond the turtle pace of incremental growth where a sizable number of people still live a subsistence standard of life. Israel comes to one's mind when one thinks of such a country of GG where often there are coalition governments, woven together by a charismatic leader to keep the country on the track of GG. In India the IAS should at least try to be like the Japanese bureaucracy which holds the country together in spite of political ups and downs. A persuasive stance with political leaders and winning them over to the agenda of GG however difficult it could be in real time - has to be attempted by the IAS. For that the esprit de core and the moral fibre displayed by the IAS has to be considerably higher. Then only 'Prashasan' could change to 'Sushasan'!

Good governance is very much there in our country, but in bits and pieces. However, India to forge ahead and meet emerging challenges particularly from China, needs Great Governance as its main response within its democratic framework.

India's strength is its youth -25% of world's youth are in India. The average Indian woman is its asset as she is by nature thrifty and has demonstrated over centuries her resilience and management of household economy in most trying of times. Women self- help groups in position have to be assigned larger role. The youth power has to be optimally used. India must start using its vast number of IT personnel of different categories - of international caliber, highly trained, trained and semi-trained.

Firstly, new and or additional governance **structures** are needed. Secondly, the **content** of governance is good, but to be great has to become more inclusive to assign larger roles to women and youth groups. Thirdly, the **process** of decision making in all branches of Government has to be much faster.

For the first issue of 'Structures', the dearth of managerial talent in Education and Health sectors in States and Center has first to be acknowledged- new cadres in States recruited for specializing and assisting in management of Social Sector Departments and institutions are needed as part of the State Administrative Services known as PCS cadre. Currently it is there for Finance, Police and General Administration.

For the second, India and its States have a host of welfare schemes already, but the contents are often hollow as detailed designing have not been done and numbers have not been crunched to implement these schemes for each Indian as promised all the year through. For the third, a bottom-up approach involving all level of officials is needed. Judiciary can lead the way by setting example of speedy disposal. Executive branch also should set itself the task of 'disposal' of a matter without procrastination. E -monitoring of the pending matters of citizen will keep everyone on toe. The Saathi Centre concept suggested in the second Annexure deserves serious attention.

And a major step will be taken in the right direction if Central Government if Central Government leverages part of its Education and Health budgets to attract flow of institutional finance enabling expansion of social goods of Education and Health for providing Standard Health Care at standard Cost through Hospital Corporation of India and Quality Higher Education for many more by setting up of more IITs and IIMs. Even the upper-poor and lower-middle class constituting the largest band of population are ready to co-share part of the cost. We should not go for the traditional PSU structures but bring in SPVs/ Management Mechanisms through PPP mode inviting our IT Giants to help in nation building.

Ultimately common man must be at the center of all Governance. The practice of treating ordinary people as passive recipient of different largesses in an uneven manner must stop. they must be facilitated and empowered through E-processes to become equal and effective partners in country's progress. We need Karmayogis in every segment of our country, be it in Government, judiciary, public sector or even private sector. The IAS should humbly lead and facilitate the way by publicly accepting the honour of announcing its acceptance and adherence to Karmayoga.

EPILOGUE

– Mission Karmayogi

Better late than never! An excellent initiative has been launched on the first week of September by Government of India, namely, the Mission Karmayogi – a serious program to improve the quality of civil servants of the country. The Cabinet Note on the subject is well conceived. The Mission aims at setting up a new national architecture to improve the training content of civil servants at various stages of their career so that they merely do not follow rules but fulfill the roles expected of them,

In 2014, Good Governance used to be mentioned as an electoral promise. It somehow took a back seat after that. Full credit now goes to our Prime Minster and his Team that they have brought back Good Governance as a key requirement of the country though initially its focus is on training and improving the knowledge and attitudinal contents of the civil servants. Good governance is more than the civil service; but then, well begun is half-done. To quote: "National Programme for Civil Services Capacity Building (NPCSCB) has been carefully designed to lay the foundations for capacity building for Civil Servants so that they remain entrenched in Indian Culture and sensibilities and remain connected, with their roots, while they learn from the best institutions and practices across the world. The Programme will be delivered by setting up an Integrated Government Online Training-"iGOTKarmayogiPlatform."

The most heartening factor is the seriousness of purpose behind this much needed effort as Prime Minister will retain the oversight

217

involvement with him as Head of Public Human Resource Council. In Independent India this is a 'first' that the human tools of governance are sought to be addressed. The 'tools' inherited from a colonial past have taken time to reorient and dedicate themselves to the sovereign citizens of a free India. Criticism of lingering feudal attitude have been voiced now and then; but, this is the first time, these issues of attitude, knowledge and modernising work processes is sought to be addressed in a holistic manner. Any disquiet about the source of funding and mentioning the value in terms of U.S. dollars is quickly set at rest when the emphasis on grounding the new knowledge paradigm on Indian ethos and culture is emphasized. We must keep open the window to the world to learn from best practices and state of the art technology of governance; but we must be clear that we shall and we can apply scintillating Indian minds together to find Indian governance solutions based on Indian socio-economic realities. 'Thought colonialism' must end.

To quote again: "Mission Karmayogi aims to prepare the Indian Civil Servant for the future by making him more creative, constructive, imaginative, innovative, proactive, professional, progressive, energetic, enabling, transparent and technology-enabled. Empowered with specific role-competencies, the civil servant will be able to ensure efficient service delivery of the highest quality standards." Excellent goals! How one wishes that, the objective of 'being more citizen and common person-friendly' could have been added to the avowed list of goals! How one further wishes that in time the leaders must realise that the goal- 'the efficient service delivery of the highest quality' still bears traces of –'Giver' [the Government and its governance through civil servants] granting concessions to citizens [the common people] by doling out good governance. One hopes that sooner than later the discourse will correct itself to bring the common man to its centre as owner and end user of this great process set in motion.

Nevertheless, it is the right response from our Prime Minister that even in the most trying of times where covid and China loom as definite threats, instead of feeling overwhelmed he has chosen to profile the right long term response- India seeks its solutions through better governance by focusing on the HR issues of Governance. It is courageous to announce right at the outset, this mechanism can gradually look at HR issues like service matters like confirmation after probation period, deployment, work assignment and notification of vacancies etc. An omission is the issue of tenure as a required input for quality of policy formulation as well as implementation. There are other important issues for HR apart from training like motivation, morale and dedication where two fundamentals are important- one is methods of increasing participation and merit bench-marking. Without objectifying assessment of 'merit', nepotism which has a strong grip on Indian Governance particularly in selection of personnel for all important top positions will demotivate the rank and file to take this noble effort of our PM seriously. The Annual Assessment Reports format, content calibration and writing should also be addressed as part of this grand effort at using Training as a tool of improving Civil Service Good governance is already there in the country in bits and pieces. The federal polity makes Good Governance uneven. However, the clarion call has been given by Prime Minister; India has to move from Good to Great Governance. The HR is the most important element in this commitment and IT tools are the best way forward for speeding up the process. The emphasis on training, standardization, sharing of learning and so on is very apt. One should however be careful to ensure the participation of rank and file while setting up the SPV of Training/learning as an external autonomous agency. As the old saying goes, you can drag a horse to the water, but, you cannot make it drink. Involving every functionary, particularly at grassroots level will remain a challenge. Reforms have been hitherto top-down; these have to become bottom-up. And the decentralized administrative set-up of India with some States not believing in 'cooperative federalism' will also throw up additional complexities. The role of National Development Council NDC has to be re-emphasized and the new effort may eventually be seen as a part of re-positioning NDC as the prime policy making body while retaining the initial emphasis and thrust that is very much needed from our Prime Minister in Chair in the proposed HR Council.

The 'elitist' India- the self-appointed guardians of the country must abandon its skepticism and come forward with constructive suggestions. The art for PM down to Cabinet Secretary and so on will be their ability to keep the activities of NPCSCB activities open in public realm and having the patience to use constructive suggestions from all layers [the argumentative Indians] including rank and file in a progressive manner and on a continuous basis.

ANNEXURE I

Hospital/Health Corporation of India: HCI

Building the Case- Pressing Health Issues at Hand

[My design of HCI involved a simulated study of cash-flow of twelve years. I have not enclosed this detailed table with all capital and revenue cost of each small and big activity daily to avoid tedium and volume. I had spent a couple of lakh rupees of personal money and studied it for 3 years with help of many CAs, Specialist doctors, many private hospitals, nursing homes, MBBS doctors, nurses, and Rourkela Ispat Hospital from 2013 to 2015.]

The improvements in public health are minimal as these are made entirely dependent on Govt. budgetary support [which has competing claims and is inflexible] while allowing the private sector to monopolize the bank finance and the growing expenditure by people. Out Of Pocket expenses for health care is increasingly crippling the lower middle class and the poor. Health insurance coverage is simply not taking off as the high cost of private care makes the present insurance products costing though some of these are – unaffordable. Along with a new public sector stream of a continuum of health care, the central govt. has to organize health insurance in an inclusive and pervasive manner to cover the majority of the population. Ayushman Bharat has to be integrated into the public health system as a Universal Insurance Scheme' with premium payment by all [different from the largess based scheme now].

The politically emotive argument is that the government must provide 'free' healthcare to the needy citizens through the budget - how can democratic govt. Charge money for health care from common people of India! The fact is that the rich and powerful monopolies the high-end care available in government and private now. The common man is the one who pays for care to access either the 'free' but extremely crowded Govt. care or, for lack of alternative, the costly private care. AIIMS like institutions as stand-alone tertiary hospitals in low performing States are unlikely to impact general health care optimally. Time has, therefore come for Central Govt. to explore alternative ways of leveraging a certain percentage of its budget for increasing the flow of more funds and new structure to increasing cost-effective health care accessible to common people by stepping in with a chain of secondary hospitals below each AIIMS. This new stream of health care has to be designed for being placed in between the 'free' and uneven care of State Governments and that of the high cost urban-centric private sector – ITS MANDATE- STANDARD CARE AT STANDARD COST.

HCI is a unique concept! It promises a watershed in the delivery of affordable and quality health care in India. It is a - commitment to creating an efficient and accountable public sector apparatus for delivery of social sector services through modern management practices. It is proposed that HCI shall be a registered as a PSU managing all Central Govt. hospitals [including AIIMS, New Delhi].

HCI Model in a Nutshell

Operational Design

HCI would constitute a network of 3-tier continuum of care. The 1st tier being 4,000 Block or Small Town level central hospitals; the 2nd tier being the 250 district level secondary hospitals [also acting as supervisory and referral for a group of 1st level], while 3rd tier being the State level AIIMS which will be acting as the supervisory and referral hospital for the 2nd tier. All AIIMS would be under a corporate structure for vigorous modern and optimal management of scale of all valuable assets.

In 5-6 years, HCI will establish this continuum of care bringing about a qualitative and quantum change in availability of standard health care to the common people at standard cost. However, for the promises to come true, considerable design efforts have to be put in place. How will the change come?

MBBS doctors at the Block/ Small Town Level Central Hospitals and Specialist doctors at the District Level Central Hospitals will be the cornerstone of HCI and its partner. AIIMS at State level will serve as apex healthcare management institution - this chain thus providing an additional spine for **CONTINUUM OF CARE – STANDARD CARE AT STANDARD COST.** The altruism of the Central Govt. from time to time about free diagnostic, free medicine needs many more functional delivery points which would be greatly supplemented through the HCI chain.

Management & Governing Structure: HCI will be professionally managed organization with top-notch MBAs in Hospital Management, Chartered Accountants, HR Specialists, Procurement & Logistics Specialists, Training, and Engineering and Maintenance Specialists holding key support responsibilities up to General Manager level only in delivering the highest level of patient care. The Directors in the Board will only be the Directors of AIIMS in ex-officio capacity. For ensuring better coordination between the three tiers of care, HCI will have Directors of State-level AIIMS as the ex-officio Chairman of a State level Board with District and Block level representation. So far HCI itself is concerned; it is to be a 'Holding' Company with all the Directors of AIIMS on its Board. It is proposed that the Chairman-cum-Managing Director of this not-for-profit PSU will be with strong 'Hospital Administration Background'. Alternatively, an Additional/ Special Secretary with aptitude could initially be posted as Chairman supported by an M.D. with Hospital Administration background.

Financing HCI: The financing of HCI establishment will be through a unique mix of central seed funding, contributions from State Governments in the form of land for the hospital campus and Bank loans. In 5-6 years, the commitment from the above partners will pan out as given below:

With Rs ten thousand crores as total central contributions in 5 years, the Central Government has to spend Rs 2000 crores (approx.) per year, which is only about 4.5% of the present annual central health budget. [Most of this equity investment by state and Central Govt. is likely to be 'redeemed' back to Govt. due to positive cash flow by 7th-8th year even after loan repayment to Banks. Detailed cash flow for 12 years has been worked out to establish the capital cost/ working capital and viability in consultation with experts who have implemented and run private hospitals.]

Output and Market Value: With a Rs 25,000 crore investments [from the Centre, States and the Banks in 5 to 6 years, the HCI chain in States will be in a position to produce medical care worth Rs 45,000 crores to Rs 50,000 crores per year [estimated at old RSBY costs/AIIMS, Delhi and rates meant for 'outsiders' at Ispat General Hospitals under Steel Authority]. This estimate does not include the value of outputs from the AIIMS directly, which together could amount to another Rs 25,000 crores. Thus, in a few years, HCI will usher in Rs 75,000 crores (market value Rs two Lakh crores) worth of medical services for the Indian people and provide a balance to run-away cost of private-sector treatment.

Boost to Insurance Sector: HCI is set to boost the expansion of the health insurance coverage from the present minuscule percentage of the country's population to an ambitious universal coverage. National insurance providers and schemes such as the old RSBY or new AB are expected to see growth and people are expected to get maximum benefits in terms of lower out-of-pocket expenses. AB has to be thus restructured immediately to create a universal health insurance product. [Premium-One day's income a year covering 100 times the premium, or Rs. 40 thousand whichever is higher]. Some amount of co-payment has to be structured in for the non-BPL category to avoid wastage and abuse. This is a win-win for all partners, including HCI which will also earn revenue from the expanded client base of AB.

Reaching out to the 'Unreached': Districts and Blocks having large tribal populations will get special attention and incentives for medical personnel to ensure basic health care to disadvantaged populations. The

Ministry of Tribal Affairs could be invited in as a Partner to invest in the assets meant for Tribal districts/blocks.

Gainful employment for MBBS doctors: The MBBS doctors who constitute more than 50% of all doctors in the country would be gainfully employed and optimally utilized in different parts of the country instead of over-concentrating in Metros and big cities only. They will be co-opted as partners at Block level hospitals. They are likely to earn about Rs. 1 lakh per month without resorting to unethical means

Operational Plan: The foundation of HCI and its entire systems, structure and pathway will be built on the learning from a series of 12 intensive studies for which the requirement framework will be developed under the collective leadership of mentors. The first step in this direction will be the formation of an elite group of mentors. This group will have distinguished and nationalistic oriented individuals from government, PSU like ESIC and private sector. The mentor group will be headed by the Union Health Minister. The key deliverables expected from this group are:

Detailing and mentoring of various technical studies that would be conducted to test key programmatic assumptions Synthesis of different studies into operational whole Finalization of the proposal document, strategies and service outputs; Buy-in of elite health technical group on the HCI model for further liaison and advocacy with Government. To assure Policy Makers that the idea of HCI is not the quixotic output from one or a few overheated minds; it is a well-considered national and nationalistic idea. This current document itself has been developed over 3 years by wide professional consultations with experts and stakeholders.

Feasibility Studies The proposed model is based on certain important assumptions. It has been planned to undertake a pre-Feasibility Study to test our assumptions and grassroots realities and thereby to build and generate evidence-based strategic cases for HCI. The snapshot of the 12 studies to be undertaken is given below. Only one sample study is detailed below to delineate the thoroughness required.

MBBS Availability Assessment Study: It is puerile to think that all of us work only driven by craze for unlimited money; most of us including the present PM work for the irreplaceable satisfaction that rendering meaningful public service offers; also that we are, as humans, should be provided with some basics needed for a reasonable standard of life along with a good chance to work for people. Primary assumption under the HCI model is the availability of MBBS doctors, especially at the Block level, to work on an entrepreneurial model. For this, a detailed MBBS Availability Assessment Study would be undertaken.

The MBBS doctor will be the cornerstone of Block level hospital-four to five of them would be inducted as 'partners'. Cash flow at old RSBY rates shows earnings for each of them to be more than Rs. one lakh per month. The purpose of this study would be to assess the current remuneration of private MBBS doctors, especially in cities and to assess their availability and interest in joining HCI. This would help us to understand what were their career motivations and aspirations. The main question would be under what terms and conditions they could be willing to relocate to Block headquarters. Would they agree to become 'partners' in HCI Block hospitals and would they agree to hold some token 'equity shares' as partners etc.

All family planning activities could gradually be handed over to the HCI chain [which will ensure a humane dignified fertility choice available in privacy to the ordinary Indian finally, rather than the 'butchering' and 'sabotage' that goes on in ill-organized State Family Planning camps] freeing the State system to concentrate on more pressing emergencies / epidemic control etc.

Expected Outcome: A customized package could be designed for actively engaging MBBS doctors at Block and other hospitals as 'partners' based on the insights gained from this study.

Study Design: The study would entail a quick qualitative sample survey. This survey would cover around 35 hospitals and 275 to 300 doctors from across 15-20 metros/large cities in North, East and Central India. This survey would mainly cover MBBS doctors working in the private sector. This may also include, in a smaller proportion, retired MBBS doctors as well who are working in the private sector.

Illustrative list of topics that the survey would cover is remunerated below:

1. At what positions are the MBBS doctors currently positioned in the private sector? o What is the current remuneration package that they are getting? o What is their current job profile? o What are the things with which they are not happy in their current position and the de-motivating factors? o What are their future aspirations? Would they be willing to work under the HCI model on an entrepreneurial model, which would assure them earnings around Rs. 1 lakh and more per month? o Would they be willing to invest 5 to 10 % as ESOP of the equity under this model as a partner? o Would they be willing to relocate to block/ tribal town locations under HCI? o Would they be willing to sign a work bond (specifying the minimum number of years of service under HCI) o What other components can be added to make HCI partnership proposition attractive to them? Could better designation and work facilities; facilitation for a Diploma in Family Medicine be the desired goal? o What would be their major apprehensions in joining HCI?

    Agency Selection: The study would be outsourced to an agency of repute. The agency should have prior experience in conducting such comprehensive qualitative health surveys across multiple states. It has to respond to our basic EOI document with a detailed response of design of the Survey along with costs for various elements to convince the selection group that among all the bidders it has understood the goal and sub-tasks of the survey and will be in a position to deliver time-bound relevant insights.

    Approximate duration for this study would be three months. At the end of the assignment, a detailed study report would be submitted by the agency.

2. **Specialists Availability Assessment Study**:

    STUDY FRAMEWORK Study Objective: There is a need for a study to test and validate assumptions regarding the availability of specialists by providing real numbers from the field regarding specialists' availability etc. in the states of Rajasthan & Odisha.

3. **Health Manpower Structural Assessment Study:** This would include following main components: o *HR Assessment for Technical Positions*: o *HR Assessment for Managerial Positions*: o *HR Assessment for Support Positions*: o *HR requirement for HCI Head office.* o *Analysis of AIIMS manpower needed for management of HCI chain:*

4. **Health Insurance Landscaping Exercise:** For this, a detailed study through a professional agency would be undertaken to develop a viable expanded RSBY and insurance products. Differential insurance and premium packages would be developed for various socio-economic classes of Indian citizens. For example for BPL families, lower middle class, middle class, upper-middle-class, different insurance packages would be developed according to their paying capacity. The analysis would include a plan for detailed income segmentation of population, preparing a roll-out plan for all-inclusive health insurance and insurance products (ranging from Rs 100 to Rs 5000) depending on the paying capacity of the consumer. ASHAs would be the frontline handler, collecting premium etc.

   Besides, current OPD, IPD, lab, medicine, surgeries etc. charges under public and private health sector would be analysed and based on it different packages for various socio-economic categories would be developed for HCI. The idea is to generate a corpus amount from cross-subsidization so that HCI could use these funds to provide standard care at standard cost. Detailed analysis of current insurance packages, how this can be expanded to include upper poor and lower middle class, financial viability, risk cover that can be offered etc. would be worked out. Also, a sample survey of current secondary care procedures and their cost in the private sector would be undertaken.

5. **Architectural Study for HCI:** *Development of a set of prototype designs for HCI Block level hospitals.* This would include detailed mapping of hospital functions, clinical services to be provided, detailing of physical infrastructure requirements, manpower requirements, equipment norms and requirements, laboratory services to be provided at block hospital, allocation of bed strength, requirements of operation theatre, list of Drugs/Lab Reagents/ Other Consumables and Disposables for Block Hospital, Capacity

Building, Quality Assurance and Quality Control of Processes and Service Delivery, Statutory Compliance, Hospital Waste Management plan, MIS, patient safety protocols etc. Besides, SOPs (Standard Operating Procedures) would be developed for all departments.

• *Development of a set of prototype designs for HCI District level hospitals.* This would include detailed mapping of hospital functions, clinical services to be provided, detailing of physical infrastructure requirements, manpower requirements, equipment norms and requirements, laboratory services to be provided at a District hospital, allocation of bed strength, requirements of operation theatre, list of Drugs/Lab Reagents/ Other Consumables and Disposables for district Hospital, Capacity Building, Quality Assurance and Quality Control of Processes and Service Delivery, Statutory Compliance, Hospital Waste Management plan, MIS, patient safety protocols etc. Besides, SOPs (Standard Operating Procedures) would be developed for all departments.

• *Referral and Linkages Plan*: Effective Referrals is an important strategy under HCI model. For this it is planned to hire services of a medical expert to chalk out Referral Arrangements from block to Dist. and Dist. to State-level hospitals, including 104 and 108 services. For this current referral mechanism would be assessed. Scope for IT-enabled referral mechanisms e.g. through SMSs; innovative models like telemedicine etc. would also be assessed.

• *Equipment planning and analysis for District and Block level hospitals.* This includes planning for diagnostics, general equipment and instruments; miscellaneous utilities and civil engineering requirements for block and district level hospitals.

• *Indicative Costing for HCI Hospitals:* Based on the architectural requirements, the agency would also come up with indicative budgets for greenfield establishment of district and Block-level hospitals under HCI model.

6. **Development of Communication & Branding Plan:** Hiring services of a communication expert/ agency to chalk out branding and marketing plans for HCI and its chain of hospitals for various stakeholders. Besides, detailed *Market Planning Exercise* would also be undertaken

7. **Financial Viability Study:** One of the lead USPs of the HCI is that it would be a financially viable healthcare delivery model. So its promise is not for overnight political decisions to indiscriminately set up thousands of hospitals using budget without ensuring viability. Hence bank loans as a major part of the funding would be a built-in safeguard feature.

8. 8. **ICT Plan:** HCI would be a highly IT-enabled healthcare delivery model. An IT professional agency would be enrolled for designing IT platforms for managing HMIS for all levels of hospitals under HCI model.

9. **104 and 108 Landscaping Study:** More importantly, use of ICT based 104 and 108 services would be done- 104 care centres and telemedicine at each tertiary level would be linked to all hospitals and ASHAs. Systems for providing medical advice/ counselling/ appointment/treatment over the phone would be developed and piloted. The feasibility and dimension of organizing this service on such a scale has to be assessed.

10. **PPP Requirement Study:** Public-Private Partnership is of utmost importance for the success of HCI. Despite all designing and planning, there would be discordance in time and readiness between Block and District hospitals coming up in a synchronized time-bound manner. Existing private hospitals have to be accredited for referral services. NGOs would be needed to mentor quality and ethical marketing of services. Technical manpower induction both in District and Block may need time and contingent situations could be there of shortage, gap, extra workload periodically coming up. Methods of buying services/temporarily inducting scarce manpower from the open market have to be planned. Certain disciplines would be in shortage- anaesthetists would be scarce in many States, so could

be neurologists. Services of laparoscopic surgeons and technicians may be needed to provide quality Family Planning services in Blocks instead of carrying huge manpower load perpetually. Training may also need a sizable element of PPP. It will be worthwhile to carry out a preliminary study about various elements of PPP at feasibility stage so that adequate designing focus is there on a detailed project report DPR stage.

11. **Study on Pre-Servicing all services-** Pre-service training and testing for all the support services like Human Resource (including recruitment criteria and mode, performance assessment system based on daily output); Finance accounts (payment, raising claims with insurance and the Govt. [where relevant] for transfer of 90% fund on daily basis); procurement and stock-management; performance record and pay bills; transport system; maintenance system for instruments and equipment, OTs etc. would be developed and made to undergo several dry-run and trials. This would be of duration of one month and would be outsourced to an external agency of repute with expertise in doing similar kinds of work. This is inclusive of launching HCI proposal documents & dissemination cost.

12. **Study for Development & Rollout of a Degree in Family & Public Medicine.** To boost the morale of MBBS doctors and to effectively leverage their expertise in the country there is need to immediately introduce a degree in Family & Public Medicine where field experience –say two thousand outpatient examinations and prescribing, five hundred day care procedures, five hundred deliveries, five hundred child emergency stabilization procedures, three hundred Family Planning operations and useful hands-on practice-based experience should be the main content of this degree in Family Medicine. MBBS doctors are precious resources; many of them are languishing and floundering around in big towns and private sector hospitals [having missed admission to Postgraduate degrees of their choice] where the specialist and the super-specialist rule the roost. But these MBBS doctors do not earn on the average more than Rs. forty thousand per month, they have no authority to prescribe, they mostly act as 'night' managers or physician assistants

to 'big' doctors. They are likely to join HCI chain if they are given the prestige, earning, designation and eventually a P.G. degree in Family Medicine which will enhance their skills and self-esteem.

The designing of HCI would be thus in two stages: the first stage is to firm up the assumptions behind this revolutionary chain, and then the second stage which would be drawing up a detailed map/ work plan of all the parameters by engaging top-notch expert agencies available in India/world. As far as possible, nothing should be left to chance; nothing needs to be commenced in the field without adequate preparation for illusory political gains. What is important is to set up a dedicated group to draw up a detailed document about all the planning and designing issues involved and draw up a comprehensive Planning and Design Document for HCI visualizing and drawing out all the operational issues that would be involved in setting up and running the HCI chain for, say twelve years including Cash Flow exercise.

This Taskforce should be serviced by HLL and chaired by Health Secretary and/or his nominee and must commence working. A consulting agency like McKinsey/Accenture/PWG/Ernest Young and the like may be engaged to assist in documentation writing and detailing.

Plan for Operationalizing HCI

Budgetary Requirement: A brilliant concept like HCI may need a sum of Rs. 3.5 crore for the 'first stage study'; it will need another Rs. 150 crore for the final designing of the actual systems. These sums of money are to be understood in the context; the final investment in HCI could be around Rs. 25 thousand crores over five years [Rs. 10 thousand crores by Central Govt., Rs. 1000 crores by States by way of land, all to be treated as equity investment] and Rs. 14 thousand crores as loan by Banks. This HCI group of hospitals [AIIMS output excluded] would be producing medical services worth Rs. forty thousand crores or more per year.

Key Lessons for Consideration

Leaders may kindly appreciate that social sector projects announced in India by whichever Govt. have failed to deliver the intended benefits to the common man due to inadequate designing of service delivery issues. Learn as you go along; let us launch the programme immediately in the field as it the core idea is good for people; we have a time limit in terms of tenure [whether as Governments or as bureaucrats], so let us take the credit for revolutionary social sector programme immediately- all this and similar approach of the past will lead us to half hazard implementation. Then the blame game will start - how could Govt. start a new PSU on health, which is again a semi-functional bunch of ill-equipped hospitals wasting the country's resources.

Indian elite traditionally delights in the non-success of various government initiatives to better the lot of the people. Let it be instead inducted into accurate designing and implementation of the HCI. Some of the key issues are reiterated below to show that design of HCI would involve very detailed thinking and innovating by a group of public health experts, administrators including retired people with a proven track record to provide the oversight needed for designing HCI so that the omissions are minimal.

- A new hospital chain like HCI dispersed in several locations would require a considerable IT-based monitoring system.

- Healthcare is highly HR intensive; monitoring the recruitment, training, performance accountability and determining reward and punishment would pose a considerable challenge.

- The flow of finance and accounts in so many locations could lead to leakage.

- Linkage to insurance claims could be weak due to some inherent indifference in the traditional public sector approach as well as widespread dispersal of locations and uneven nature of individual claims and the paperwork involved.

- Treatment quality could vary and become non-standard, particularly in outlying Block hospitals.

- Logistic difficulties of stock of consumables, medicines and other materials needed in different locations could cause dislocation in rendering care.

The above set of right apprehensions need to and can be addressed through an extremely detailed set of it based systems which will ensure standardization, speed, objectivity, efficiency and transparency. It is proposed that about 6 months are devoted to developing these systems through the engagement of the best information technology organization like TCS has recently done for issuance of passports.

Proposed Plan of Action for Enhancing Efficiency of AIIMS It is easier to declare AIIMS like institutions of each State as the Apex management institution for the HCI chain in the State than to ensure effective leadership from AIIMS like institutions who are in nascent stages themselves beset with their teething problems. There are two answers to this very important operational issue.

- Firstly, able consultant groups must be engaged to study and prescribe the processes involved in detail and the managerial and other skill sets needed on a daily and periodic basis in-house in each AIIMS to provide the managerial oversight.

- Secondly, we should engage for 3 years an Implementation Agency of a proven track record for each State for operationalizing the key assumptions of the HCI chain and act as eyes and ears of HCI Head office as well as that of the Health Ministry.

- The fidelity and flexibility of the IT platform created for each important sub-group of activities itself would need periodic updating and modifications.

- Construction: Implementation of AIIMS like institutions has thrown up several lessons about efficient civil construction at different locations. The proposed HCI chain involves even more dispersed locations.

- If we are to start with six States, we should distribute these States between CPWD and NBCC. HLL can act as the oversight agency for developing prototype designs and be the monitoring agency for HCI and the Ministry.

- Sites may vary in contour, shape, and soil condition; yet, standard designs should be created for guiding field layout. The HCI chain is about standardization and building up of Brand equity. The view and layout of the hospital buildings must promote the efficiency of circulation and the Brand HCL.

- A three-months' time should be devoted to design the set of prototypes suitable for HCI chain. A dedicated group of civil architects with hospital experience have to sit together to thrash out the broad parameters.

- The challenge is to provide a modular approach with provision for expansion. Tenders are to be prepared and floated after all detailed drawings are available. This will avoid hold-ups and ad-hoc approach; execution efficiency will be ensured.

A reader may get bored with this Annexure with so much micro-detail. However, it is a fact that designing for a large country like India, particularly for social sector goods needs considrable patience and attention to details for eventual success. Details are immense; but I have avoided jargons and obfuscation.

ANNEXURE II

SAATHI CENTERS

I have not carried out as intensive a study for this concept as I have undertaken for the HCI concept. However, leaders and colleagues may find it worth their time to take this concept seriously and operationalize it for ushering in Good Governance far and wide of India. This concept has struck me not out of my original introspection- I have picked it up by observing what is going on in the small towns and Block headquarters. Stray facilitation activities are happening in District towns through individual Cyber Cafe owners etc. to facilitate travel, education [admission] transfer of money and so on.

Involving The Larger India

Some States would continue to perform poorly for some more years as they have traditionally lacked implementation structures. Some improvements in some sectors have taken place. Resources of different Departments at grass root level often are scattered; if enumeration and integration of these assets take place under a District Development Officer, much more optimal utilization and results could be expected. **In fact, enumeration of existing assets and putting them to optimal use through e-platform is as important as adding/creating new assets for service delivery.** However, distortion in human resource management in Central and State bureaucracy for decades have led to such complexities that the feeble attempt at reforms in personnel policies have had very limited impact.

IT based Facilitation Centres - Saathi Centres:

Knowledge is power; so the new discourse will do well to improve access of the dispersed 'key' population to knowledge based economy by setting up a chain of IT based Facilitation Centre in small towns through PPP with the large number of young technical manpower available even in small towns. Most of them are unorganized and semi-employed after acquiring their degree/diploma at considerable cost. The Saathi Centres can have nodes in each village through Anganwadi /ASHA/Gramasevak. So an IT based network will be at the disposal of all; survey work of different departments at field level can be assigned to these Centres. In a few years, even the census work can be assigned to these Centres saving costs and time. These Centres can be hubs of agricultural input/marketing for the Govt. and common people. And Centres can also be the gateway of large private sector FMCGs/ E-Commerce set-ups to rural markets. These will also usher in cost-effective marketing of insurance products including health insurance. The potential is immense. The Centre is to be seen as a great addition to the existing District administration and private efforts. Designing these under a visible brand, operating smartly after training under supportive supervision at regional hubs would be a great challenge; but some result oriented mid-level bureaucrats/technocrats could be given a five year mandate through a Mission/Corporation structure to design and implement this under the Dept. of IT of Govt. of India. These will be the mini Stock Exchanges of real India trading in knowledge, information, finance, commodities, marketing and so on.

Ordinary Indian as Game-Changer:

It is time that we recognize and facilitate the ordinary Indian to be a 'Game Changer' in the Development agenda, and not direct most of our policies to only 20% of the population. The larger mass is not waiting for hand-outs; it seeks participation. The high-end urban economy can and has done much, but only so much. Global inflow has benefits and issues. It is the ordinary Indian who could contribute significantly to GDP, if his social goods are assured and his entrepreneurial skills are unleashed through policy and special infrastructure facilitation. Transactional speed has to go up substantially throughout India. Velocity of access to information has to be substantially enhanced; increase in velocity of money will follow. Surpluses and purchasing power at the bottom of the Pyramid will buoy up the entire economy.

A chain of Saathi Centres should be established- initially one at each Block headquarters. Let us take Odisha - my cadre- as a case study; there are about 320 Blocks. In each Block headquarter. a State Govt. owned semi-used or unused building has to be located. A refurbished space of about 2500 square feet is needed. Reliable internet service is now available in all Block headquarters. This space has to be designed as an IT centre with 12 to 16 work stations. Most of the small towns also have trained and semi-trained computer literate young men and women who are doing all sorts of jobs at often very low salaries in big towns. Many of them will be happy to go back to the Block headquarters of their village and work there for a reasonable income. Many of them have spent a lot of money acquiring IT skills but do not have suitable jobs. They will be interested to join Saathi Centres as executives. They can even bring in 'refundable' equity of, say, Rs. fifty thousand each to give them a sense of belonging and partnership. The capital investment for the space, the work stations and computers are likely to be around Rs. thirty lakh per centre. The work force can work in shifts. There can be several types of service rendered like applications for Tehsil [even the simple task of paying the land revenue could cost a huge amount of time, PDS and Block work. Seeds and fertilizers could be ordered, State and Central Governments have to empower these Centres by making the Collector of the District the Chairperson of the Management Committee of Saathi Centres in a District. Field offices under the Collector will have to be made duty bound to respond to queries and applications made through these Centres by citizens in a time-bound manner. We have already Suvidha/Grahak Seva Centres in many urban areas; but these lack empowerment and vigorous management framework to be effective. The farmer, the artisan, the handicraft maker all could use the Saathi Centre to access information of market and benefit. These Centres should have SOPs, standard dress code, logo of the Centre etc. to establish the brand. The States could be divided into groups and the Saathi Centres there could be established on PPP mode. **Our renowned IT firms like Infosys, TCS, WIPRO and the like could be given the responsibility of groups of States to establish and manage these Centres, recruit and train the personnel and set up a few central problem solving and maintenance Cells to back up these centres. These Saathi Centres can and will function as the eyes and ears of the Central and State Governments to throw up real-time data on a continuous basis. Census and NSSO type of organizations and their costs and inaccuracies can be bid 'good bye' within two to three years once the Saathi Centres get going as all verified data will be on the system of Saathi Centres.**

Rural and semi urban people are eager to welcome this facilitation by paying token fees as they would save time and their information levels would go up to access better choice for all types of activities like ordering inputs, interfacing with distant institutions for their child's education, health, travel etc. The advantage is that they could use mobile telephony to access service and payment wallets can be created for collection of the fees.

An example of the benefit of this Centre:

A woman from a village can ring up the emergency Helpline of the Centre late at night and requisition the service of a nurse to come to her home to treat her child having acute diarrhoea or fever etc. when she has no one to help her, nor does she know to which hospital she can go at that hour arranging a transport. The Centre would be maintaining a master list of such medical personnel and transport available in the area [including Govt. ambulance if there]. It could arrange emergency help; the medical personnel would earn a standard fee, the Centre gets a small fee and the woman in distress gets service in time within reasonable cost. This chain over a period of one year can generate a lakh of jobs directly and another two lakh indirectly; more than that it can stimulate and increase income for all in small towns by increasing the reliability and speed of access to information for the common people. After the first year, all these Centres will generate enough income through fees to sustain themselves. I talked to some traditional but capable farmers of my and nearby villages. Most said that they were uncomfortable with the indifferent attitude of Block and Tehsil employees to their requisition for seeds, fertilisers and similar inputs and other matters. The Tahsildar make people run for dozens of times for even ordinary work. The Saathi Centre will reveal the ground level reality to the Collector etc. on real time basis as the transaction will be recorded in an e-process. Petty corruption is the order of the day. I have experienced it personally now. Even a reputed Chief Secretary failed to rectify the mischief. The Addl. Tahsildar passed a back-dated order on my mutation application for parental property. OSD to Chief Secretary who had seen the case record orally agreed that there was no order when he saw the papers in June; but he was helpless to declare the order passed a day after his examination back-dated to January as illegal as there was no way he could prove. If my application would have been filed through a Saathi Centre no nonsense like this dare happen. Similarly, the Block Office provides no marketing information etc. to farmers on a guaranteed basis. Something like Saathi Centre will help the District Magistrate get recorded and verifiable ground data, increase accountability and reduce endemic corruption going unchallenged at Tehsil and Block levels. A combination of ASHAs and Saathi Centres could be a great platform for marketing Health Insurance products. Ayushman Bharat can be a real universal insurance scheme by premium contribution of at least 70% of Indians of the rural area once the systems become operative.

Saathi Centre is an idea of scale; it has to be designed carefully. It has to be implemented through PPP model, not like some of the semi-functional Government run Suvidha/Grahak Kendra. Velocity of information exchange and access will widen choice for the ordinary man and increase the velocity of money in rural area. It can act as a game changer for rural and semi-urban India's ambition to integrate with the metro India with dignity, equality and efficiency.

ACKNOWLEDGEMENTS

I acknowledge the help and advice I have received from many friends, colleagues and seniors which has enriched the book. Mr. B. K. Chaturvedi, former Cabinet Secretary, alerted me to the dynamic nature of the concept of good governance. Mr. D. P. Bagchi, former Chief Secretary of Odisha moderated my excessive frankness and made me realise that the book is not meant to name and shame anyone; it is meant to stimulate thinking about concepts of good governance in action. Mr. Anil Swarup, former Union Education Secretary, helped me rethink some concepts. Prof. Sudhakar Panda former Chairman of Odisha State Finance Commission gave me sagacious advice on the publication aspects as well as about the contents. He was the exception who app the concept of 'skill-balance' as essential for the implementation of large programmes. Ms. S. Rao, former Health Secretary made me realise that perspectives on efficiency differs. Prof. R. N. Mohanty provided the Educator's view of an IAS officer. Mr. Malay Chatterjee, CMD of many PSUs gave me invaluable insight into PSUs. There are other innumerable personalities, particularly the top Bankers of the country who have coached me to do financial analyses of my work; because of them this small saga of an individual IAS officer could assume a larger than life shape.

I have also benefited by reading the books on governance by several eminent IAS authors like late Mr. U.C. Agarwal, Mr. M. Godbole, Mr. Sovan Kanungo, Mr. P. C. Hota [for stimulating my thinking on our Judicial system] Mr. B.K. Chaturvedi, my esteemed batch-mate Mr. P. C. Parekh's book on role of Agencies in Coal allegations;

Mr. Amitabh Kant, Mr. Anil Swarup, and the book 'Governance -Issues and Challenges' edited by Prof. A. P. Singh and Prof. Krishna Murari. I am grateful to the Librarian of the Administrative Reforms Department for permitting me to use the books available in the library. I am ever grateful to Mr. Jagannath Patnaik former Minister who insisted that I write the book instead of moralizing and lamenting all the time about state of governance in India verbally. I benefited considerably by discussing the manuscript with Mr. Mukesh Shivdasani who displayed great patience in correcting some omission and commission in the writing.

Above all, I acknowledge the invaluable guidance I have received from Mrs. Almitra Patel who read each word the first draft and alerted me to the several errors of facts and spellings etc. She is the first Indian woman to get an M.S. Engineering degree from MIT, Boston, USA. I am ever so grateful to her for writing the Preface of the book.

I am grateful to daughter, Tanmaya for letting me use her laptop and niece Vaishnavi Mishra for teaching me patiently the use of Google Docs and handling the laptop. I thank Mr. Rajora from heart.

I have to remember and thank each of my office colleagues, the senior to the junior-most. From each I learnt and got support. I remember the famous wrestler of my childhood Cuttack; we lived in the same neighbourhood. He was a lion; I was a mosquito in awe. Later the role reversed; he was the 'Sardar' of the group of Safai workers of the Municipality and I was the Collector and Chairman. The cleaning staff worked only 3-4 hours in the morning. I requested that the city would be cleaned twice a day. Municipal officers were wary about the Union. But the workers agreed. On a Sunday afternoon, it was launched formally. There were some soft drink bottles; I was offered one, drank half and kept it down. I picked up a broom and started sweeping. My childhood lion appeared from nowhere, roared at the fellow workers and drank from my left-over bottle, took the broom from my hand and led the sweeping. Through him, I beg forgiveness of all my co-workers whom I haven't named. They are the silent heroes of this book.